Advance Praise For

FROM PEBBLES TO PATHWAYS

"Though a memoir of an individual journey, *From Pebbles to Pathways* reveals universal truths about the human condition. In relentlessly questioning the meaning of relationships, emotional responses and life experiences, the book's raw honesty and innocence give it an unusual, page-turning power. Not only does the past not make us, it says, but trust in the strange but wondrous ways of the universe will reveal a perfect pattern to our lives. In the author's case, this only became fully apparent in the process of writing. Yet in the tradition of great spiritual auto-biographies, deeply personal insights in one can trigger insights and realizations in the many. An exemplary 21st century spiritual work."

~ Tom Butler-Bowdon, author of *50 Self-Help Classics, 50 Spiritual Classics*

"An intimate and powerful memoir that catapults the reader through an insightful journey. The depth and honesty of this book surprises as it exemplifies one woman's real process of coming to terms with herself and healing the heart. *From Pebbles to Pathways* is a compelling glimpse into the journey of a formidable woman whose early life was spent struggling to find security and safety, losing herself along the way. Through her relentless commitment to well-being, and her riveting inner and spiritual journeys, we watch her courageously create a life of fulfillment. The stories in each chapter, and the profound insights that follow, inspire the reader to find the good in oneself, the courage to love, and recognize the endless opportunities life has to offer, regardless of circumstance."

~ Margaret Paul, Ph.D., author and co-creator of Inner Bonding® and
SelfQuest®

"All teachers must first be pupils. As they grow, the blank slate with which they began life becomes colored in hues often dark—the ragged scars of growing, learning, and loving. The trick, Donna Thomas tells us in her sometimes harrowing memoir, *From Pebbles to Pathways*, is to divine the lessons from the damage, the light from the sorrow, and to absorb—and, ultimately, impart—the wisdom that ensues. Somewhat to her own surprise, Thomas evolved into one of life's teachers, a healer of uncommon grace and intuition. As readers will discover, her path to that point was never assured, given her troubled, emotionally removed parents and the litany of abuses and calamities to which Thomas was subjected. What is striking about the book is not just the clarity the author brings to her own healing, but her talent in discerning the lessons all of us should be learning."

~ Nick Madigan, former correspondent for The *New York Times* and The *Washington Post*

"*From Pebbles to Pathways* reads like a fascinating and spellbinding novel, but with the added benefit of life lessons. It may be 'one woman's journey of healing the heart,' but the candid, personal stories are so profound that anyone can experience similar breakthroughs and paradigm shifts from them."

~ Heather Vale Goss, a.k.a. The Unwrapper™, Author and Interviewer

"At a time when fewer and fewer people have time to read, *From Pebbles to Pathways* is a must-read. Fascinating and compelling, it's an exhilarating ride to growth and awareness—an educational and evocative journey to greater enlightenment."

~ John Donley, Writer/Producer

"Donna Thomas tells her story with honesty and sincerity, drawing the reader into her transformational experiences. *From Pebbles to Pathways* will inspire and encourage those who are on a journey of personal enlightenment to find the good in all of the steps on their path."

~ Ron Scolastico, Ph.D., Author of *Doorway to the Soul* and *The Mystery of the Christ Force*

"Author Donna Thomas has created a biography of her life in a new work intended to offer guidance to those on a quest for spiritual awakening. It is an engrossing and intimate read of her journey through 38 years of life in a search for Grace. Reading *From Pebbles to Pathways* is like reading a woman's diary. It is jaw-droppingly honest and straight-forward...eye-opening and a testimony to her simplicity, honesty, and courage—the result of practicing what she preaches and the deter-mination to learn the lessons life teaches her. What you read is what you get—a level of insight to mind, thought, and essence that exposes her fully as she constructs herself into an integral whole from the elements life gave her.

"The fathers of daughters would do well to read this book as it may add dimension to how young girls come to grips with their dads. Likewise, smart men would read *Pebbles* with a view toward learning what better women want from better men. One seeking pathways through their own life would be blessed to find Thomas' *Pebbles*—if only to discover what a contemporary woman has done for herself on her own with her own resources. Perhaps that's as good as finding oneself gets."

~ John Rippo, The Espresso Café Newspaper

From PEBBLES to PATHWAYS

Suzanne !
All good to you
now and always,
Donna Thomas

Sage House Publishing, Santa Monica, CA
http://SageHousePublishing.com

ISBN: 978-0-9859390-1-4

Printed in the United States of America

First Edition
10 9 8 7 6 5 4 3 2 1

Cover photo "Montana Love" by Donna M. Thomas
Cover photo of child courtesy of Jason Noffsinger
Cover photo of woman courtesy of iStock Photo

Book design by Stacey Aaronson, www.creative-collaborations.com

In an effort to raise awareness and funds to help those suffering from
hunger and malnutrition, Sage House Publishing donates
ten percent of the sales profits of this book to these organizations:

SHARE OUR STRENGTH
NO KID HUNGRY

EMBRACING THE
WORLD®

http://ShareOurStrength.org

http://embracingtheworld.org

Get involved today.

From

PEBBLES *to*
PATHWAYS

A Journey *of*
Healing the Heart
One Insight at a Time

DONNA M. THOMAS

Sage House

In honor of my mother and father.

~∾~

May the insights that took place in this story and in the telling of it bring healing to the seven generations before and behind me.

CONTENTS

INTRODUCTION

☙

*B*efore delving into this book, it is important, I think, to clarify my meaning of *Grace*. *Grace is the power of the omnipresent, exquisite Divine (the governing force that lives in and through all things), revealing itself as supreme love by which one can find guidance, support, and inspiration as well as healing and regeneration. Simply put, Grace is "God" in action.*

This is an intimate account of how I was guided by Grace through the first thirty-eight years of my life, during periods of awareness and willingness as well as times of being oblivious and thickheaded. In fact, a strong contender for the subtitle of this book was *How Grace Guides the Thickheaded*.

Just as there are no short cuts to spiritual evolution, emotional (also known as personal) development requires dedication and consciousness. Both spiritual evolution and emotional development are vitally important to a deeply fulfilling life. This story is ultimately about the spiraling path of spiritual and emotional growth, and what happens when one brings awareness to one's life experiences, and how from these experiences—at times plea-surable, but more often challenging—profound insights are realized, and depth and growth are inspired. It is these insights that pave the pathway of our lives.

At the end of each chapter you will find sections called "Pebbles." These sections contain the insights and/or revelations that I gained from my experiences. For the earlier pebbles, because I was young and not yet practiced in self-reflection, they are my current insights into how each experience was important to the evolution of my life. The later pebbles give current insights in addition to awareness gained from the experiences as they occurred.

Alongside my stories, the intent of the pebbles is to exemplify four things: 1) the progress of bringing awareness, honesty, and intimacy to one's life experiences; 2) how one can find deep meaning, growth, and healing by this process; 3) how the meaning we attach to our experiences creates the life we are currently leading; and 4) how, if one is not satisfied with the life they now lead, by making a different body of choices, this body becomes what theorist Buckminster Fuller referred to as a Trim Tab[1] for our lives—the tiny, trailing part of the ship's rudder, which with a low amount of pressure, changes the direction of the ship (one's life). Once the rudder turns, the ship, no matter its size, makes a change in direction.

The pebbles are not intended to rob you, the reader, of your own insights. Rather, they are to augment what you take from the stories, given your perspective. They could also be thought of as me standing on top of a hill saying, "See me up here? The view is great!" as well as, "See the path to your right? Because of a, b and c, that is the path I took. Consider taking it. It could be easier for you." Still, if the pebbles don't resonate with you, skip them and simply read the stories, for they, in and of themselves, exemplify evolution.

This is a heroine's journey. It is not to say that my journey was more challenging than another's, as I am certain that each of our journeys is truly heroic, some in mythic proportions. Nor is this a whiny story of how life is just plain hard. For one person's challenge could just as easily be another person's defining moment. This book honors the journey of life itself and all that it offers. It attempts to embrace all experiences as offerings from the Divine and opportunities for growth. It is meant to encourage our trust in the guidance that is always waiting in the wings for our permission to rush forward on our behalf. It is a confirmation that fulfillment is often only a choice away.

I have heard that for some, the first fifty or so pages of this book can be somewhat reactivating to read, as I write in detail about personal experiences that were less than desirable. If you find this is the case for you, I encourage you to just keep reading. Everything turns out well in the end. You will see!

The reason for writing this book is simple. With the fear, suffering, and unrest in the world, I had to *do* something, *offer* something. I have found that one of the most potent actions to take in healing oneself of emotional pain is to tell the truth...the authentic truth. When one splays herself open so that all can be seen, even though it may not always be easy, deep and lasting healing can then occur. With my desire to inspire and guide others to achieve more peaceful and fulfilling lives, I offer this book as an exemplification of this powerful and sometimes harrowing process.

Most of the names in this book have been altered to respect the privacy of the people portrayed.

"Let your teacher be love itself."
Rumi

Chapter One

INNATE KNOWING

∞

I was born to a mother and father who loved me utterly, the best way they knew how. Here begins my journey, one pebble at a time …

I recall, as a young child, experiencing what I believed to be the true nature of human existence. In my naturally joyous state, I experienced regular moments of what I perceived as expanded consciousness and interconnectedness. During these times of heightened awareness, usually in my bed, just before sleep or after waking, I felt myself release into a state of utter union with my body, the world around me, and another dimension of consciousness that I could not name but saw and felt clearly.

As I began to release into this state of awareness, I would see my body expand and think, *I look like a balloon. Wow, look at my toes. I wonder how much bigger I'm going to get.* Then I would watch objects and what seemed like different forms of consciousness float around and through me. My body continued to expand until it filled the room. Then I disappeared and became at one with everything. There seemed to be no separation with all that was around me. I simply became the witness. My sense was that this state of being was just another aspect of my innate nature, and I felt an unspoken invitation to simply stay there as long as I wanted.

I would feel butterflies in my stomach each time one of these periods began. I sensed that something wonderful was about to happen to me, even though there was nothing actually happening *to me.* It was more like stepping into another aspect of my *beingness* that was every bit as real as my earthly experience, but at the same time more essential.

I was fortunate enough to have these experiences regularly until I was, I believe, six or seven years old, at which time I felt my more earthly self begin to take over. I never questioned why they stopped; it simply felt like the natural course of things.

PEBBLE

These experiences shaped my primary awareness and fundamental understanding that at my essence, I am at one with a world that is utterly loving and interconnected. These moments of connection allowed me to have a very different, and more personal, experience of spirituality than what I was taught in the Christian Sunday school I attended. In fact, I didn't associate my experiences with the church at all. They seemed completely unrelated. Such is how I began the first steps of my spiritual walk.

Chapter Two

LIFE HITS THE FAN

❧

*W*hile still quite young, I became aware that my parents were having problems and that my mother in particular seemed troubled. I often heard them argue, and on one occasion I saw my father slap my mother across the face. Another time I saw him become very upset when he discovered a hidden bottle that belonged to her in the linen closet.

My father often traveled on business, and while he was away my mother drank something that made her act different and disconnected. In bed with pneumonia at age five, I saw a glass of what looked like water on the bed stand. Being very thirsty and seeing that my mother was tending to something, I reached out through a slit in the plastic tent surrounding my bed and took a drink. I felt my mouth and throat burn and thought I would wretch. How could something that looked so pure taste so terrible? My mother quickly took away the glass and told me that the drink was for her and that I should not have any. I realized then that it was my mother's drink that made her lose track of me.

Unattended, I would often walk the far reaches of our neighborhood wearing nothing more than a t-shirt and panties. One time my father found me and walked me home. With my small hand holding his large index finger, I looked up and saw his disturbed face. For a long time I believed I had done something very wrong to make him look that way.

This was just the beginning of the hardships I experienced growing up in a troubled family. During this period, I watched my parents' relationship deteriorate. My father disowned my funny and charming older half-brother, Ronny, because they had a terrible fight. Don, Ronny's older brother who was very kind and loving toward me, had just become a police officer when he was tragically killed in a motorcycle accident. And because I was often on my own, I was sexually molested several times by neighborhood boys. The first time was when I was five.

I was playing up the street by myself when the older brother of one of my school friends approached me and asked if I wanted to play cops and robbers. It felt great to be asked to play by someone *older*, so I happily agreed. He told me that he wanted to be the police officer, and he made up a story that I was a bad person and he had to arrest me. He lured me into a group of trees and told me he had to tie my hands so he could take me to jail. Innocently, I held out my wrists for him to bind. He tightly tied them with what looked like a phone cord and said, "Now you have to do exactly what I tell you to do."

I said, "Okay."

He unbuttoned my pants and began to pull them down. I didn't understand how this was part of the game and began to protest.

"Shut up!" he yelled, and pulled my pants down to my ankles. He put his hand between my legs and ran his fingers along my labia. A surge of fear overcame me, and I screamed for help. He tried to convince me to stop but he could not. My scream must have scared him because he finally ran off. Fearful that he would return, I frantically struggled to untie my hands, but they had been tied very tightly. I finally got my hands free, pulled my pants back up, and ran out of the trees, cautiously looking around to see if he was still there. Seeing that he wasn't, I ran home. I told no one about what had happened because I thought I would get in trouble.

The next incident began a year or two later when I was in the pool playing with several kids. One of the boys, Billy, was a friend of my brother Stuart, who was five years older than me. Billy paid a lot of attention to me in the pool, but I thought nothing of it and played and teased with him. A few days later he came over to my house and asked if I wanted to come out with him. I asked him where we were going and he said, "Over to my house." I happily followed him. We walked into his large home, and he guided me into his lavishly decorated living room with a marbled fireplace hearth. I didn't see his parents and asked him where they were. Pulling some brightly colored pillows off the couch onto the floor, he nonchalantly said, "They're at work." He then motioned for me to come to him and sat me down on the pillows as he proceeded to take off his pants. He sat down in front of me, pointed to his penis and asked, "Do you know what this is?"

"Sure," I said. "I've seen my little brother's."

He then asked, "Do you want to touch it?" I didn't really want to touch it, but I didn't know what else to do, so I complied. I was curious about how it could grow and get hard like it did, but a part of me was also disgusted by it. I thought it smelled weird. Even though I wanted to stop, he encouraged me to keep stroking him. I was curious about the slimy stuff that came out of the opening, but I didn't ask him what it was. Then he said that his parents would be home soon so we had to stop. He put his clothes back on and walked me home.

For several months, he came over to my house and in some way or another he let me know that he wanted me. I would follow him from place to place—at his home or to a local field—and fondle him until he got slimy again. He would also fondle me. At some point I began to have bad feelings about him and didn't want to do it anymore. But he continued to come over and would look at me hard if I didn't want to go with him. One day we were out in the field in a large fort someone had made. My mother had evidently seen me walking to the field from the kitchen window. She went to our neighbor and asked him to help her find me. While we were in the fort, we heard my mother calling me from far away. Billy ran away, but before he left, he warned me not to say anything to anyone about what we were doing. Confused and scared, I stayed in the fort until my worried mother showed up a few minutes later, asking me who I was with and what I was doing out in the field. I lied and said, "I was just playing with Billy, but he left." I was grateful that she found me. Even though she didn't know what had been going on, it was comforting that she cared enough to come out to the field to find me. I was also grateful that from that point on, she would not let me go out and play with Billy.

Another incident occurred after we moved to a new neighborhood. An eighteen-year-old in our complex heard me say a curse word and threatened to tell my mother if I didn't have sex with him. My fear of being scolded was huge, and since I thought I was already somewhat familiar with what I understood as sex, I thought it would be less horrible than being told on, so I complied. Over a period of months he fondled me, I fondled him and he tried to have intercourse with me. I say tried because he was either too big or too inexperienced and could never achieve penetration. I hated what he would do to me, but I didn't know how to stop him. Eventually, I found relief when he moved away with his parents to another town.

PEBBLE

I am grateful that there was no penetration by any of the boys who molested me, but this is not to say that their actions didn't leave scars, as you will see further down my path.

Two scars I will mention now are that I believed I somehow deserved what had happened, and that this was what boys did to girls. Thus these became my expectations. Because I knew nothing else, and because I felt I could talk to no one about it, I silently tucked away these beliefs along with the unpleasant memories.

Chapter Three

DADDY DOESN'T KNOW

⁂

$\mathcal{L}$ate in 1965, while traveling to Arizona from California with my father and two brothers, I discovered my reason for living. One night during the trip I was sitting in the front seat of my father's car listening to the radio. While singing along with Jackie DeShannon's "What the World Needs Now Is Love," I felt the song ring deeply inside and felt my body and my being expand. I turned to my father and said, "Daddy, you know, this song is true. Love is the most important thing. It's the only thing we need. Love is *everything*." At that moment I was overcome by the immense power of Love, and I knew with all my being that what I was saying was "truth." To this he said, "Honey, there's a lot more to life than love. What we need is more understanding," and then he went on to tell me how simplistic, unrealistic, and just plain wrong my reality was. I was flabbergasted. How could he not see the truth? How could he not feel the Love that to me was so palpable? I thought to myself, "But Daddy, Love makes everyone *want* to understand. It's what makes everything in this world work right!" But I didn't tell him this. He didn't seem to want to know what I knew.

Although I could not articulate it, I knew that this higher Love I was trying to speak about was the true or "real" reality, and it was the only truth I knew. It was the water in which I swam. I felt that anything other than this, including my father's thoughts, was not true. All at once I felt the weight of the world on my shoulders.

PEBBLE

This was my defining moment. At age eight I discovered the truth about Love, and resolved for the rest of my life to live my truth and to love this world to the best of my ability, and in whatever way I could, into a better place. Although I didn't realize it as such, I had discovered my life's purpose.

Chapter Four

DOING TIME

∽

$\mathcal{H}$aving come to understand that Love has the power to transcend everything unlike itself, I had no idea how this knowledge would be tested again and again over the next several years.

What I had not known during the trip to Arizona was that my parents' relationship had unraveled. Later in my ninth year, because my father wanted to remove my brothers and me from the toxicity of my mother's alcoholism, my parents divorced and my father obtained custody. He moved us to Corona del Mar, where we lived for a year or so.

I recall our last day at home with my mother. I was standing in my bedroom, looking at my bed, and I thought, *I'm going away and I won't be living with Mommy anymore.* I remember how surreal it felt. I loved my father. I was Daddy's little girl, his "princess" as he would say. I loved how he let me watch the cream flow into his iced coffee while I ate ice cream every Sunday morning after attending our Evangelical church. I loved how he sang to me. I loved his smile and how he let me sit on his lap. I knew living with him must be better, or he would not be taking us away from my mother. But I didn't want to go. I wondered what she would do without me.

After moving, we saw very little of my father. He traveled for days and sometimes weeks at a time selling life insurance, leaving Stuart to care for Nate—two years my junior— and me and to ward off bill collectors. It was during this period that I began to experience a deep and pervading fear at night. I believe my fear was triggered when Stuart walked into our living room one night while Nate and I were watching television. His face looked disturbed and he seemed agitated. I asked him what was wrong and he said, "I just caught someone trying to break in through your bedroom sliding glass door!" I jumped up and asked him how he knew this.

"I was in my room," (which was right next to my bedroom), "and I heard someone walking on the outside patio. Then I heard someone fiddling with the lock to your sliding glass door. I jumped into your doorway to see who it was, and I scared him off." This shook me to my bones and I had great difficulty sleeping in my room afterward. My brothers also liked to scare me in the dark, like many kids do, and I remember that each time they would jump out from behind a door, or turn out the lights in the room I was in, I felt as if my heart might stop beating. From this time, feelings of panic at being alone and an immense fear of the dark haunted me. I could never sleep unless there was a light on nearby, and while I was a child I often ended up sleeping with my younger brother.

Along with the difficult times, I also have wonderful memories of living in Corona del Mar. I often explored the beaches, rocks, and caves, and even got over to Balboa Island and experienced my first-ever frozen banana. (There's something incredible about the combination of a crunchy chocolate candy/nut topping over a fresh frozen banana that still makes my body hum.)

Also, I was a big lover of music and listened to everything that was playing on the radio in 1966—The Beatles, The Beach Boys, The Monkees, The Supremes, The Mamas & Papas, etc. (essentially, all the groups starting with "The")—and then there was Nancy Sinatra who sang one of my favorite songs, "These Boots are Made for Walking." I owned a pair of go-go boots that I wore daily and a mini-skirt outfit to match, which I wore several times a week.

A highlight of this period was my fourth grade teacher. I can still picture her kind and vibrant face. I wish I could remember her name. She was, in a word, wonderful. She kept a close eye on me, and although I was reprimanded from time to time for giggling in class, she seemed to sincerely care for me. She was also responsible for introducing me to classical music. On one occasion our class went to the symphony, and she made sure I sat next to her. I remember her loving gaze when I began to cry as the beautiful sounds drifted into me. I had never been touched like that by music before; it felt uplifting and freeing. I felt my spirit soar as if there were a full wind and I had wings. I will be forever grateful to this wonderful woman for giving me this experience.

Then late one night, after about a year of living in Corona del Mar, my father woke my brothers and me after coming home from one of his trips. He told us that we were leaving our home, that we could only bring what could fit in the car, and that we had to leave quickly and quietly. I was confused and didn't understand why we had to do this, but I accepted it like everything else that had happened in my life before that moment. It felt like an adventure... until I realized later that I had left behind my favorite beatnik doll and the flag that was part of my departed half-brother Don's police burial ceremony. I no longer had anything in the physical realm to connect me to Don, nor did I have my faithful sleep mate, and this deeply saddened me.

I learned much later that my father had not paid the rent for some time and that he saw no other way of freeing himself from his debt than to steal away in the middle of the night.

We ended up in Las Vegas in a motel-apartment complex. We had nothing to play with and no yard to play in. We had no friends or family, no support system, no car, and no church to attend. So being resourceful as children are, Nate and I got paper, scissors, and tape from the front office and made an elaborate paper dollhouse, complete with furniture and a family of handmade paper dolls. The fantasy lives we created enabled us to play in harmony with each other for countless hours, and it was in this way that we coped with living in that dreadfully hot, barren, and lonely place while our father traveled.

Within a few months of moving there we were put into an orphanage. Stuart had already left for school one morning when Nate and I missed the bus. Not having another way to get to school, I decided to go to the office to ask for money for a taxi. As Nate and I walked to the motel office, I felt that what I was about to do would probably get my father in trouble, but at the same time I knew in my gut that it was the best thing to do. When I asked for the money, the people in the office asked me where my father was. I told them the truth—that he was away somewhere doing business and that I wasn't exactly sure when he'd be back. Someone called the police and reported that my father had abandoned us. We were picked up early that evening and taken to the orphanage where we would spend the next month.

As one can imagine, my brothers and I were not happy being taken away. Stuart was angry. Nate was traumatized and stayed close to my older brother. I wanted to make the most of this new adventure and have as much fun as possible. I spent many hours playing with the younger children and enjoyed visiting and holding the babies. I also tried to be helpful to the adults running the place. I *knew* my father would eventually come get us, while the other children there would not be so fortunate. Some of the older girls had a strong dislike for me and came to my bunk at night to pick on me after everyone had gone to bed. They told me I wasn't worth anything and that I was dumb and ugly. They wanted me to know they were the bosses and threatened to hurt me. This frightened me, but nothing of consequence came of it. Oddly, it is not them or their mistreatment of me that I remember most, but the tenderness I felt for the other children that most moves my memory…and the Grace I felt while we were there.

Upon my father's return from his trip, he was jailed for child abandonment, which we found out later was why we were in the orphanage as long as we were. I can still picture the pained but joyous look on his face when he eventually came to get us. For me, it was bittersweet leaving that place. I had grown very fond of the children and felt bad leaving them there.

After our reunion we went back to the motel-hotel to pick up our things and then drove to our new home in Incline Village, Lake Tahoe.

PEBBLE

As a child, while going through these experiences, I was simply "in" the moment, doing the best I could without thinking much, which is not unlike how most people live their lives on an ongoing basis. With no thought on my part, my life unfolded depending on outside circumstances and how I responded to each moment as it arose. Luckily, I felt good about the choices I made while in the orphanage: being helpful to the staff, loving toward the orphans, and hopeful about the future. These allowed me to keep my loving and positive nature intact.

Chapter Five

TAHOE, A WHOLE
NEW WORLD

∽

I felt truly blessed to live in such a pristine place as Tahoe. I still remember the magic feeling in realizing that God (what I had naturally come to understand as the presence that lives in all things) was especially alive in the water, rocks, pine trees, aspen trees, and birds. The grand lake and magnificent mountains with the backdrop of the change of seasons— the quiet splendor of the snow, in particular—was a source of great peace. I felt that the beauty of my surroundings matched my inner world. Even though my family life was far from stable, I felt very happy living in the mountains.

Upon arriving in "Incline," my father took us to the local Presbyterian church and we became members. It was important to him for us to attend church again as we had not gone to one with any regularity since my parents' divorce.

My father could no longer leave us alone as he did before, so he hired live-in babysitters to stay with us while he traveled. I missed him and my mother greatly. My mother had recently re-married and she and her new husband, Rick, continued to live in Southern California. Because of the distance, we saw her just twice a year— at Christmas and in the summer. The pain I felt not having her near me, even though she was troubled and sick, was excruciating. Underneath her pathology, I knew her love for me was deep and unconditional, and I loved her in return. Every day I longed to see her wavy, auburn hair and hazel eyes, and to hear her gentle voice, to have her feminine presence reflect beauty back to me and to show me how to grow up. I also felt the loss of not having my father, the strongest male figure I knew, to guide me on a daily basis.

Although I was usually very adaptable, my social integration into my new school was not smooth. Entering fifth grade in the fall of 1967, I felt unsure how to connect with my classmates. I had spent most of the last couple of years with my brothers and was naturally more comfortable around boys. I soon reached out to a cute boy named Bobby, a fellow fifth grader. I wanted to let him know that I really liked him, so I wrote him a note asking him if he would have sex with me. I was obviously confused about boundaries. Bobby gave our teacher the note and I was asked to go to the principal's office. The principal asked me a few questions about why I had asked Bobby such a question. I responded by saying that I thought that was what people did when they liked someone else. At the time, schools had very little experience in dealing with victims of child abuse. Had this happened now, I imagine there would have been a larger conversation and perhaps my molestations might have been uncovered. But with a light reprimand and a statement that "little girls don't ask boys to do such things," he sent me back to class. For a while some of my classmates teased me about the note and kept their distance, but in time I integrated more normally into this new chapter of my life.

The fall and winter brought heavy snows that year. It was freezing, and I loved it. The snow in our front yard was a good foot or two taller than I was. I carved out secret hiding places in the walls of snow that marked our path from our front door to the street. My brothers and I spent hours and days sledding down the surrounding hills, and we made gigantic snowballs by rolling balls of snow up and down the streets.

That winter, I got pneumonia for the second time. My father was out of town and so the live-in babysitter admitted me into the hospital down in Reno. I was there for a week, at the end of which my father returned from his trip and brought me home to finish recuperating. It was then that he taught me how to play cards. His favorite game was gin rummy, so this is what he taught me. I loved it. We would play for hours. He also taught me blackjack—he said it would help me with my math—and other games, too, but gin was our favorite. Playing cards with my father became something I cherished.

After the snow thawed in the spring, we made forts and climbed trees (one of my favorite things to do). When summer came, I spent many warm nights, with the fragrant smell of tree sap and pine needles gorging my senses, sleeping out under the vivid stars behind our house with my neighbor and first best friend Valerie and her brothers. I felt very much at home being in the woods or swimming in the lake with my friends. We played, fought, and laughed like children do. We had snowball and cake fights, skied, and made long and scary sled runs; and, if we didn't have sleds, we pulled our parkas low in the back and slid down on our backsides, all in the name of fun.

My first lifelong friend was Bill. He had a huge and devoted heart and he treated me with nothing but love and kindness. Our fathers worked together, and we spent virtually every day of our eleventh year together. We climbed mountains looking for gooseberries and ate pine nuts out of pinecones. We spent hours in his bedroom talking about everything, drinking Lipton iced tea by the gallon, and eating fresh-baked cookies (that Bill baked) by the dozens. We listened to the Shirelles, Little Eva (The Locomotion!), and other sixties greats on four-track tapes, and we listened over and over to the soundtrack of *Paint Your Wagon*, our favorite movie. We even attended a Presbyterian church camp together. We were happily connected at the hip. He even rescued me when I got locked out of a place where I was babysitting, which would have been difficult if not for the fact that one of the children had locked me and her toddler sibling out on the deck of their second story house. As always, he was there for me with an open heart and without judgment. He was the first male to leave a positive lasting impression on me. He was also the first person, other than my family, to show me unconditional love. I gave him his first back rubs and his first kiss.

The summer of my twelfth year I began competing in our local swim team. Being a bit taller and stronger than many of the girls my age, as well as being quite agile, I was good at athletics and was adept at swimming. It felt very satisfying to do something at which I excelled. It also felt great being a part of something. Not only did everyone work very hard together, but we cared for one another, too. I was used to being on my own, and to me the team felt like a big family. I spent most of my splendid summer days in the pool, at the beach swimming in the lake, and eating piping hot French fries with my friends. Life for me, in this arena, was very good.

I won all but two events I swam in that summer, and when it came time for the end-of-the-year awards, I was named the Most Valuable Swimmer in my age group, barely inched out of being the most valuable swimmer on the team. I was so proud of myself. This was the first real thing I felt I had ever accomplished. I loved my coaches and teammates and felt their care for me. It was suggested at one point that I be groomed for more serious competition in the Junior Olympics, and this sounded fantastic to me but there was no indoor swimming pool where we lived. We would have had to move to a larger city to have access to year-round swimming, and by that time my father had a solid job in Tahoe. Moving was out of the question.

The next summer, I moved up an age bracket though I was smaller than many of the other swimmers. I was still very good and competed well, but knowing that I could never train to be a truly great swimmer, I began to lose my edge and my heart was less and less in it. Over time I became more interested in hanging out with my friends and began to sporadically miss practices. My coach came to speak with my father about it, telling him that he felt I was too talented a swimmer to let it go. I appreciated that he cared enough about me to come and persuade me to be dedicated again, so I finished out the season mostly for him, but no longer with the burning desire I once had. By the end of summer, I completely let it go.

PEBBLE

I feel very fortunate that I had the opportunity to find and participate in something I was good at that I loved to do. Up until then, most of my daily life had been about other people's needs. I feel Grace definitely had a hand in helping me discover something in which I could have personal pride. I was able to see that I could rely on myself and produce something that was meaningful to me. These memories—those of swimming and of Bill—are some of my happiest from childhood.

Even now I believe it's important for me to always have my hand in something that I thoroughly enjoy, that is just for me—even if no one else appreciates it to the extent that I do. It keeps me open, with my mind at peace and my heart happy.

Chapter Six

DOWNWARD SPIRAL

✐

*A*s I moved into puberty, the effects of my earlier childhood experiences began to take their toll. Even with my experience of the profound truth of Love and the nature of my existence, I began to lose confidence in myself and how to live in the world. In the three years since moving to Tahoe, we had moved five times and had not settled into a stable place to call home. Then my father brought home a new wife. She was much younger than he and very jealous of my relationship with him. There were many arguments between them and much anger directed to me from her. Her uncle was the last person to molest me. I didn't tell anyone because, like many who have been molested, I didn't know if I would be heard or believed. I kept my anger and disillusionment inside and began to withdraw.

To make matters even more challenging, I was extremely sensitive, loyal, open, and naive, which caused me much pain in my school life. I loved my peers, but found many of them to be unethical, insensitive, and just plain mean. I think that because of my sensitivity, I became a regular target for pranks and the brunt of many jokes. Male schoolmates put tacks in my seat, a girl took a photo of my naked butt in gym class and circulated it, and others made fun of my very crooked teeth and later my braces, among other insults. I took these things personally and began to shut down.

On several occasions, while sitting in school or in my bedroom, I felt the intensity of my internal storms whirling around. As I allowed myself to sink more deeply into these feelings, I had an insight that I interpreted in this way: *If I could learn to love others more deeply, then I would be able to transcend the pain both in myself and in those around me.* I wished for this on many occasions and prayed for my liberation from the agony that also seemed to enshroud others. But as I would go to school day after day thinking I would love them more, I became more and more disillusioned. I saw no change in my peers' behaviors, and, if anything, I became more sensitive to how much they didn't want to be loved—by me, anyway.

PEBBLE

Years later I realized that I had only partially understood the insight I had as a young child. Although it was about loving more deeply, it was specifically about loving me more deeply and attending to my own well-being first. As long as I remained dependent on others to stop doing things so that I could be happy, I was setting myself up for more pain. Even though I didn't understand this completely at first, the seed had been planted.

Chapter Seven

HITTING BOTTOM

∞

$\mathcal{T}$he deep fear that was triggered by the earlier attempted break-in intensified drastically during the early 1970s when the Zodiac serial killer was on his rampage in San Francisco. I had no framework to understand or process such appalling acts of violence and felt petrified by them. There were many nights when I was too afraid to go to sleep until the sun began to rise. I can vividly recall seeing the rays of sun peeking up from behind the mountains and feeling a sigh of relief that I could finally sleep. The fear became so overwhelming that I eventually made a bed for myself in my closet (behind the washing machine that was being stored there) and I slept there for months. It was the only place I could feel safe sleeping until the killings ceased. The embarrassment and shame I felt about having so much fear contributed to the erosion of my self-confidence, which naturally affected other areas of my life.

Around this time I began to have serious doubts about the purpose of my life. There were many times that I couldn't understand why my inner life (what I believed I was capable of, and what I felt life was meant to be) didn't jibe with my outer, or actual, life. It felt as if some unforgiving force was slowly driving strength, faith, and trust out of me. I began to feel more and more like a victim, and this mentality catapulted me into certain behaviors and actions that I didn't like but felt I had no control over.

Like many teenage children in my hometown, I experimented with marijuana and other drugs. I was fifteen. During this time, I was introduced to some twenty-year-old men with whom my girlfriends and I got high on occasion. They also engaged in a range of sexual activity. Being a virgin, I wasn't comfortable with that, but Gary, the man I was spending time with, understood and didn't press me. We would kiss and pet each other, which went on for many weeks.

One night I had a profound experience. We had been on Gary's bed for a while when he got up to go to the bathroom. While he was gone, I had a luminous moment imagining myself becoming pregnant by virgin conception. One moment I was looking around his dimly lit room filled with East Indian window coverings, musical equipment, and candles, and the next moment I was hurled into a vision, seeing myself being chosen and accepting a holy child into my body with great reverence. The part of me not currently in the vision knew that it had not actually happened, but I also felt certain that I had somehow experienced it indirectly, perhaps in some other time. During the vision, I felt a deep and pervading love surrounding me. After being "in" the vision for some time, I came to the understanding that it was telling me I was meant for something larger than the life I was currently living. I asked, as if something inside me would know the answer, "Tell me, what am I meant for?" *More than this*, I understood in my heart. I had not yet contemplated the concept of reincarnation, so I had no frame of reference or explanation for my vision of becoming pregnant other than that I was high. Still, the inner *knowing* stayed with me and I felt my mind and heart expand. I left his home soon after. What I was doing with him seemed to pale in comparison.

My experience of this vision was so powerful that I could not let it go. Later, it became one of many experiences that helped me piece together an understanding of my strong connection to The Christ force—the consciousness of Divine Love, outside the dogma of the church. (More on this as we move further down the path.)

Another unexpected outcome from my association with Gary and his friends was the unmasking of my second lifelong friend, Laura. She and I both liked Gary, and we both became very territorial over him. We were actually mortal enemies! He told me he liked me and that Laura meant nothing to him, while saying the same thing to her about me. We both felt claim over him and neither of us would budge. Shortly thereafter, I came to the realization that I didn't like him that much, and I no longer wanted to see him. Coincidentally, she stopped seeing him as well. Once we both decided he wasn't worth fighting over, our friendship began.

Laura was the most vibrant and intelligent person I knew. Her short, blond, perfectly coiffed hair, and five foot one shapely frame was quite a sight alongside my Amazonian reddish-brown hair and six-foot-plus, fine-boned frame. She was about eye to eye with my navel, with a heart twice her size. She was the first female in my life (other than my mother) to show me what loving unconditionally was, and the first person ever to show me what really being there for someone looked like.

One day, Laura called me up and said, "Let's go hike up to the water tower and do our homework." I thought it sounded like a great idea, although I had no idea how to get up to it. I needn't have worried, though; Laura knew the way. In fact, she seemed to know how to get anywhere. I met her at her condominium and with books in hand, we piled into the car and she drove us to the base of the mountain we were about to climb. It was a gorgeous Tahoe day in late spring, the bright sun casting diamonds onto the lake while at the same time revealing the surrounding snow-capped mountains. The lightly scattered clouds passed freely overhead and a warm and gentle breeze caressed the trees. Perfection exemplified. I looked up to where we were headed and saw no visible path. "How are we going to get up there?" I asked.

"Don't worry, I know the way." *Of course you do*, I thought.

We started the climb up and through the ocean of manzanita bushes, which are characterized by their stiff red branches that scratch you like crazy when you're walking through them. Laura navigated through and around them as if it were effortless. We made it to the top without incident, other than the myriad scrapes on our arms and legs, and climbed onto the water tower. The view was breathtaking. Being on top of the tower, with no people around, gave me a sense of power and connection to God and nature that was elating. We laid our towels down, took off our shirts and bathed ourselves in the rays of the sun. Laura had brought sunscreen and made sure it was on the places I couldn't reach. After we had been studying a while she asked, "Do you want a mango?"

"What's a mango?" I replied.

"Oh, you'll love it. I was raised on them." (Laura's father was a pilot and was stationed in Guam, where she was born and raised before moving to Lake Tahoe.) She effortlessly peeled one and handed it to me, giving me my first exotic fruit experience. As its sweet, fragrant juices ran down my chin and fingers, I knew I must have died and gone to heaven. She looked at me with a Cheshire cat grin and giggled. "Told ya."

It was primarily her friendship and nurturing that helped me through the challenging experiences that transpired over the next couple of years.

I was sixteen and wearing braces when I was asked to be a participant in a high school version of *The Dating Game* during a pep rally. The young man chosen to be the "bachelor" was a football and basketball star and very popular. I'm not sure why I was chosen to be a "bachelorette," but I was willing and thought it would be fun. I sat with two other girls, older and more popular than I, and I answered "the bachelor's" questions with charm and lightness. Not knowing who I was, he chose me as his date. As the school cheered and laughed, he jumped over the partition separating us. When he saw me he buried his face in his hands and yelled, "Oh no!" I felt my face burn in humiliation as I sat on stage watching him act out his displeasure, but at the same time I felt pleased that even though he wasn't happy that he chose me, it was *me* that he chose. Who I was in some way touched him. Still, it was painful having him act that way toward me in public. Laura came to me afterward and said, "He's just a jerk, Donna. What he did is about him, not you." Of course, the young man and I never went out on the date. In fact, he never spoke to me again.

Early in my sixteenth year, I hit emotional bottom. For months, I had a secret crush on a classmate named Sam, who I thought was the cutest boy in my class. One night I asked him to drive me home from a pool party so that I could spend a bit of time with him. He said yes, and when we got in the car he told me he wanted to take a drive before he took me home. I took that to mean he liked me as well and wanted to spend time with me, so I eagerly agreed. He drove me to the top of a mountain, parked the car, and said he wanted to have some beer. He proceeded to open a bottle of Budweiser and began to drink. Because of my history, I didn't drink, nor was I comfortable being around alcohol, but in that moment I wasn't sure how to deal with my discomfort.

Shortly after he started drinking, he asked me if I wanted to have sex with him. I was shocked, scared, and flattered that he would ask me such a thing. I told him I had never had sex and that I didn't want to. He said that *he* really wanted to and then spent the next hour or so trying to coerce me. I thought about just getting out of the car and walking home, but we were miles away and it was very late. His most compelling argument was that he would take me home after we had sex. So many thoughts were going through my mind from utter terror to curiosity to just wanting to do whatever it took so that I could go home. At this point I thought, *Maybe it won't be so bad.* I reluctantly said yes and he proceeded to lie on top of me, in between the front seats of his car, and burst through my hymen. I was in intense pain, but he didn't care. He just kept on thrusting himself inside me. I knew this was going to get me home, so I endured it. There was no kissing or tenderness expressed from him. Afterward, I felt dirty and demoralized. He never spoke to me again.

The days, weeks, and months to come were profoundly difficult. I experienced intense humiliation, guilt, and sadness over the incident and in losing my virginity in that way. Then there was the matter of what he told our schoolmates and their disrespect toward me afterward. While in the lunch line one day, two boys from my class were talking. One of them glanced at me and said in a volume that I and everyone else in line could hear, "Hey, did you hear about Thomas and Sam? He balled her on Friday night." Just about everyone in the line turned to look at me with silent judgment and amusement in their faces. And to make matters worse, most likely due to stress, I didn't menstruate for three months and therefore wondered if I was pregnant. Word got around school that I *was* pregnant and that brought a deeper level of humiliation. When I finally began to menstruate again (albeit irregularly), I was relieved, but mostly I just felt gaping wounds in my heart.

A few months after this incident, Nate and I went to visit my mother in Los Angeles for our summer visit. While I was there, I briefly saw another boy I liked and who I thought liked me, but I later realized he also wanted me not for who I was but for what he could do with me. Again, I submitted, and again I felt devalued and ashamed. I continued to spiral downwards emotionally, feeling worse and worse about myself.

I had trouble finding my way through the pain and started smoking marijuana to numb myself. I didn't like the feeling of being in an altered state, but I disliked the feeling of despair and humiliation even more. Most of my friends smoked pot, and after feeling the pain of rejection and the burn of being ridiculed, I wanted desperately to fit in somewhere. I joined in and convinced myself that this would allow me to feel accepted. Living this way didn't feel natural though, and I often thought that what I was doing was foolish. Still, I wasn't yet ready to let go of my pain.

One night, I was at a party with friends and some older schoolmates. While smoking, I began to feel much higher than usual and wondered why. I heard someone say that the marijuana had been laced with something. Shortly after this I felt unstable, and I lost my hearing. I didn't want to talk to anyone about what was happening to me, and when I began to get very scared, my inner guidance—which I hadn't heard for a while—took over and I got a strong message to walk home. It was a brisk fall night. There was no moon out, and I could see millions of stars. I had always felt a special affinity for trees, and on my long walk home I gazed up and felt, as I always did, their loving and protective presence around me. The freshness of the air and the beauty of the night woke me up on many levels. By the time I got home, I was unaltered, my hearing had returned, and I was filled with feelings of love and gratitude.

This experience seemed to prompt me to reconcile with myself and to reconnect with my true nature. I began to take small steps to regain my openness and to be willing to trust again. While in my re-opening process, and with the coaxing from Kim—a classmate and close friend of Laura's and mine—I began deepening my relationship with Spirit and mysticism. Kim was (although she didn't admit it) a Wicca, and she introduced me to the Tarot and the mystery and power of the supernatural. This was utterly fascinating to me. She acquainted me with things that felt absolutely true and natural, yet they were things I had never heard of. She gave me oracle readings and talked about being in tune with nature; we danced under the moon and discussed what it was to be at one with everything around us. And even though it was never named, she introduced me to the concept of the Goddess. With my Christian indoctrination, I had never heard mention of a feminine face or counterpart to the stern-faced, law-making God, and I was fascinated by the notion. I easily welcomed these concepts, especially the rekindling of my sense of an all-pervasive fundamental interconnectedness and the Love that I felt was the underlying creator.

PEBBLE

The time with Kim and the seeds that were planted became the inspiration, basis, and foundation of my later journey into a more mystical awareness.

To me, this is a perfect example of how Grace steps in when one is able to open her heart. I said "yes" and chose to open again and to trust in the goodness that I believed was there (even though it was not plainly visible), and in came insight into how to live a more fulfilling life.

It took me years, but I finally felt at peace with the fact that challenging and painful things will always happen, just as easy and happy things will happen —they are both part of the human condition. I prefer the happy experiences, of course, but I am aware that it's important to embrace the painful times, because not only are they part of the same extraordinary life, they are actually interdependent with one another. What I learn from each of life's challenges guides me into a deeper and more meaningful life—maybe not immediately, but always eventually.

Then, of course, there's the notion that one's responses (trusting, fearful, etc.) can be present with both positive experiences as well as negative. I have found that my inner peace depends on how I choose to respond to anything at any given moment. The responsibility inherent in this knowledge is annoying at times, but it doesn't change the fact that it's true.

Something else I took away from that time was a conscious realization that although I had deep fears of the dark, I didn't have them when I was out in nature. On the contrary, I always felt protected. This knowledge began to give me a deeper insight into my understanding of interconnectedness.

Chapter Eight

DEEPER THAN SKIN

✑

℘aura stood close by me with a few other friends as I went back to school after summer break. I received many looks and questions about whether or not I had been pregnant and gotten an abortion. I chose not to let other students' shallow curiosity derail me and focused on what I was happy about—that I had great friends, I was feeling good about myself again, I had finally gotten my braces off, and I had started to grow into my body.

I was very slow to bloom, not starting my menstrual cycle until a few months before my experience with Sam, and I was painfully aware that with braces and my tall, thin body, I seemed much younger than I was. But during summer, after years of feeling awkward, I blossomed into a young woman, and with this it appeared that I had graduated, seemingly overnight, into a different existence. I began to receive positive attention from the kids at school, mostly from the boys.

I found it fascinating and curious that boys now noticed me and seemed to find me attractive. I was no longer the one being made fun of, but rather the one who was wanted. Did I relish that! But while I enjoyed my newfound attention, I also wondered why *who* I was had not been enough before. I was much more proud of who I was on the inside than what my body looked like. I concluded that this new "popularity," although much preferred, was shallow. This understanding kept me humble and gave me the awareness that looks will always be just skin-deep. And with this came the insight that my physical appearance was mutable and my youthful beauty temporary. I imagined that this would also be the case with my popularity and thought I should enjoy it while it lasted.

My junior year went more smoothly than the previous year had gone. With my newfound acceptance and without the ridicule, I was able to settle more into myself. I focused on singing and dancing, two things I enjoyed. I sang in chorus and was cast in *The Mikado*, although I later backed out because I felt too shy to be on stage. I also earned money with a thriving babysitting business and was enjoying more freedom now that I could drive.

I spent a fair amount of time with Laura. We had a profound connection and trust in one another, and our acceptance and encouragement of each other carried us with strength. Her mere presence seemed to affirm that whatever I wanted was possible. We spent many hours out in the mountains, at the lake communing with nature, and hiking up to rocks and other remote places to do our homework.

During this year, and for a few months, I had my first boyfriend. Bart, who was two years my senior, had been a football and basketball star at our school and had graduated the year before.

Our first and only "date" was going to a friend of Bart's house. We went there with Mary, a close friend of mine, and her boyfriend. Bart brought beer and even with my aversion to alcohol, I drank with them. I liked Bart and wanted him to like me back. Since it was my first time drinking, after a few cans I was quite intoxicated. Mary and her boyfriend eventually went into a bedroom and left Bart and me alone. I wasn't sure what to do at that point. I didn't know what one did on a date, especially with someone older than I. Too inebriated to talk with clear coherency, I figured all he probably wanted was to have sex. I had just finished my period, so I knew I would be safe. (We didn't talk much about sexually-transmitted diseases back then.) So, I allowed him to kiss me. We began on the couch, and then after a while he led me into the bedroom where we continued. I could hear the bed in the other room banging against the wall and felt embarrassed by it. It appeared that Bart didn't seem comfortable either, because shortly after the banging began, he said he wanted to take me home.

The next day he told Mary that he didn't want to see me again because he didn't like that I got so drunk. She explained that I had never drunk beer before and didn't know what I was doing. She assured him that I had more class than it appeared, and that he should give me another chance.

The next week he came over to my home, and we watched TV and talked. We had a very nice time and decided to begin to see each other. I was so honored that someone of his "caliber" would want a relationship with me that I didn't hear him when he told me that while he was seeing me, he was also waiting to hear if Anne, his previous girlfriend (whom I didn't know well, but in passing had experienced as rather unfriendly and not interested in much more than herself), was going to move back from living in Hawaii. He told me that if she returned he would likely go back with her.

This being my first relationship, I wasn't sure how things were supposed to go. There were a fair amount of tender moments with Bart; he seemed to truly like me. But I also felt ambivalence from him. This was confusing and didn't sit well with me. Then, sure enough, after a few months Anne came back and he dropped me like a hot potato. I felt sad because I quite liked him and my ego was bruised, but he *had* warned me. After shedding some tears, I came to the realization that if Bart really wanted to drop me to be with someone like Anne, then they deserved each other. This outlook helped me get over the hump, so to speak.

Later that year, I developed a friendship with Jake, the younger brother of Sam, the one with whom I regretfully lost my virginity. There was a point when we considered getting into a relationship (he was actually a very nice person), but eventually I realized that my real motivation was to try to heal what had happened between his brother and me. I believe that was part of his motivation as well. He had been very apologetic for what his brother had done. We both realized in time that we didn't have a real spark between us, and so we didn't continue exploring a relationship. We did, however, remain friendly and this was in and of itself healing.

PEBBLE

This was the beginning of my healing what had happened with Sam. From my experience with Bart, I learned that just because someone is popular or handsome doesn't mean they will treat you well.

Although it didn't feel good being dumped, I understood that Bart's choice to leave was about him and not about me. It felt good to know this. And though I had not yet fully wrapped my mind around personal responsibility, with this insight about Bart I began to vaguely see how some of the choices I had made (including choosing to be with someone who was waiting for someone else) caused things to happen that were not pleasant. This was an important pebble to begin to build on.

As I continued to stay open and curious, I felt better and better about myself, and although nothing monumental happened in my junior year, I felt that I was gradually healing.

ADDENDUM

Here is a note on how healing events of the past can take just one weekend. Recently (and after I wrote this chapter and pebble), I went to my thirty-third high school reunion. Because our classes were so small, ten years of graduating classes were included. I spoke with several people I hadn't seen or talked to since high school. In chatting with my old schoolmates, it was glaringly apparent that during our school experience, many of the students were going through very difficult times—from family members dying, to getting kicked out of their homes, to rape, to abortion. I even spoke with Bart. I was laughing with him and another classmate while telling my story that Bart was my first boyfriend and that he had dumped me. I no longer felt bad about it and could talk about it as if it were a story that happened to someone else. After the other person left, Bart looked at me squarely and said, "I didn't dump you."

I said laughing, "Sure you did. But it's okay, Bart."

Again, more seriously than before, he said, "I didn't dump you."

Later that night as I went through the evening in my mind, recalling all the stories I had heard, I realized that it seemed to be important to Bart to let me know that he had not dumped me, and that moved me. It occurred to me that there was evidently another side to the story, and I decided that if I saw Bart again, I would ask him to give me his version of what happened.

Sure enough, the next night of the reunion I saw Bart, and I walked straight to him. I was not going to let this opportunity slip past. I told him I was surprised to hear what he had said the previous night and asked that he tell me, from his perspective, what had happened. He looked a bit hesitant, and I assured him that I truly wanted to know his side of it. He complied and told me that several things were at play back then. His father had recently died, Anne had broken his heart before I came into the picture, and his closest friends were giving him a hard time about dating me. He went on to say that he felt conflicted because he liked me very much, but he didn't know how to deal with everything that was going on. He admitted that he didn't handle things well with me, but what was most important to him was that I know he had liked me and that he was sorry.

After hearing this story and all the other tragic and challenging stories from others, it occurred to me that as children we have profound experiences that shape our lives and who we are. We think we know why they happened. We think we know why people do what they do, but actually we don't. We have only our limited perception. Many of the difficult stories I heard were from people I didn't necessarily like when I was in high school. Yet in hearing their tales, I came to a place of absolution and real inner peace with them. We were all doing the best we could, given our circumstances and our perspectives. This even applies to Sam and the many students who constantly picked on me in school. I know that Sam had a very hard life and had virtually no adult supervision. I now understand why he acted in such a hurtful way, and I feel compassion for those I believe treated me poorly and release any residual negative thoughts.

Another person apologized to me at the reunion—the student who chose me in *The Dating Game*. He felt bad that I might still be hurt and/or holding a grudge. He said that he was actually quite shy back then and didn't know how to deal with the situation. He knew he didn't handle the game well and apologized for whatever pain his actions caused.

PEBBLE

These insights have proven to me that many of the painful experiences I have written about had very little to do with me—except, of course, the feelings that I carried away. This has brought me a new sense of freedom. As I sit here now, any pain I had in the recesses of my mind that was associated with these experiences has been, by and large, healed.

Chapter Nine

THE MIRACLE OF LOVE

∽

*S*hortly after the start of my senior year I began to date Trent, an African American, who was very handsome and intelligent. He was new at the school and was unaware of my experience with Sam. With the strength I had begun to develop, and with his lack of knowledge of my past, I felt as if I had a blank canvas with him. We dated for a few months and had some very nice times together. He was kind and vibrant and he treated me with respect. He opened doors for me and was authentically interested in what I thought and what I liked, and he didn't attempt to push me into having sex right off the bat.

His father liked me and I liked him too, but my father had a problem with the color of Trent's skin. I can remember the day I brought him home after school to meet my father. I walked in the front door with Trent behind me. My father was standing just inside the front door, ready to greet me. But as I went to hug him with all the excitement of having him meet a boy I was interested in, I watched his smile fade and his face turn ashen as he saw Trent. I introduced them anyway then motioned to Trent to follow me into the living room so that we could talk for a while. It was obvious to Trent that my father wasn't happy with me, and after a short time he said he thought he should go. The moment Trent left, my father informed me that I could have a "colored person" as a friend, but not as a boyfriend. I protested, proclaiming that there was absolutely no difference between us, but his resolve was unrelenting. Given my father's background (growing up in the deep south, and some of his family members still referring to African-Americans as n****rs) I understood why he said what he did. From his perspective, I'm certain he felt it was for my own good, but I resented the prejudice and secretly saw Trent for a while longer until the tension became too challenging for us to deal with. We came to the mutual decision that because of my father's feelings and the resentment it was causing for Trent, it was best that we stop seeing each other, though we remained friends.

Late in autumn, nestled in a sweater with frost encircling my breath, wonder of all wonders and as a gift from God, I fell in love. I remember the first moment I saw Fernando; he felt like…home. It was as if I were looking into a mirror at another aspect of myself. He was so familiar and exquisitely beautiful to me. He was a foreign exchange student from Guadalajara, and I exuberantly volunteered to teach him English. The depth and sweetness of our friendship was something I cherished from the moment we began spending time together.

We had our first and only misunderstanding a month or so after we met. It was just before Christmas vacation, and I was going to visit my mother. I was sad to leave and wanted Fernando to know that I really liked him. I didn't know how to show him, so I bought him a pen. (Laugh you might, but it was made of wood and quite beautiful.) I gave it to him sincerely with a hug goodbye. After three weeks of torture at not being able to see him, I came back to find him pursuing another girl. I was crushed! As a result of the language barrier, he misunderstood my goodbye and thought I was moving away. To my delight the girl he liked wasn't interested in him (I never understood how that could be and thought she must be blind, but was grateful for it!), and we quickly resumed our budding romance.

One night after a month or so, we were sitting next to each other in front of the fireplace at the home where he was staying. As we gazed into a low-burning fire, listening to Roberta Flack on the radio singing "The First Time Ever I Saw Your Face," I began to feel something happening inside me. I didn't know what it was until I looked into his eyes. At that moment I felt my heart open so wide that I thought it would burst out of my chest. While feeling this sensation and falling into his eyes, I realized that I had entered into the glorious, joyous state of being "In Love" and told him that I loved him. He looked as if someone had just handed him a million dollars. His eyes glowed as he said, "Donna, I love you, too," and we kissed tenderly. A few minutes later he slowly took the gold ring that he always wore and deliberately placed it on the ring finger of my right hand. With joy-filled tears in my eyes, I asked, "Where is this ring from?"

"It's my family ring," he said. "I want you to wear it." And I collapsed into his arms.

I clearly remember having the feeling that what I was experiencing was a *true* miracle, and that my life would never be the same.

Now that I was older and able to take care of my brother at home, my father began to travel again. He was not around much and so he never met Fernando. I also had no idea if my father would accept him or reject him as he did Trent, so when he was around, I wasn't going to take a chance he'd find out we were dating.

The next few months, we were inseparable. I could hardly live a moment without him. This was the greatest journey of human joy that I had known, and I fully immersed myself in its magic. Our first time making love was sweet and comical. I was only somewhat experienced in sex, and he was a virgin. He had no idea how to move, and I was too shy to tell him what to do. His body was completely rigid as he floundered around and I blushed, not knowing what to say. He was bewildered but open, and eventually we both saw humor in the moment and laughed, after which he loosened up. We found our way through and entered into the world of being lovers.

The next months were bittersweet. I had many wonderful times with both Fernando and Laura—loving, laughing, dancing…living, but this period also had its challenges.

In late winter my father moved to Southern California. He could not find work locally and decided to leave Nate and me alone at The Lake to finish out the school year. (Stuart had moved to Los Angeles for college years before.) He sent us money from time to time, and I had a part-time job at the local Hallmark store to bring in more. Always there for me, Laura showed up at my doorstep on many occasions with groceries in her arms and a smile on her face. Although we ran in separate circles, Nate and I were very close to one another, as we always had been, and during the next few months we depended heavily on each other for strength.

With the encouragement of a friend's mother, I entered a preliminary Miss America pageant. I was told that she had called the Miss America office to have a pageant started in our hometown so that I could participate in it. I felt flattered by this but it didn't feel like…me. The secure part of me didn't like the idea of being put on stage in that way, but at the same time the insecure part of me was attracted to it, so I agreed to be a contestant.

My mother had won a beauty pageant when she was young, and so I wanted her to come and watch me. She could not afford to come to both the pageant and my high school graduation, so I had to make a choice. I figured my father would only attend my graduation, so I asked her to come to my pageant. I hoped she would see me win, just as she had won so many years before.

What an experience the pageant was! Some who I thought were uninterested in me turned out to be wonderful allies, like the participant who knew I was coming straight from work to the rehearsal and brought me a plate of food for dinner; and some who I thought were allies turned out to be unfaithful and unethical. I overheard the president of the local woman's association that sponsored the pageant tell the judges after my preliminary interview that I was not serious about going to college, that instead of focusing on my studies in my senior year, I was working after school and on weekends. The thing was, not only did my brother and I need the money I earned from working, but I also worked for her in her store! It was painful to be the brunt of such underhandedness and malice. I had had a feeling that she wanted another girl to win the competition, but I had no idea she would resort to this. Still, I gave it my all. It made me more determined to do my very best. I borrowed a bathing suit from a friend's mother —one that looked "Miss America-ish," and another friend made me a beautiful gown. For my talent I sang "Sunshine on my Shoulders" while wearing a cowboy hat and boots and a western blouse that I wore years before when I had a job at the Ponderosa Ranch. When I think back, I smile at my innocence in my dressing up in "country" clothes to mirror John Denver and his song.

Well, I didn't win and I didn't place, but my mother was there and very proud of me regardless. Even though the nights were filled with alcoholic storms, I appreciated her coming to see the pageant. It was nice to feel her support as well as the undying encouragement I always felt from Bill, Laura, Fernando, and Nate. Many may not have loved me, but a few loved me very much.

It was disappointing and embarrassing to lose in front of my peers and the community, but I also realized, at some level, that I was in the pageant for the wrong reasons. I had hoped this event would be a vehicle to heal residual pain from my early high school years and to earn respect from those with whom I still had various issues. But of course I could not have found it there, even if I had won.

Summer was quickly approaching, and Fernando would soon be returning to Guadalajara. The harshness of this reality weighed heavily on me. I could not imagine living without him, but I also had no idea how to keep our relationship going with us living in different countries.

Around that time, the car my father had left for us was repossessed. Nate and I had no way to get around and had to walk or rely on friends to drive us.

Everything that was happening contributed to a deep sense that the end of something big was coming, and even though I desperately wanted to hold on so that my life would stay the same, it all seemed to be falling away.

Our vice-principal, Mr. Corley, was a godsend during this period, as were my friends. He somehow knew that my brother and I were struggling and he kept a watchful eye on us, mostly me. Sometimes it was a look, sometimes a word (or a few of them), but his love-filled firmness always kept me on my toes and in line. I knew he cared for my well-being, and I was grateful.

When graduation day arrived, for a reason that I cannot recall, my father didn't make it. So there I was with Nate and Fernando watching, and with Laura at my side, on the celebration of our biggest accomplishment. I felt so much pride, so much disappointment, and so much sadness that day, but with the strength of love that surrounded me, how could I pity myself? The one man I thanked that day was Mr. Corley. I acknowledged his importance in my life and thanked him for caring for me. I knew that he was a large part of my success in graduating.

With the end of school came the completion of this chapter of my life. During one of our last outings together, Fernando and I declared our everlasting love for one another and made promises to keep in touch. I returned his family ring that I had so lovingly worn, and we cried in each other's arms. The day he left, I thought my world had ended. My beloved had gone, and I was about to move away from Laura and The Lake down to Southern California.

PEBBLE

Falling in love with Fernando was more like a diamond than a pebble. I feel now, as I felt then, a deep gratitude that my heart was able to experience such a thing, and "do" such a thing! I had loved another person with my entire heart and soul. This was truly one of the most profound experiences I have ever had, and I am eternally grateful and feel graced to have had it.

Another byproduct of my experience of romantic love was the realization that this "personal" love was the physical manifestation of the "impersonal" and all-pervading Love that I had always sensed in the unseen world. I therefore understood that it was also eternal and unending. I knew that the love we created together would never die and would live forever in my being, as it thrives now with my telling. Loving Fernando became an affirmation of the power that Love has, whether it be romantic, familial, or platonic—to change a life, to heal a heart, and to create color in a world of black and white.

∽

Looking back over my first eighteen years, I see that what changed my life then, and continues to guide me still, is a combination of my inner knowing, my day-to-day choices, and last, but most of all—Love.

Chapter Ten

LIFE ON PLANET SCA

∽

$\mathcal{S}$hortly after graduation, Stuart had come to fetch Nate and me. We all crammed into a U-Haul truck with our dog, Prince, and left our beloved lake. The drive was a sad one. Even if I had tried, I couldn't have kept my thoughts away from the boy I so cherished. How was I to go on living without him? How was I supposed to let go of something so immensely powerful? How was I going to get through the grief I felt in losing that kind of love? Would I always feel the agony and nausea that seemed to engulf me?

Then I began to worry about how Prince would live in a city. Prince, who was a mixture of Alaskan malamute and collie, had been our dog for four years. He had grown up in the mountains in a sparsely populated area. He was high-spirited and not good around cars. He proved this on many occasions when cars would come down our street and he would chase after them, barking at their tires. Sure enough, while staying in a motel our first night in Orange County, he ran off. We found him a few days later in a dog pound, and I assumed we would bring him to our new home in Irvine. At the pound, however, my father informed us that it would be better if we left him there for someone else to take home. He explained that because we only had a small patio in the back where we were moving, Prince would likely escape again, and given that our new place was next to a major thoroughfare, he expressed concern that Prince might get hit by a car. I felt crushed by what he was saying and protested. "Why can't we rent a home with a yard?

We can't just leave him here! We've had him his whole life." I argued to no avail. In the end, my father's rationale won as he assured us that someone else would adopt him.

As we all began to walk out of the kennel, I stopped to look back at Prince. Through my tears, I saw him sitting in his cage looking at me with his princely smile and his golden coat. Then he anxiously put his paw up on the cage door as if to say, "Where are you going? Aren't you going to take me with you?" I didn't know what to do. My father was supposed to know what was best, but leaving Prince there felt so harsh and inhumane. I began to open my mouth in protest again, but in a moment realized that my arguing would do no good. I said a forlorn goodbye and cried hard as we left. It still wrenches my heart not knowing if he was adopted or put to sleep.

I cried for months after moving away from Tahoe. My life held no joy as I mourned the life and loved ones I had left behind. I kept my love alive by writing to Fernando the depths of what I felt for him and about my new life. I called Laura often to connect and catch up.

Each day I would take a deep breath as I looked on my bedroom wall at my favorite poster of bright yellow lemons dropping onto a man's spigot-shaped head, quoting the proverb, "When life gives you lemons, make lemonade." I knew I would have to "make lemonade" if I was to bring happiness into my life again. At some point I began to adopt this attitude, and I started to understand that it was far better to have loved Fernando and lost him than to not have loved. In time, I began to make friends and create a new life for myself.

One of my first friends in the neighborhood was named Virginia. She was in her seventies or eighties and lived alone. She seemed like a jolly grandmother, and I grew very fond of her. We spent many hours talking and telling stories to each other while sharing tea or hot cocoa. I still smile thinking about her and what a gentle soul she was.

My father was encouraging me to look at continuing my education, and although I agreed with this in theory, I was apprehensive. Much of my high school experience was neither pleasant nor useful, to my reckoning anyway. I saw very little application for what I had learned. I could not understand how dissecting a frog would further me in life, nor did I see how learning shorthand would contribute to my long-term success. And even though I had no evidence to the contrary, I felt that the "history" I had been taught was very one-sided and therefore not true. I remember often asking myself, *What is the meaning of all this?* In addition, I was very shy speaking in public and was not good at reading out loud, so of course I was called upon often to read. My stumbling over words only confirmed my opinion that I was not a good reader. I scarcely studied and cared very little about school. I knew it was important to get good grades and therefore applied myself just enough to get by. Needless to say, even though I graduated with a B- average, I didn't feel good about my educational experience or what I thought my level of intelligence was. I felt dumb, and that encouraged negative thoughts about my abilities.

Despite those feelings, my father wanted to see me get a college degree (no one in our family had ever earned one). He said that even though I couldn't see it, getting an education was important to my future. At his insistence, I applied to the University of California at Irvine but got a letter back stating that I didn't have a high enough GPA to get accepted. They suggested that I attend a junior college and work my way up from there. After a fair amount of contemplation, I concluded that I needed to create a new life for myself and this was as good a way as any to begin. So I enrolled at our local junior college, taking on a full load and throwing myself into my schoolwork.

From time to time, Stuart brought his friends around. Some I had known from Tahoe, and some were new to me. One day he brought Daniel to our home. He was a nice young Russian man between Stuart's age and mine. Stuart and Daniel worked in the parts department at a local car dealership. Daniel was quick to laugh and had a kind way about him. During their visit, I overheard a conversation about a party they were going to in Laguna Beach and begged for them to take me. I had never gone to a party with my "big brother" before, so this was a major request. Stuart reluctantly caved in with a little help from Daniel's encouragement, and I quickly got myself dressed up as "cool" as I knew how. We all piled into Stuart's pickup truck, with Daniel and me in the back, and made the trek through Laguna canyon. It was a wonderful drive in the warm California air, getting to know Daniel while gazing upon the beautiful Canyon.

We found the home nestled in the hills. I was struck with the beauty of the spacious-looking, two-story home with its numerous large windows and myriad lights. I noted a fountain and the lush surroundings and thought, "They must be artists or something. I'll bet they're really interesting!" Excitedly, I hopped out of the truck and waited for my brother to lead the way. We walked into a loud room full of people dancing and drinking. What a scene—I was in awe of how remarkable all the men and women looked. Never had I seen so many tan, beautiful people in one place before. Many of them were scantly clad and in black. I scanned the room and it appeared that they all had tight bodies and the women had beautifully made-up faces. Daniel asked if I wanted to dance. This was music to my ears given that I absolutely love to dance, and I hadn't done so since I graduated from high school. I eagerly nodded yes and began to move my body to the sounds and with the energy in the room. As we were dancing, I continued to look around to take in everything when all at once I realized that the beautiful women...weren't women. All the people in the room, except me, as far as I could see, were men. I looked at my brother with surprise and exclaimed, "Stuart, these are all guys!" Evidently, he had noticed the same thing in the same moment. Looking stunned, he called out to Daniel, "I think we should go," and then made a motion to leave. We made our way out of the house, in shock from what we had just seen. As we got to the car, we all broke out laughing. Being from Tahoe, I had just barely heard of gay men and didn't even know if they really existed. Certainly I had never met anyone who was gay (that I knew of). Stuart and Daniel laughed about how embarrassed they felt. I watched them and laughed out of discomfort at not understanding the world we had just walked into. As I was laughing, though, I remember feeling that something inside me wanted to understand "gay" and not just throw them out of my realm of what should be accepted. I sensed that this lifestyle was just a smattering of many lifestyle choices that I would see in Southern California, and that the more accepting and at peace I could be with others' choices and our differences, the better.

PEBBLE

This was my initiation to the new planet called Southern California where the lifestyle felt like being in the fast lane or at a 24-hour amusement park. Everything was fast—drivers didn't seem to know the speed limit, and even the pedestrians all seemed to be in a hurry. I remember often thinking, "Where is everybody going?" Then there was the wide array of colors, sizes, shapes, and styles of the people, and the myriad ways that they chose to express themselves, from the homeless man yelling at a tree, to the Angelyne in her slinky pink attire, to the Newport Beach residents privileged in their Porsches, Izod shirts, and diamonds, to the surfers and their bleached-out hair living for the next big wave, to the Buddhist monk walking down the street in his saffron-colored robes. It all seemed so much larger than life. Of course, my naïveté and ignorance were quickly cured, living among this wonderful variety of people and belief systems that made up such a place.

Chapter Eleven

THE PROVERBIAL REBOUND

∽

*A*fter a few months I began to spend more time with Stuart's friend, Daniel. I was still very much in love with Fernando and felt a terrible emptiness. I felt I was not yet ready to move on to another relationship, but as the weeks went on and we saw each other more regularly, Daniel wanted us to become more than friends. One day, we were alone at my father's home talking and hanging out when the topic turned more serious. He said he wanted to be closer with me…and he wanted to have sex. I tried to explain that I believed I wasn't ready to have sex with someone else, but he felt he knew better. "You have to move on, Donna. You've been sad for six months."

"I know Daniel, but I just don't feel ready."

"Come on. It'll be fun," he reasoned.

"I don't know. I just…"

"Please?" And with each minute that passed I felt his questions turn into pleading. Against my better judgment, I conceded, and thus began my first "rebound relationship."

Spending time with Daniel seemed to somewhat help ease the pain of missing Fernando. We went camping and to car races; we had outings at the beach and took day trips up and down the coast. We also traveled fairly often to Woodland Hills to spend time with my mother. Even though I felt ambivalent about being with him, we slowly began to function more and more like a couple. I even began to include Daniel in family events and holidays.

We had fun together, but in the two years we dated I never fell in love with him. He was in love with me, though, which in time made being with him harder and harder. I liked him, but my strongest feeling for him was one of friendship and reciprocity for his generosity and love. I had not yet learned how to tell a man the truth when I knew it wasn't something he wanted to hear, so I chose to stay with him out of obligation. I wanted to say to him, "Daniel, you're a great guy, but we aren't cut from the same cloth." Although very sweet and accommodating to my wishes (probably too much so), he was all about racecars and parties. Instead, I wanted someone strong and deep and solid.

In time, I became very unhappy, and as an attempt to create distance between Daniel and me, I began to have affairs. I knew what I was doing was unethical, but I didn't know what else to do. For seven months I lost myself again (as I did at age sixteen) while I lived a double life—going from man to man, hiding my every move from Daniel. At one point I think I was dating seven men. It became easier for me to have affairs and lie about it than to tell Daniel the truth about my lack of love for him.

PEBBLE

One of the pebbles from this experience painfully rattled around in my shoe for years. It was not until fairly recently that I was able to lovingly place it on my path and leave it behind. The first wound of love was very deep, as it usually is for most people. This wound set a pattern in my life where I yearned for the unattainable, or, stated differently, where I believed that any man I felt deeply passionate about would somehow be unattainable. Either way you look at it, I was set up to lose. It was not unlike yearning for my father when he left us as children for his business trips, crying night after night for him to tuck me in, then resigning myself to the fact that I would just have to comfort myself to sleep. These two are not unconnected. But even though my father's lack of presence was painful, not being able to live out my love with Fernando cut even deeper, or at least that is how it felt. There is a lot to be said for healing old wounds (a pebble), for as you will see much further down the path, I continued to live out this wound over and over and over again.

Add to this my fear and unwillingness to tell the whole truth so as not to disappoint others, as well as my ability to have affairs, and you have a recipe for disaster. It was as if I was walking down a path of thousands of tiny marbles under my feet…not a travel-friendly path.

Chapter Twelve

MY FIVE LIVES

∽

$\mathcal{E}$arly in my nineteenth year, Laura invited me up to visit her in Tahoe and I stayed with her and her roommate, Larry, for a few days. I felt I needed to be free from Daniel if only for a week, and I jumped at the chance to get away. During my stay, I had an experience that had a big impact on me. One night Larry and another friend, Beth, wanted to go to the other side of the lake to go dancing. I didn't particularly want to go and decided to stay with Laura and instead go dancing with her. Later that night, Larry and Beth got into a head-on collision. They came out of it alive, although deeply cut and bruised, but the car was destroyed. When I learned of their accident, I was hit hard with the realization that this was the fifth time I had been "saved" from being hurt or seriously injured, if not killed.

The first was at age five when I was playing on the center divider rope of a pool. I lost my grip and began to drown, drinking in water as my arms flailed. Luckily, my brother Stuart was close by. He saw what was happening and saved me.

The second time was when I was around seventeen and was being driven by a friend of my father's from Redding to Tahoe. It was nighttime. The friend was passing a truck and hadn't given herself enough time to get around it before being overcome by an oncoming car. When she slammed on her brakes, her Ford Ranchero pickup began to fishtail. I remember feeling utter terror seeing the headlights barrel down upon us from the front and seeing huge truck tires going full force directly to my right. I don't know how it happened, but at the last moment everything passed us by and we were unharmed. Although deeply shaken by the experience, I had a feeling that we, by all intents and purposes, should not have survived and felt that we had somehow been protected.

The third experience was with Laura when we were eighteen. We were driving from Reno to South Lake Tahoe to go see some friends of ours who were playing in a band. I was driving her Volkswagen Bug, doing about sixty mph. As I was coming around a large bend, I saw a car off to my right that was supposed to be stopping at a stop sign before coming onto the highway...only it wasn't stopping. The car began to pull out in front of us to turn left onto the highway. When I saw the car, I froze. I saw what was about to happen, but was unable to move my arms to react. Laura saw what was happening, yelled "No!" and before I knew it, took hold of the steering wheel and swerved around the car just in time. As we passed the car, I realized that if not for Laura, her Volkswagen would have gotten demolished and we would probably have died. I thanked her and pulled over to let her drive.

The fourth experience was when I was nineteen. I was boogie boarding and got disoriented when a wave came crashing down on top of me and pulled me under. Struggling to reach the surface, I kicked and kicked in an attempt to find the ocean floor. Eventually, I exhausted myself and ran out of air. The struggle drained out of me and I let go as I saw my life beginning to end. I felt my lungs ready to drink in the all-encompassing water and surrendered. Without realizing it, in my letting go I began to float to the surface. As I began to breathe in water, I felt a cool breeze on my face and I lifted my head out of the ocean, gasping and coughing. Exhausted and frightened, I limply swam back to shore and collapsed onto the beach.

PEBBLE

All five experiences of narrow escape had their impact on me, but the last made the strongest impression. It was as if I finally received a message that someone or something wanted me to understand: that I was meant to do more before I die, and this is why I was still alive.. It was not the thought that I must be so special that some great, unseen force was sent to protect me. It was more like: Wow… I've been given another chance to live…Perhaps I have something to do before I leave this planet…I should get to it. With this realization, I consciously chose life, to look for more meaning, and to be safer.

This realization stayed with me for a long time, and I relished the gift of being able to continue living…though I had no idea yet what to do with it.

Chapter Thirteen

A FATHER'S HOLD

∽

*W*hile up in Tahoe, Laura and I talked about her moving down to Southern California. She wanted to move there to go to school and be close to me. I found a great little apartment on Balboa Island and made arrangements to move in so that we could fulfill one of our dreams and live together. But when I told my father, he said emphatically, "Absolutely not."

"But I really want to move in with her!" I pleaded.

"Why do you want to move in with her?" The tone of his voice made me think that he was taking my request personally.

"Because she's my best friend and we want to have a place of our own."

"You don't have the money," he said, shaking his head.

"I have a job."

"You're not ready." Something made me think that *he* wasn't ready. "You're not old enough or experienced enough to live on your own."

"I *am* ready. I'm eighteen," I tried to reason, feeling myself begin to falter.

"No, you're not ready." Again, I sensed that it was he who wasn't equipped to let me go.

"Dad, *please!*" I said, pleading for his blessing. Although I didn't technically need my father's approval, I could not imagine leaving home without it.

Then he pulled out a new strategy that stunned me. With a threatening look, he said, "Remember, I'm the only father you have." I took this to mean that if I moved in with Laura, he would disown me as he had my older half-brother. I was devastated. I felt the energy drain out of my feet and as if duck tape had just been securely placed over my mouth. I desperately wanted to live with Laura, and with a little help I had the money to do so but didn't know how to stand up to him. So, I acquiesced to his will…again. I felt like I was in a cage. I judged myself as weak and saw my situation hopeless.

Reluctantly and sadly, I called Laura to tell her that I couldn't live with her. Understandably, she was very unhappy with this news. She had already made arrangements to move and couldn't alter her plans. I couldn't leave her hanging, so I put out the word to everyone I knew to find a roommate for her. Someone I worked with was looking to move out from her boyfriend's home and agreed to be Laura's roommate. Soon after, they moved in together, having never met.

Laura forgave me, like the saint she was, and I helped her move in. It was a rocky beginning, but eventually she settled into her new life on Balboa Island. It was a great place for two nineteen-year-olds to sun and play. We took full advantage of the California weather—and the men—and opened fully to the wild and crazy adventures presented to us. We had barbecues, went to nightclubs to listen to music, and we danced.

PEBBLE

Although thrilling in many ways, my eighteenth and nineteenth years were challenging to live through, and surprisingly, this period has been very difficult now to write about.

Being desired by many men and seeing several men simultaneously temporarily fed my searching ego. And even though it was exciting for me to see these men secretly (in a perverted way, this helped me feel in control and it allowed me to rebel against my father), I didn't feel good about what I was doing to Daniel, and this further eroded my respect for myself.

Clearly, I was struggling between what was perhaps the best thing to do—leave my father and Daniel and move in with Laura; or do the safe thing and stay. I had not yet begun to understand the hold my father had on me. Even though I knew he was flawed, I loved him, as most girls love their fathers. He was the only strong male presence I had. But I also feared him. I was desperately afraid of displeasing him and possibly losing him as a father, and this fear transferred into my relationships and into most aspects of my life. I felt that what I needed and wanted didn't matter to him, and because of this, I felt that I must somehow not deserve what I desired. As a result I had not learned to stand up straight and pursue what I yearned for. What was expected of me, as far as I could see, was that I was to simply follow my father's lead, however misguided, and remain in want, relying on his pity from my emotional manipulation to get what I wanted. But then pity didn't always work, so I found another way—doing things secretly and sometimes taking quite a chance, like having sex with Daniel in our open patio just outside where my father was watching television. I felt the stakes were getting much higher and more dangerous, yet didn't know how to approach change.

Given that I had not yet begun a life of self-reflection, I was unaware that the experiences from these last two chapters were opportunities to awaken me to the option of choosing my own life. They kept being lovingly offered to me, but I was unaware of their presence and I didn't take the baton, so to speak. As Grace would have it, soon I would be given another chance to make a shift in my consciousness, and I would take it.

Chapter Fourteen

HELPING HANDS

∽

$\mathcal{L}$aura and I spent more and more time together. As always, her inherent goodness and presence helped ground me. With Laura, I felt that I was *home*. She knew my depth, my desires, and my secrets, and she also understood my struggles with my father and mother, which was freeing. We lived on the wild side, and in some ways we lived on the edge, but even as we did so we lived in deep love for each other: the love of sisterhood.

It was during this time that I first recognized my ability to help someone other than a member of my family. Growing up, I was the one Nate always came to when he wasn't feeling well. Usually, I would simply rub his back or stroke his face, and he would feel better. My father also asked me to rub his back from time to time. I never thought twice about it. I just knew my touch helped them.

Laura had periodic headaches and would ask me to put my hands on her to help her with the pain. I don't recall when it was established that I could help her in this way, but I was always happy to be asked, and usually after a few minutes of massage her pain would decrease. One night, we were in her apartment with a few friends, and she said that her head felt like it was going to split in two. She begged me to get rid of her pain. I said sure and casually sat next to her, massaging her neck and shoulders in places I felt would help. After a few minutes she thanked me and said that all the pain had gone. I didn't give these interactions much thought, but I did come away from the experiences with the knowledge that something about my touch could help "heal" people.

PEBBLE

This is a priceless pebble. It is clear to me that even through my wild times, Spirit was working through me and inviting me into another realm of awareness. It was largely from my experiences with Laura and others that I would much later welcome the notion that love is a healer, or more specifically, that my love heals.

I find it fascinating that these experiences were not happening while I had a clear head and a clear heart or while I was in meditation or in contemplation. I was all over the place...literally. They were happening simultaneously with my confusion, my frustration, my searching, and with no consciousness around them.

Spirit is now, and always has been, right here moving through me, whether I have been aware of its presence or not, whether I think I deserve it or not, and even though I may not have had the consciousness to understand what was going on, or why.

I now clearly see that if we can be present to what is happening around us, or through us, in the moment, eventually the puzzle pieces will all fit together. It may take moments, days—or as in my case, years—but they will come together...in a profound way. We must simply be aware...and patient. Being willing is also helpful, but not a requirement.

Chapter Fifteen

PIANO MAN

∽

*A*round this time I also began to feel strongly that I had to break up with Daniel and wondered how to do it. One night in October of 1977, I decided to go out with Laura and her boyfriend to listen to music. She had heard that there was a great band playing at the Studio Café, a little restaurant and jazz club at the base of the pier on the Balboa Peninsula. Little did I know, as we rode the ferry across the channel, that my life was about to be transformed.

We walked into the dimly lit club and took our seats in three short director's chairs around a small table. It was a comfortable place—natural wood decor with plants throughout and conversation surrounding us—and we settled in and ordered our drinks. The band was on break, so we talked to pass the time. After about ten minutes, three band members walked over to the corner where a piano, drum set, and bass were huddled. They began their first song, and as they played it felt as if their music was emanating from my own heart. I had never heard anything like it, nor had I ever had a response like this to music. Similar to the classical music experience I had as a child, the music was deeply moving, but this also felt *intimate*. I sat back in my chair with my eyes closed, and I felt the pianist's fingers, the drummer's rhythms, and the bassist's strings running through my being. Moved and inspired, I asked our waitress the name of the band and found out that they called themselves Odyssey.

"Odyssey," I thought, "How perfect. A fitting name for such a talented group of jazz musicians."

It was quite late, but we stayed until they ended their set. My mind was dominated by one thought—I had to meet the pianist. I needed to see what kind of man could create such beauty. As the band finished, they walked out into the audience, and I eagerly approached the pianist and introduced myself to him. He introduced himself as Sean and began to answer my questions about his music. I asked if he supported himself solely by playing music. He said that he augmented his income by teaching piano. As I heard this, my mind and heart reeled. I had always wanted to play the piano but never had the opportunity. After taking a deep breath, I heard myself say, "Yes!" and I asked him for his phone number.

I called him the next day and asked when I could have my first lesson. He asked if I had a piano, and I said no. He said I would need to be able to practice if I were to take lessons. I thought for a moment and said that I would ask if I could practice on the piano at the Methodist church we had been attending. This sounded acceptable to him, and he agreed to teach me. He seemed authentic and friendly and his warmth came through the phone. I remember liking the sound of his voice—slightly deep and rough. We talked for a while longer and eventually set up a time to meet the following week.

I was very excited to go to my first lesson. I showed up at his small, two-bedroom home on Balboa Island ready to jump in. I wanted to fill my own heart the way his music so brilliantly had the night I met him. The lesson went very well. It turned out I was a quick learner, and I was thrilled when he began to teach me one of my then-favorite piano songs, the theme to the movie, *The Sting.*

After the lesson, we decided to take a walk around the island together. The day was warm and breezy, and as it softly tossed our hair we talked—all of it feeling oddly familiar and comfortable. At one point, I began to talk about my love for the mountains. "I miss them so much." I sighed.

"So, you're a hick, huh?"

"No! I'm a mountain girl! I can read as well as write," I answered with a smirk. He laughed.

"Don't mess with me, I have brothers," I threatened lightheartedly. I noticed how much I liked his gray-blue eyes, full lips, and genuine grin.

Later, as we continued our walk together, I noticed a cozy-looking home on the waterfront, with abundant plants growing around it, natural wood beams, large bay windows, and a huge fireplace inside.

"I like that house. I'd like to live in a place like that," I said.

"It's a nice one, isn't it? It reminds me of some of the homes near my parents' place in Alaska."

"You lived there?" I asked, interested.

"Yes. For ten years my family lived there," he said, still gazing at the home.

"Oh, so you're a mountain boy!" I teased.

"Why, I guess I am." He said with a chuckle.

"So you love the mountains, too?"

"Yes, I do. I like to camp." This was like music to my deprived ears.

Even with our age difference (he was six years my senior), we seemed to see many things similarly and our conversation flowed easily. After a couple of hours, we somehow got on the subject of massage, and we lightheartedly flirted as he showed me the canal surrounding the island and other houses he liked. We sat on a small pier and continued our conversation about massage. At some point, he asked nonchalantly, "Would you like to go back to my place and play with some oils?" I blushed. Shyly, I said yes, and we spent our first evening together.

This was the beginning of a grand love affair that spanned almost ten years, and a deep and abiding friendship that has continued another fifteen years.

Once I began a relationship with Sean, I could no longer see Daniel, or anyone else. In my eyes, Sean was one of the most extraordinary people I had ever met, and I could no longer divide my affections. So one day I called Daniel over to my home, and although I would not yet tell him about Sean or my infidelities, I thanked him for his love and generosity, explaining that I wasn't in love with him and could no longer continue a relationship. I imagine he had seen it coming because although he was very sad, he didn't put up a fight. We tearfully hugged each other and he made his way to the door and out of my life.

PEBBLE

I felt relieved to end my charade with Daniel and my other lovers and was excited about my new relationship. Again, and at a new level, I began to feel myself return. Of course, when I did, what came rushing forward were feelings of shame about how I had lived for the previous couple of years. I knew I was "better" than that—or, at least, I wanted to be, but I didn't know how to make amends with Daniel and myself. I didn't yet know how to create the life I wanted. I only knew two things: that I no longer wanted to feel powerless living under my father's thumb, and that I wanted to see Sean. I felt incredibly drawn to him—his easygoing intelligence, generous smile, and quick wit. And there was something else about him that I sensed but didn't yet understand. All I knew was that I wanted to be more...like him. He seemed to me to be happy in his own skin and confident in who he was. I wanted that kind of peace.

This was a good start.

ADDENDUM

A few months after I had split with Daniel, I asked him to come over so we could talk. Because I was his first love (and his first lover, as I found out much later), and because he didn't know about what I'd done while we were together, I knew he was still hoping that we would get back together one day. I wanted him to take me off "the pedestal" I knew he had me on and to let me go; I didn't want him to immortalize me in that way. I didn't deserve it. I wanted him to see the truth about who I was during our relationship.

When I answered the door, I could see the hope in his face. Feeling awkward, I asked if we could take a walk. He agreed, and I closed the door behind me. As we began to walk, I looked over at him. I saw the sincerity in his eyes and felt the fragility of his heart. He seemed to fumble as he attempted to hug me and be physically affectionate. Full of remorse, I began to explain what happened between us. I informed him of my infidelities, and I sincerely apologized for taking advantage of his trust and for treating him in that way. He remained quiet while I spoke, nodding every now and then and trying to maintain a smile. Then, as the sun began to set behind us, he stopped, took my hand, and guided me around so that I would face him. He looked into my eyes and said, "I forgive you and I understand."

I shook my head and said, "Daniel, how can you understand? I don't even understand. And you shouldn't forgive me so quickly. There were more men than the ones I've told you about."

He considered this for a moment, and then said, "Sometimes people do things because they're trying to figure things out. I know you'll figure it out. You're smart." He went on to say that he hoped some day we might be together again. At that point, I knew no other way to respond except to implore him to let me go and to tell him that I was seeing someone I really liked. With this, I saw his hopes disappear as his face registered my conviction. I apologized again and hugged him goodbye.

I had hoped that exposing my unethical behavior and explaining my internal struggles would help Daniel release me; it appeared I was correct. Before leaving, he expressed his gratitude for my honesty and said that our conversation had helped him resolve his feelings. And although I didn't confess to him to benefit myself, an unexpected byproduct occurred: it was cleansing for me to tell the truth, and as a result, a feeling of self-forgiveness ensued. It also prompted a small spark of awareness within me of issues surrounding the fear of disappointing men, of not asking for what I wanted, of putting men's needs before mine, of needing to be in control to feel safe, and of wanting to be independent. In my naïveté, I believed that my awareness of these issues meant that they no longer had power over me. Little did I know that it was only the beginning of my work in these areas, and that this work would span for over a decade.

Chapter Sixteen

SHIFT HAPPENS

✺

ot long after we met, I asked Sean, "How did you become such an amazing person?" (Amazing as in embodying innate qualities of intelligence, kindness, compassion, and the like, as well as being articulate, wise, generous, positive, honest, and having a great sense of humor.) Once his face returned to its normal hue, he told me that for the past year he had been involved with a group doing self-growth work. In the following weeks, he introduced me to the organization with which he had done his work.

I opened myself to their teachings and began to understand that my childhood experiences—or rather, the residual pain I experienced from those experiences and the fear that developed to protect me from possible future pain—had been making many of my choices. I also learned that given the proper attention and consciousness, these experiences and my pain and fear surrounding them could become building blocks for my personal healing. I learned that I was responsible for the choices I made and for the shape of my life, and that any "victim consciousness" I had didn't serve who I was, nor was it useful or empowering to me. I began to live knowing that I was in charge of my life and my destiny, and that I was more than my thoughts, or better yet, my pain or my fear. I began to live in the "present"—and my entire world changed course.

We did several seminars together and our relationship blossomed and began to thrive. We gave ourselves to each other in deep friendship, and when the two of us weren't working, we were inseparable. Like best friends, we told each other everything and listened eagerly for what the other had to say. I felt safe with him and adored by him. I respected and felt inspired by him, and I began to fall in love with him and all that he was.

Sean was a bit more...shall we say...slower to jump in. There were several women who would have loved to be his woman, and they called him regularly. A couple of them came to see him play at the club on separate occasions. It was clear that they were interested, and although Sean didn't return their advances, he didn't discourage them either. One day Sean said that he wanted to spend an entire day with Terry, one of his woman friends. I knew they hadn't had sex, but I also knew he felt attracted to her. He said he was telling me because he wanted to be honest. We hadn't talked about being exclusive, and although I wasn't interested in seeing anyone else, I understood that he wanted to see her and said he should do it.

We checked in with each other after his day with Terry, and he admitted that they had sex. It hurt to hear it, but I knew it was important to just be present to all of what was happening. We talked for a long time about it, and he explained why he wanted to be with her in that way. He said that he felt for her and the difficult life that she was leading; she seemed fragile and so sad. It was like expressing comfort and affection as loving friends. Oddly and interestingly, after he finished his explanation, I actually felt for the woman and got—from his perspective—why he did what he did. Afterward, though, I made it clear to him that if he wanted to continue with Terry, I could not stay with him. He said he didn't feel that he wanted to, but he wanted to think about it. A week or so later, he came back to me, saying he had made a decision. He realized that he no longer wanted to see other women and that he wanted to see only me. He paused for a moment, clearly thinking, and then looking at me with great glee he asked, "Will you go steady with me?" I laughed and said, "Yes, I would love to go steady with you."

A month or so later, I had a moment where I thought I might have to choose between Sean and another man. Dancing was the one thing I did where I felt totally uninhibited. I went out to dance as often as I could. Sean didn't particularly like dancing, so when I got the bug I would either go with friends, or I'd go out alone. One night I went solo to a small local nightclub. It was a place professionals went after leaving the office. I was having fun dancing with a conservative looking man wearing a suit and tie when I noticed another man. He was tall, dark, and handsome in the truest sense of the words. I was drawn to him and thought it was odd that I would feel such a thing, given what I felt for Sean. I saw him look at me and felt shy and excited when he walked up to ask me to dance. As we danced, I became more and more elated. We looked into each other's eyes, and as we did, I felt lightning in my heart. I thought, *Whoa! What's going on here?* He felt like a tractor beam for which I had no defenses. At some point, we decided to take a break from dancing. We found a quiet corner and talked about who we were and what we did for a living. His name was Michael. He was an actor, and he had recently completed a small role in a Bond film. The more we talked, the more we became enthralled with each other. We went out on the dance floor and moved together effortlessly. After the song, we hugged each other, and I felt like I had been in his arms for a thousand years. *What's happening?* I wondered. It was the first time this type of thing had ever happened to me. I felt complete and utter passion for a man I didn't even know. I yearned for every inch of him.

It was getting late, and it was obvious that a choice had to be made about what was going to happen next. He looked into my eyes and said, "What I want more than anything else right now is to take you home with me, but I'm not going to, because I like you and respect you."

I responded with a smile, "Good."

"Let me take your phone number and I will call you. I want to get to know you."

"Yes, please do," I said, nodding in agreement, and we said goodnight with another embrace.

I left the nightclub wondering what had just happened. I loved Sean, but I also yearned for this man I didn't know. I thought, *How does this happen? And, what does one do when this happens?* When I talked to Sean the next day, I told him that I met someone I had a great time with. I decided in the moment not to discuss the intensity of what I felt. I wanted to wait until after I spoke with Michael.

The next day I told the women at the office where I was working what had happened. I told them I had given Michael my work number so I could be sure to get his call. In the early afternoon, one of the women brightly told me that Michael was on the line. My heart leaped and I had to force myself to breathe. I picked the phone up giggling and said, "Hi, Michael!" I heard him say hello and begin to say something. Then, in all of my excitement, I accidentally dropped the receiver. As the phone dropped, it hit one of the buttons on the phone and disconnected him. I frantically tried to get the line back, but he was gone. I looked at the receiver, devastated. Pleading, I thought, *Michael, call me back. Call me back!* But he never did.

In an attempt to find completion, I gave a fair amount of thought as to why Michael didn't call back. I guessed a few different scenarios. The two that seemed most likely were: He thought I hung up on him on purpose and that I was insincere; or he was in a relationship, as I was. Whatever the truth, he didn't call back.

PEBBLE

The pebble for this chapter—things happen for a reason, and/or depending on one's orientation, there is opportunity in all situations.

If Sean had not had sex with Terry, he would not have come to the realization that he wanted to be with me. So, were Terry and Sean guided to each other for the lessons they would learn? Or was it just happenstance, and then they made the most of their experience? I believe that there are no accidents and that all things have a reason, meaning, or lesson. Whether or not you jibe with my beliefs, in order to be with me, Sean needed to make a choice. His experience with Terry gave him the opportunity to do so.

Another byproduct of their experience was that I matured as I came to understand that everything is not always black and white; people do what they do for many different reasons. Also, what may look bad or wrong to one person may not be either to another. I got to know Terry and discovered that she was quite wonderful. I came to like her very much. She respected Sean's choice to be with me, and I respected their affinity for each other. We stayed close friends with her for years.

A few pebbles came out of my experience with Michael. First was my understanding that a relationship with him was not meant to be—otherwise, things would have happened differently. The blessing in the experience was that it helped me choose Sean.

A pebble I didn't see then but am grateful to understand now is that my experience with Michael was an outward manifestation of my core belief that I could not allow myself to be with a man I was deeply passionate about. Although I loved Sean, I didn't have that kind of passionate yearning for him. With him it was more like an inner feeling of profound happiness, that he was the one I most trusted. Of course, these are important factors for a successful long-term relationship, but with my (unconscious) belief, I could not be with a man I both loved like Sean AND felt deeply passionate about like Michael. My past experiences had told me that men I loved or were passionate about were either untrustworthy, like my father, or unattainable, like Fernando, and with this belief I invited the unattainable Michael into my life. As fate would have it, I was being shown the beliefs I had, but I was not then able to recognize them. Had I been more conscious and courageous to delve more deeply into what was being shown and why, perhaps I could have avoided the future that I would eventually create.

But before I take you there…

Chapter Seventeen

COMING HOME

∽

*O*nce Sean and I chose to be with each other, we settled into a relationship that felt real and good. It was just so *easy* being with him. I felt like we were two peas in the same pod, often having the same thoughts. I respected him immensely and couldn't wait to hear the next thought to roll out of his mouth. Even his goofy sense of humor and dumb jokes were music to my ears. I would groan when he did his lame impression of Alfred Hitchcock, puffing out his cheeks and sticking out his skinny belly, but secretly I could not have loved it more.

One day, after Sean and I had been together for about two months, I was sitting at home having a quiet moment sewing and reflecting on Sean. We had seen each other almost every day since we met, and in that moment of quiet I didn't see that changing. I wasn't thinking of marriage or commitment, I just didn't see an end to our time together.

Evidently, Sean had a similar experience around the same time. Within a couple weeks of my insight, we were driving up Bayside Drive in Newport in his vintage and barely running Jaguar. We were having a great time together, like we usually did. The sun was bright as we talked about anything and everything when he nonchalantly said he wanted to tell me about a realization that he had had. He explained in a very matter-of-fact way that he saw us married. He said he was not asking me to marry him; he just wanted me to know that he saw it as something that was imminent for us.

As he continued to drive, I felt my brain cease to function. I couldn't think or talk; I simply sat transfixed on the road for a minute, five minutes, ten minutes. I must have looked comical, because Sean began to laugh at me. His laughter broke my trance and I, too, began to laugh. We laughed long and we laughed deep, and for a time we didn't say anything else about his statement. We went back to his place and as we walked in, I asked if he had something to drink—somehow, our conversation left my mouth feeling dry. He said, "I don't think we have much in the fridge, but you're welcome to look." I opened the refrigerator door and gasped, "Oh!" when I saw a block of moldy cheese, an opened box of crackers, a wilted head of lettuce, shriveled-up tomatoes, and a carton of milk. I went for the milk, opened it, and closed it quickly so as not to faint from the smell.

For a couple of weeks I was in a state of shock. I had never seriously thought of marriage. After all, I was only twenty and still lived at home. Marriage was something adults did, and I certainly didn't see myself as such, nor did I want to. I liked being young, and I liked my freedom. To me, marriage was something done in another world, and I wasn't at all sure that I wanted to welcome it into mine ... and certainly not with him. After all, he was a slob! I mean, who in her right mind would marry a man who never made his bed and had fungus growing abundantly on his cheese and milk that had expired a month before in his refrigerator? Not me. No way could I marry this man! I resisted as best I could and groped for whatever excuses I could to justify my position. I even told my mother that he had essentially asked me to marry him. When she asked me what I wanted to do, I said that I could not and would not ever marry him. No way and no how! Then I gave her my list of very real reasons why it was not possible.

But try as I might to fight, and with my heels dug in deep, I was lovingly yet strongly being pressed by some unseen force. And as real love can do, it eventually wore down my resistance. After a few more mental gyrations by each of us over the next several weeks, we settled into the notion of marriage, and Sean officially asked me to marry him on bended knee, under the moonlight, in a gazebo outstretched over a charming little lake. Wholeheartedly, I answered, yes.

Shortly after I accepted Sean's proposal, I realized that I needed to drop the bomb with my father. Oddly, I felt a sense of calmness and certainty that gave me the strength to approach him.

One afternoon in March, my father was ironing in our living room. I took a deep breath to center myself and told him I had something to speak to him about. I rarely approached him in this way, and I noticed him preparing himself for what I was about to say. Though he continued to iron, he was alert and focused on me as I began to speak. I decided that the best way to tell him was to just come out and say it. So I said, "Dad, you know that Sean and I have been spending a lot of time together. Well, we love each other. He asked me to marry him, and I said yes." There was a stilted silence. I thought he might burn a hole right through his shirt. It appeared that he was gathering information for his best argument against my proposition. When he spoke, he did so deliberately, alternating his glances between his shirt and me.

"He's a nice man, Donna, but he's smaller than you, and he's not strong enough for you. It won't last." Of all the things I imagined I would hear, I never expected him to say this. Yes, I was several inches taller than Sean (he being five foot seven), but height had never been an issue with me. It's nothing I even thought about. Oddly, not in judgment of the pettiness of his statement, I simply thought to myself, *What a strange thing to say,* and his words seemed to roll off of me—even when he followed with an insinuation that I was making the mistake of my life. It was as if I had become impenetrable to his will. With the new strength I felt, I told him that I disagreed with him. I knew how good Sean was for me and there was nothing he could say to dissuade me. I watched my father's ship begin to sink and his words become less and less audible. I had reached the end of my desire to listen to his counsel, and his threat of abandonment no longer had a hold on me. I said, "Dad, I love Sean, and I'm going to marry him." A bit shaken, he asked me when, and I answered that it would be soon. In his most concerned and dramatic voice he offered, "Okay." At that moment, I had a surge of compassion for him. I knew that he adored and needed me, but I no longer needed him. I hugged him and told him I loved him. And that was that.

PEBBLE

By this simple yet powerful act, I felt freed from the cage that had kept me captive. Not what one feels from leaving something behind out of anger or loss, but the feeling of freedom that comes from moving toward something out of expansion and inspiration. I had made a paramount choice from my own resources, my own love, and my own will, and I felt resolute. I felt empowered. I was excited by the inner strength I had cultivated from speaking my truth in the face of adversity. I was grateful for the deep and abiding love and support I felt, for the first time in my life, from a man—my man, Sean.

Chapter Eighteen

SPEAKING OF ORGASMS:
A CHAPTER OF PEBBLES

✑

*S*ean and I participated in several seminars, focusing on various aspects of living more conscious lives. We continued with these seminars during the five months before for our wedding. Some of the subjects we studied were communication, self-expression, keeping one's word, going for it in life, contribution, being present in the moment (e.g. releasing mind chatter and accepting what is), and sex. Focusing on each of these subjects profoundly affected my moment-to-moment experience, and they helped shape my newly forming life path.

Communication

What I discovered was that relational love that thrives is a function of good communication—"good" meaning clear, honest, authentic, and complete. Throughout most of our relationship, Sean and I spoke about everything—the harder the subject, the more in depth the conversation. We spent many hours, and sometimes nights, talking through feelings and fears. If we were dealing with an issue and I felt "incomplete," although it seemed as if there was nothing more to say, I would state that and we would know there was more to heal. We trusted our communication, and our relationship thrived as a result.

One of the other extremely valuable byproducts of this work was for me to learn what it was to listen without adding any of my own "stuff." With this work, I became adept at hearing people without filters or commentary of my own. I became a better listener and a better source of support. I discovered that when I was able to set my own agenda aside, I then became more available to whomever I was with. Most importantly, I learned to truly hear what people were telling me. As I became better at this process, I noticed that I was able to intuitively feel others' emotions and into what they were communicating underneath their words.

Full Self-Expression

Part of full self-expression is communication, to be sure. But the full scope of this work showed me that if I was not expressing myself, whether it be my creativity, my feelings, my dreams and desires, my insights and wisdom, and my love, then I was not fully living.

I realized that in much of my life up to that point, I had suffered from a lack of confidence, and this stopped me from fully expressing myself. I was afraid that what I said or did would be squished, dishonored, and/or unacknowledged, so I often disregarded my own ideas and gave up on desires before I ever got started on them, which further eroded my confidence.

Being given "permission" in the seminars and by Sean to more fully express myself, in whatever way that felt good to me, seemed to provide the freedom to be more of *me* and to discover what I was impassioned and inspired by.

The more I expressed myself, the more I was met with unfathomable acceptance and acknowledgement. I began to be regularly approached by people who would say that something I said or did affected them in a positive way. This was very affirming to me.

Keeping One's Word

Keeping one's word could also be known as being accountable. This, too, was a foundational discovery for me. I learned from my father to lie and manipulate in order to get what I wanted. I learned from my mother that I was a victim and not responsible. The notion of keeping my word and being accountable were very foreign concepts to me, yet I welcomed them like a plant that had not had water for months. I knew that there was something missing in my life and these concepts seemed to be integral parts of the puzzle. I drank up the fact that my word and my actions really were who I was (in the physical world), pure and simple. I saw that my life was a reflection of the choices I had made. Yes, I had a history, but my history was only the foundation for my life work. What I built on top of that foundation was my doing, my responsibility for which only I was accountable.

This brought many things to the surface for me. I saw that being impeccable with my word was important to how people and the world responded to me, and how I responded to myself. Every time I hedged either in what I said or what I promised, I sent myself a message that I could not be trusted. Then I would begin to feel bad about myself and believe I didn't *deserve to be happy and to have good things come my way*. What I noticed was that the more authentic and truthful I was, the better I felt about myself; and of course the better I felt about myself, the more joy I felt; and the more joy I felt, the more goodness I attracted. As simple as this concept is, I had never heard it before. This was quite an eye opener for me.

Going for It

I had never really gone for it because much of my life was spent being afraid—afraid of what people thought of me, of causing pain, of my pain, of being criticized, of my inadequacies, and of my power. In this work I got a glimpse into my fears and saw where they stopped me in life. Because of my youth, my malleability, and my willingness to see into the center of my fears, they seemed to quickly evaporate. As I continued to welcome this process, I felt an invitation to step forward and do what I was afraid of. I began doing what I loved most, whether it was singing, playing piano, dancing, or being involved in the organization with which I was doing seminars. I felt alive and impassioned in going past what was comfortable into what was charged and inspired. I even began to write, which was something I had never been interested in doing. I had always been terrible at reading and writing. It felt like hard work, and I saw no joy or creativity in it. But once the block was removed, I seemed to want to express myself in more creative ways. This brought me a new type of fulfillment.

Contribution

Once I knew my own emotional and physical needs were being met and I began to go for it, I saw that going for it meant very little to me if the thing I was aiming for had no meaning. It was at this time in my life that I became conscious that other people had far worse childhoods than mine, if they even survived. Sean and I became involved in various causes from ending world hunger with the Hunger Project, to sponsoring a child in India with an organization that was known as Foster Parents Plan, to organizing events to support more personal/local issues. We also helped create a human chain and held hands with thousands of others for Hands Across America, a benefit for charities helping with hunger. It was refreshing to take the attention off myself and to focus on others, being part of the effort to find solutions for some of the turmoil in the world.

Being Present in the Moment

As I mentioned in Communication, the beauty for me about being present in the moment was the ability I gained to more fully feel what was happening around me and to be able to empathize with people. For those who relish intimacy as I do, being present is a key to success in this arena. Learning to be truly present also allowed me to not miss what the Universe (divine intelligence) was showing me. I am one of those people who you just about have to hog-tie to go to bed—I don't want to miss a thing! Before I learned to be present, I was always on the move and rarely just "with" myself. With this work, I discovered that the more I ran around from this thing to the next, the more I missed. John Lennon said, "Life is what happens when you are busy making other plans." I realized that if I was not present—with myself, or with those with whom I was interacting, with each step I took—then I would miss the power of that *now* moment, and that *now* moment was so full and had so much to offer if I would just give it a chance.

With this new understanding, all desire I had to alter myself, for recreation or for numbing purposes, was gone. At any given moment I found so much pleasure in my skin and in my soul that there was no longer a desire or a need to do anything but feel the moment.

I also learned—and this was key to my learning to live in the present—that no matter what I thought about something or how much I disliked it or wished it were different, *it was what it was*. I discovered that the greater my capacity to be at peace with what was, the greater my capacity for joy. This is not to say that I learned to be complacent—on the contrary. I saw that my willingness to embrace things, my circumstances, and myself exactly as they were was *key* to taking responsibility in my life. Then, and only then, was I effectively able to make the shifts I wanted.

Another aspect of being in the present and at peace with what is, is the notion that if one is not in that place, whatever is being resisted (not attended to) will stick to us like gum on the bottom of our shoe. There was a great saying that floated around our group: "What we resist, persists." No matter how much we may try to avoid an issue, it isn't going anywhere until we address it.

Oh yes, Sex...or rather
The Orgasming Pebble

We were in a seminar about sex and sexuality. Mostly I was thinking, *so, what's the big deal?* I mean it's fun and all, but what's all the hooha about?

For all the reasons one can probably imagine when reading my story, by the age of twenty I had never experienced an orgasm. I had no idea what one was or that orgasms even existed, though it wasn't for the lack of trying by some very determined fellows. The ones who come to mind tried long and hard to give me this experience. I wondered what they were doing and why they were spending so much time in certain practices. I would think to myself, *Hmmm. This feels kind of good, but it's pretty messy, and for the life of me I do not understand why they like having their faces down there.* Since I had not yet experienced real intimacy with sex, with the exception of Fernando who knew less than I did, I never felt *safe* to let go in this arena. Therefore, their efforts were fruitless.

Then smack dab in the middle of the series *it* happened, in a way that I never would have guessed (of course).

Making love with Sean was always a loving experience. He was practiced sexually and his heart was very open to me, and I trusted him more than I had ever trusted any man. On this particular night, I was a bit shy because I was menstruating (although very lightly) and I had no experience making love during this time of month. I noticed that he was just as present and engaged with me as he always was, which surprised me. Then, he wanted to go *you know where*! I resisted because I was embarrassed, and I couldn't imagine why anyone would want to do that. He didn't seem to care, which surprised and pleased me, and he began to lovingly caress me with his tongue, first fast and then slow. He touched places that I didn't know were there and after a time, the combination of the sensations and the trust and love I felt for him caused an explosion in my entire body. Talk about shock and awe! Since I didn't know what an orgasm was, I didn't know what had happened. All I knew was that I felt elated in my whole body and in my heart. I laughed and cried at the same time at my new revelation. Unable to string coherent words together to adequately express my feelings, I muttered as best I could ebullient thanks to him for giving me such a precious gift. Of course, Sean was feeling quite the man at that moment and reveled with me.

At the next seminar, I raised my hand and shared my experience and my newfound pleasure. Everyone celebrated, then laughed when I exclaimed, "Why didn't anyone ever tell me about this before?!"

PEBBLE

These insights and the practices I embraced were the holy waters that blessed me and brought profound change into my life. Actually, it was the first time in my life that I felt I was truly living.

I am eternally grateful for the opportunity I had to take these seminars at such a young age. Not only were many pebbles acquired during that time, but a large part of the fundamental foundation on which I still live had also been laid.

Chapter Nineteen

THE MIRACLE OF AUTHENTICITY

∽

A testament to Sean's and my communication and ability to be present in the moment lies in a story that happened about two weeks before we were to be married. Sean called me at work one afternoon and said that he had something important to speak with me about. His voice sounded hesitant and unsure. I knew something was up. But because I was so happy in my bones and sure of our love, I wasn't shaken by his request. I wanted to be available for whatever was happening with him and agreed to meet him that evening.

It was a beautiful night in early August when we met at sunset, at the park next to the gazebo where he had proposed and where our ceremony was to take place. He looked disheveled and nervous, and he hardly made eye contact. He paced to calm himself before he spoke. Once he settled in, he began to tell me that he had been feeling concerned about something. "You see," he hesitated, "the thing is…is that…I don't think you're *The One* for me…you know, my Fairy Princess." He cleared his throat, then continued. "I think that maybe Gina (someone he had dated before me) might be my Fairy Princess, but I'm pretty sure you're not." Then, he dropped the bomb. "I think…that we should call off the wedding."

As he spoke, I took a deep breath. I listened to him, and I heard him, *really* heard him. I took it in… but I didn't take it personally. Surprisingly, as he confessed his feelings, I was completely open and utterly devoid of pain, and it wasn't something I had to fabricate. I focused on him and had no attachment to what our relationship needed to look like. I knew our love existed, and no matter what he said or did in that moment, I knew that it was just part of our path, and I was all right with that. The foremost thought on my mind was, *All right. The invitations have already gone out. I wonder how we can let everyone know that we're not getting married. Maybe we can call everyone…*

Then, something happened. In that moment of Sean communicating truthfully and authentically, and of me hearing him and responding from absolute certainty and love, a miracle occurred—he shifted. One moment he was sure that he didn't want to commit to me, and the next moment he wanted nothing more. As the shift happened, we both felt it. We looked at each other musing over what had just transpired, then broke out into laughter. We embraced with our love fully intact and our commitment refreshed.

PEBBLE

This was yet another diamond for my path. What stood out to me most about that moment in time are two things: First is that Sean had the integrity to say what he was feeling, even though the outcome could have been very uncomfortable and painful. He didn't have to act out, as he might if he didn't have the courage or the strength to tell me. He honored me, and he honored himself with the truth. This was something I was very unfamiliar with. It was so simple, yet so powerful, and I was grateful to be a witness and a student of it. Second is my openness. I could have reacted in anger or out of fear, but I didn't. And it was not a choice I made not to react; it was a state of being. In that moment I was in the state of utter love and openness to Sean. I rode the wave of trust and landed in the land of Grace. I knew no fear, only love. Rarely in my life before Sean had I experienced such surrender. I realized that I was capable of trusting love and trusting a man to tell me his truth.

It was with this kind of authenticity that we intended to live our life together.

Chapter Twenty

INTENTION TO FRUITION

∽

In planning our wedding, we didn't want to obligate ourselves to tradition or what we "should" do. We felt that what was most important in creating our celebration was to be clear about what our intention was. If our intention was clear, we knew that opportunities aligned with our intention would find us. We wanted only to do what inspired us, and what inspired us was to give our guests a glimpse into our love and for us to express our love for them. When pressure was placed upon us to do something a certain way and it didn't feel right, we said no thank you and moved on to something that did. Sean's parents weren't altogether pleased with our choices, but we were clear that our wedding was about us and not about them, so we gently and firmly let them know that we were going to do things our way. From our invitations to our departure, we planned our day and our honeymoon with love and much forethought of our desired outcome. Sean had a hand in designing my ring and I designed my dress and my bridesmaids' dresses. We asked several friends to be our wedding crew. It was perfect. Their job was to set everything up so that the only thing we had to do was show up and enjoy ourselves. Before the wedding, Sean and I had a thank you dinner for these friends, and at just the right moment we instigated a spaghetti fight. It was sticky and messy, but the clean up was a small price to pay for the laughs.

Then came the night before our wedding. As the night approached, I began to be filled with doubt—not doubt about marrying Sean, but doubt as to whether or not I would survive. I was the happiest I had ever been and happier than I thought was possible. I realized that I had no frame of reference on how to live so happily. Along with this, and probably because of this, I had a foreboding feeling that something was going to happen to stop me. I actually thought that somehow I would not survive the night. This feeling was so strong that I chose not to go out with my friends after the rehearsal dinner. My foremost thought was to get home and to be safe. I remember my journey home being harrowing. I looked both ways before crossing every intersection, and went exactly the speed limit as I nervously avoided everything that looked remotely dangerous. I was very grateful when I finally crawled into my safe and comfortable bed.

The next day, I awoke relieved and delighted that I made it through the night alive! I thought to myself, *I did it! I made it through. I guess I can live happily ever after.* I felt I was given the gift of continued life so that I could begin to truly live.

Laura, my maid of honor, and my bridesmaids arrived at my home and we played and laughed and celebrated while getting ourselves ready for the big day. While we engaged in our feminine rituals, my brothers and father watched amusingly from the perimeter until it was time to pile into the car and head to the wedding site.

The entire day was infused with effulgent joy. I walked down the aisle with my father and two brothers to a prerecorded piano suite written for me by Sean. The ceremony began with us walking around and greeting each guest in his or her seat. We wanted to make sure we connected with everyone before we got caught up in the festivities. Then, on that breezy summer day with swans paddling freely around the white gazebo surrounded by a tree-encircled lake, we wholeheartedly offered our vows to each other.

The first half of our reception was spent in the park next to the gazebo. My mother, who was a masterful cook, baked our three-layer wedding cake—banana, carrot, and zucchini. Sean and I didn't drink alcohol, so we toasted with our favorite drink, orange milkshake. I ceremoniously smashed the cake in and around his mouth, and with threat of retaliation, he playfully and gently fed me my piece. For the second half of our reception, we caravanned to the local university Sean had graduated from, where we hosted a concert for our guests. As always, he and his group wowed the audience with their incredible groove and melodic instrumentations. For the show finale, Sean invited me up on stage to dance to their music.

With a trail of birdseed in our wake, we left the reception in my graffiti-ridden car and the traditional cans clanking behind us, feeling like we had just robbed a bank. We were full to the brim as we recounted to each other our favorite moments of the wedding.

Still in our regalia, we drove to Ventura for our wedding night. We were received as royalty, and we reveled in our fortune. Our dinner was complete with exquisite food and impeccable service. Each bite we took seemed to melt into utter joy. We laughed, we cried, we celebrated each other and the moment.

Before going back to our room, we walked to the beach and lay for a while listening to the waves. Since we were headed to the Sierras to camp, we had sleeping bags in the trunk of the car. Sean brought one to the beach, and we crawled inside and fell asleep in each other's arms. We woke up hours later surprised at our sleepiness, and after a good laugh we walked back to our room and made love.

PEBBLE

This was another diamond for my pathway. Thirty years later, this day still registers as one of the most pure of all the days I have lived—purity of heart and purity of expression of joy. It was as if magic had revealed itself through the power of our intention and we were deeply grateful to be witnesses to this potent example and lesson.

ADDENDUM
...because it's a story worth telling...

The rest of our honeymoon was just as magical. When we left Ventura, we drove to Tuolumne Meadows in Yosemite National Park and camped out in its beauty and majesty. The weather was perfect, the air was clean, the scents were vibrant—it was a pristine setting. We made love in the meadows. The rocks and trees were our threshold.

Our final blessing came when we decided to go listen to Carl Sharsmith, the local ranger-naturalist who was loved by many, speak at a campfire. We weren't quite done cooking dinner when we realized that his talk was about to begin. He was getting along in age and this would be our last opportunity to see him for some time, if ever again, so we popped our beans and hotdogs in the tent and scrambled to the fire site.

The talk was wonderful. Carl so loved the mountains; I doubt anyone knew more about Yosemite than he did. He was both passionate and peaceful as he spoke of the history and the nature of the land. It felt like we were in a dream as we walked back; the sun had set behind the purple mountains and the subtle nighttime sounds had begun. We switched on our flashlights to find our way back while expressing our gratitude for having had such an experience with Carl. When we reached our tent, three things startled us out of our dream—a loud hoarse grunt, seeing the back of a bear's butt walking away, and discovering what was left of our tent. It was ripped to shreds. The bear had probably been in the trees waiting for the dumb tourists to do exactly what we did. Realizing what we had done, we nervously sniggered at each other and at our stupidity, wondering what to do next. We figured the bear would not return, but we were still somewhat frightened at the thought that it might. We looked in the tent, expecting to see our dinner eaten, but the pan was still there and the food was untouched. We looked at each other and said, "Hm. That's strange." We decided we must have scared it away before it had a chance to eat. We then looked around to see if anything else had been touched and saw that our cooler was open. We walked over and looked inside to see if anything was missing. Something was missing all right—the bear had actually opened the cooler and made off with our milk and chocolate syrup! At that point we lost it.

After a good laugh, we packed up all our things, piled into the car, and headed for our next destination, Lake Tahoe, which I'm happy to say was just as pristine, but not as eventful, as Yosemite.

Chapter Twenty-One

FRANNY WAS RIGHT

∽

*P*rimary in Sean's and my relationship was the profound love we had for each other. Rarely in my life have I experienced the kind of *complete* love that I felt for Sean. When I say complete, I mean I loved his mind, his body, his spirit, his creativity, his heart, his really dumb sense of humor, his funny looking toes, his ability to procrastinate, and all ten hairs on his chest. I loved everything he was and everything he was becoming. We were best friends and partners. I respected him and trusted him, and I loved and honored him.

The strong foundation of our emotional relationship and the financial stability that Sean soon began to provide allowed me to feel *safe* in the world. This enabled me to complete my childhood and to begin to live as an adult. I discovered that I had my own voice and acknowledged that I had my own desires. With this, I began to have a small glimpse into who I was (albeit defined by who I was in relationship to Sean and within the confines of marriage).

I learned what it was to talk issues through until we felt clear, loving, and connected again.

There were many nights that we worked on issues where one or both of us wanted to check out, but we didn't. Sean was famous for starting to fall asleep when the conversation got too intense or too lengthy. That is when the squirt bottle came in handy. He had given me permission to squirt him to help him stay conscious...and although I didn't enjoy it (much), I did it when necessary. He may have a different memory of (and a good defense for) this, but I believe I only had to use the bottle a few times before his subconscious learned that I wasn't going to let him check out while we were working through things. We were committed to keeping the love connection clear, and we did whatever it took to get there —including, but not limited to, drenching the other if need be. Of course I don't remember him ever having to use the bottle on me...

We both learned to let go of our pasts. We felt that being present in the moment was of utmost importance in living a powerful and contented life. If we questioned the past or tried to keep it alive, we felt that it was robbing us of experiencing the now and creating a future.

We spent hours upon hours on this, going through photos and things that had been given to us by past lovers. We wanted to start with a cleaner slate, so to speak. If we had any sentimental attachment to a thing, we put it in the "to be tossed" pile. If we had no real attachment but enjoyed a thing just for what it was, we allowed ourselves to keep it. If one of us thought we had no attachment to a thing but the other was not convinced, we would place the thing in the toss pile and see what the reaction was. If feelings of loss resulted, then we would take that as a sign that we had some letting go to do. We disposed of quite a pile of things.

Although I believe the essence of what we did was very valuable, I did wish later that I had kept a couple of photos of Fernando and me. There was one photo in particular of the two of us snuggling in a quiet room in the library and one could see the look of first love in our eyes. Our radiance was truly magnificent.

I learned several valuable lessons here: that I don't always make the correct choice, that I don't know everything, and that what I believe to be appropriate in one moment can, and often does, change at some point. The best we can do is our best in each moment.

We saw how it was possible to succeed just by being ourselves and enjoying the moment. One day while we were over at Sean's parents' house for a visit, his dad told us that he had read in the paper that *The Newlywed Game* was having auditions for their show. We decided it could be a blast, so we called and set up a time to meet with the show's casting directors. We arrived at the audition in awe of the goings on around us. They sat our group in a room and asked us all sorts of questions. We felt shy and a bit out of place. Everyone else seemed much more animated and interesting than we did. After about ten minutes, they excused everyone and we walked out, relieved that the audition was over. We felt that there was no way we would get chosen, so we let it go.

A week later we got a call from the casting people saying that they would love to have us on the show. We thought they had probably gotten us confused with someone else, but we accepted their offer anyway.

In preparation for the show, we felt it was important to do our "homework," so we watched the show several times to practice and to see how well we would do. We could not match each other's answers to save our lives. In fact, in all the episodes we watched we only matched one question and answer—What is your husband's favorite food? Easy. Frosted Flakes. We knew for sure that we would come in dead last. Because we were certain we wouldn't win, we decided to do two things: 1) Have as much fun as possible and enjoy this crazy thing we were doing; and 2) If they asked anything negative or embarrassing about either of our families, we would answer, "Muffin" (his parents' dog).

Then came the day of the taping. We were excited and feeling shy about being on national television. Before the show, they put us in a room with the other contestants and a person who was there to loosen us up. I noticed that she was also writing notes from time to time. Sean and I were content watching all the other couples working out their nerves by being goofy. We simply trusted that we would have fun, no matter what. Before we left the room, the show's representative coached us by saying that we should be as animated as possible and poke at each other and even get mad at each other whenever possible. I didn't like the thought of having to poke at Sean to make the show more entertaining.

When it was time to start the game, they brought us onto the set and I looked around. Off to my left was the familiar white latticework behind Bob Eubanks' podium, and in front of me were the swivel seats that the four couples sat in behind the circular score panels. Then I looked out into the crowd and saw our families sitting in the front. Lastly, I noticed the cameras. *It looks so small compared to how it looks on TV*, I thought to myself.

We sat down in our seats and they began taping the show. Bob introduced the couples, and for the first round, the women were taken to the "soundproof room" while the men answered questions. After our husbands were finished, we were led to sit down next to them and began to try to match their answers. It was fun, and Sean and I did fairly well, only missing the question, "How many edges do you have on your dining room table?" Sean answered, "Two—the top edge and the bottom." I answered "Zero" because our table was a circle. I know. An edge is not a corner. I tried to poke fun at Sean a bit when he answered a question that was way off base, but I didn't feel good doing it, so I decided I would not do it again. I also noticed that the camera and the host seemed to give more time to the people who had been most animated in the room. They also cut to the next person if the current person answering the question wasn't interesting, and a light bulb went off in my head: *That's why the woman was taking notes!* I decided after this realization that I was not going to play the way they wanted us to but rather to simply love my husband and enjoy our time as we had agreed. I also decided, so they would not cut me off, to give my explanation before answering their questions.

Then the funniest thing happened, probably because we were so relaxed and because we weren't concerned about winning, we started getting all the answers correct. We missed just one question in the second round: "What is your husband's least favorite spice?" He answered, "Allspice," but I answered, "Pepper" because he didn't like it. We didn't make a big deal out of our miss, and they quickly went on to the other couples.

It was finally time for Sean to answer the final "bonus" question. We were shocked when Bob told us that we were ahead! I couldn't believe we had done so well. I felt little jitters in my stomach when Bob asked, "Does your husband shake hands the *old way* or the *new way*?" He asked the other couples to answer before coming to us. I knew Sean would answer as I had, and I pumped up and down in my seat as Sean matched my answer with "the old way," winning the game. Our family erupted and so did we, kissing and hugging and openly expressing how much we loved each other.

The prize we won was small and inconsequential, but the lesson we learned was significant. Although winning is always fun, it truly is not whether you win or not, it's *how* you play the game that brings the most fulfillment. In our case, loving each other and enjoying the moment helped us win.

In watching Sean write and perform his incredible music I learned what true creativity is. I also came to understand through him that being creative (whatever the mode of expression) was a natural state of existence, and since that was the case with him, it must also flow through me. Over the years I learned that I simply had to allow the juices to flow and be witnessed, if by no one other than me. This took some doing, because I had virtually no confidence in this arena.

While pressing through my fear to invite my creativity to surface, I uncovered a memory having to do with a painful experience around my artistic abilities. I was around three. My family was at my uncle's home for a party. Someone must have given me some colorful crayons, because they inspired me to draw a very beautiful and very large mural on the wall behind my uncle's favorite leather chair in his office. It resembled one of Jackson Pollack's more colorful pieces. Well, my uncle evidently didn't know how priceless my mural was, because upon discovering it, he hit the ceiling. I can still remember my uncle's red face yelling at me and the feeling that my art was very, very ugly. I came away from that experience thinking not only that I was bad at art, but also that creating would get me in a whole lot of trouble. To this day, I draw not much more than stick figures.

With Sean's example, I learned to trust my creativity as well as to learn various modes to express it. I can still remember clearly the night I learned that I loved to write.

We had been married for about a year. I always accompanied Sean to the club and watched his sets. I felt it a privilege to be with him while he carried people's cares away with his music. On this night, though, I felt very tired and decided to go home before he finished. It was a cool and windy night just before fall. As usual, I crossed the canal on the ferry and began to stroll along the walkway around the island toward our home. The air was thick with a salty mist. I absolutely loved walking at night and did it often no matter the weather. The boats were swaying and the masts were clanking. As I strolled, I felt this feeling of wonder at what all my senses were taking in. It was as if my pores and my mind were open like never before, and I could actually feel everything that was happening around me. I heard words begin to bubble up into my consciousness. They were describing what I was seeing, thinking, and feeling, but in a way that I didn't normally string words together. I felt a sense of newness and freedom come over me and a surge of inspiration to write down what I was hearing, so I dug into my purse, pulled out some paper, and began to write. Below are the very first words I wrote while in a creative state.

On my way home I am thinking of you…
The half-bent moon appeared like diamonds as the current carried them down the bay.
But there are no stars out tonight. Oh, wait, I see one sending out its signal to me.
The man in the window didn't see me waving.
I think of us.

But the wind chimes do not care. They keep on with their songs along with the fern's dancing legs that seem to be enchanted.

The masts seem disturbed by the clanking of the buoys, but the buoys can't help it. It's that damn wind.

Is that the ocean I hear? Yes – yes, I believe it is. It's the ocean throwing shells onto the shore.

I long for you.

I'm getting cold now, but can't I stay here just a while longer?

The bugs like to come out at night—no one will challenge them.

My feet await the warmth of our bed and my mind awaits rest.

I await you.

The wind grows silent behind me. Do not walk too fast. The sounds are almost faded.

A familiar sound—Ah, yes, he's at it again cricketing to his heart's content. Do not listen to the cars. Keep going…

Ah, there it is, but should I sit and listen for more?

Coziness always wins.

The door opens. It's empty.

I think of you.

Goodnight.

This was my awakening to trusting the free flow of creativity. From that moment on, whether it be journaling, letters, poems, songs, or anecdotal stories, writing became one of my most cherished expressions of creativity.

PEBBLE

Grace is the pebble to end this chapter of many insights. As Sean's friend Franny used to say, when I would ask the heavens what I did to deserve such a man as Sean, "There's no deserving here. It's just pure Grace."

Chapter Twenty-Two

REWRITING THE PAST

∾

$\mathcal{L}$ate in 1981, after much consideration and conversation with Sean, I decided to go back to school. Community college had felt more like high school than college to me, and after almost two years of taking classes, I quit. Now, I wanted to have an educational experience with people who actually wanted to learn and with teachers who loved to teach. I wanted to see what I could accomplish. The following spring, I applied to Long Beach State University and was accepted as a sophomore.

Walking onto campus the first day of the first semester felt incredibly exciting. I could not wait to walk into my classes and absorb new ideas and concepts. I took geology, mathematics, philosophy, and an introductory acting class. My teachers were passionate and that made it easy and surprisingly fun to learn.

As the semester progressed, I could see myself continuing on with any of the subjects I was taking, but the classes that surprised me most were psychology, philosophy, and acting. I had always loved thinking things through from various points of view, so I found I was a natural in philosophy, and I excelled. Since my first personal-growth seminar, I had been quite interested in what makes people do what they do, and so the idea of psychology fascinated me, too. The acting surprised me as well because I had been so shy about speaking in front of people. I loved the exercises, and I adored improvisation. I delighted in feeling the creative juices flow. I threw myself into the class and blossomed.

All in all, my first semester was a smash. I succeeded in that I lived the educational experience I desired, and I loved it! I ended up receiving all A's and getting on the President's Honor List.

PEBBLE

For the first time in my life I actually felt 'smart'. It was empowering to see myself thrive in an educational environment, and it was healing to build a feeling within of rightness where there was once falseness, doubt, and self-criticism.

The pebbles here are application and re-creation. By applying myself 100% in this educational experience it felt like my past was re-created, or re-written. My high school was what it was, but it no longer was my frame of reference for my level of intelligence or my ability to learn. It was as if my high school learning experiences were no longer my history. This transformative semester at Long Beach State had become my new history. It has been affirming to know that this kind of re-creation can be applied in other areas of life.

Chapter Twenty-Three

INSPIRATION AND
CONFIDENCE

∽

*A*s it is with many relationships, during the course of our marriage, Sean and I had much love and expansion as well as several deeply challenging times. About a year and a half into our marriage I was fortunate that Sean made enough money at his day job of computer consulting that I didn't need to work at my day job any longer. This allowed me to spend more time working with him on his music, exploring songwriting and singing, as well as doing other things that inspired me. Besides writing, at this point in my life I also loved crafting and baking, especially at Christmastime.

As I had witnessed throughout my childhood, Christmas and Thanksgiving seemed to be times when my mother was most contented, and some of my happiest memories of her are during this time of year: the elaborate and unbelievably delicious meals she lovingly created for us; her Christmas cookies, unlike anything I had ever tasted before or since; how she always seemed to know what I wanted for Christmas; her festive home always filled with the smell of holiday time; the sounds of her most recent favorite Christmas music filling the air (one year it was Yogi Yorgessen singing, "I Yust go Nuts at Christmas"); and her special holiday decorations placed throughout her home (among them was a collection of nativity scenes inside of actual eggs that she made by hand). All were things she offered with great love. In my adulthood and going into my own holiday preparations and focusing on Love, which was the true meaning of Christmas for me, I felt my heart renew itself.

One year when Christmas was coming, I got a spark of inspiration. I always looked forward to this time of year because to me, Christmas was a time when people seemed to set aside their "regular" lives and settle into peace, love, and the spirit of generosity. It was the time of year that I felt the world around me living in the kind of love and goodwill that I had envisioned as a child. It was also the time of year when my mother had taught me how to bake. Those moments are still the ones I recall most fondly with my mother. The year she shared one of her secret recipes and lovingly taught me to bake her Walnut Snow Storms, I wanted to eat the entire first batch I made (what thirteen-year-old wouldn't?), and she let me! Baking was our time to create love together, and because of this, baking is to this day therapeutic for me. The heirloom recipes she handed down to me are of my most cherished possessions…along with the Christmas ornaments I have collected through the years.

From these treasured memories, I came up with the idea of selling Christmas-oriented items in our home. My idea was to ask friends to contribute their handmade things and we all would sell them in a bazaar of sorts. We lived on Balboa Island, where tourists and walkers were abundant, so all I would have to do for advertising was make signs.

The idea inspired me, so I sat down with Sean and shared my intention. I wanted to turn our home into a Christmas paradise. I envisioned my "Christmas House," complete with a real Christmas tree decorated with handmade ornaments, the fireplace going, hot spiced tea being served, my home-baked cookies to sample and sell, a variety of other handcrafted house decorations on display, and Christmas cards made by a friend who was an artist. I wanted to share the joy I felt at Christmastime with all who entered our home. The idea easily took off, and I threw myself into planning, making ornaments, and baking dozens and dozens of cookies.

I greeted all who came to the door with Christmas spirit. When a police officer came knocking, I walked outside with him and openly looked into his eyes as he asked me what we were doing. I believed I was doing nothing wrong, so I happily explained. He then looked straight at me while shaking his head as if to say "no" and asked if I was making a profit from the sales. Getting what his concern was about, I indicated that a portion of the money would in fact be donated to The Hunger Project (an organization Sean and I supported that was dedicated to the sustainable end of world hunger), leaving the rest up to him to decipher. He seemed to be satisfied enough and walked away with a knowing smile.

The weekend was a huge success and we sold much of what we offered for sale. We made a bundle of money for my charity and for ourselves.

PEBBLE

This was my second experience of having a vision for something and organizing it and seeing it through (the first being our wedding). It was enlivening for me to watch something I created in my mind's eye come to life exactly how I intended. From this came a confidence in my ability to materialize my visions, and it felt empowering.

Chapter Twenty-Four

WAKE OF PAIN

∽

*T*he first Christmas House was so successful that the next year I decided to have another one. I gathered some of the same friends from the previous year and put it together. It was as wonderful as the first one had been—until the last day.

My mother said she was going to visit during the day, that she had made some holiday cannoli she wanted to contribute to my baked items. I was excited by the idea of her presence and her offer, and I expected to see her at about 2 p.m. At 1:30, I got a call from a police officer who told me that my mother had been in a car accident. I abruptly left the Christmas House to my friends and went to the scene.

When I arrived, I saw her looking very upset. I walked up to her and noticed the familiar smell of alcohol. She had hit another car at an intersection and both cars were somewhat damaged. Thankfully, no one was hurt. I was very upset thinking that her being affected by the drinking was most likely the cause of the accident. I realized that she could have seriously hurt someone. I thought, *I have to do something*, so I walked up to the officer, out of earshot of her, and asked if he had tested her for alcohol. He seemed taken aback that I would ask such a thing, but he casually walked over and asked her if she had been drinking. While looking at me, obviously upset by the question and knowing it had been asked by me, she said no. He seemed satisfied, took her word for it, and didn't give her a Breathalyzer test. I thought to myself, *This is unbelievable. He's taking her side.*

I was disgusted by what I had witnessed and felt that I had had enough of the many effects that her drinking had on my life. I didn't want her or this incident to impact my weekend, so I told her that I needed to get back to the house and said she would have to handle this on her own. She and the police officer looked at me with obvious judgment; oddly for me, I didn't care. I knew I needed to take care of myself and turned to walk to my car. Before getting in, I remembered the cannoli and asked my mother if she wanted to keep it or give it to me. She went to her car, got the plate and handed it to me. A wave of guilt came over me. I thanked her and told her they looked wonderful (which they did) and got in my car and left. On my way home, after a good cry, I regrouped as I had learned to do so many times over the years.

Again we finished the weekend with great success. We sold just about everything, with the exception of one item: the cannoli. Not a single one was purchased. When my mother asked over the phone if they had sold, part of me wanted to lie and tell her that they had sold like gangbusters. The other part of me, the angry part, wanted to hurt her and tell her that none sold. The angry part won out and I told her, in a rather businesslike way, that they hadn't sold, and I asked her what she wanted me to do with them. She told us to eat them.

They were delicious, of course, but as I chewed and swallowed I felt great regret at my anger and how I had expressed it to her.

PEBBLE

Along with the love I felt so deeply for Sean and the joy I had begun to find in living, I also felt deep sadness and pain for my mother on a continual basis. I could feel her blood run through me, and it was extremely uncomfortable knowing that this person, this highly dysfunctional person, was the one from whom I sprang. It felt too close for comfort, and although I felt much guilt about it, and at times I felt quite heartless, I simply had to separate myself from who she was. It turned out it was a healthy choice for me to make. I found that my backing off and allowing her to live her life, while reminding myself that I had no control over her, was what kept me sane over the next couple of years.

Even though I know I was doing the best I could at the time, I still carry sadness that I chose to tell my mother the truth about the cannoli, and it's almost twenty-five years after the incident. Another pebble here is that saying things to hurt people, or saying things in an angry way and not caring how they land, hurts oneself in addition to the one intended. Neither person leaves happy or nurtured and only a wake of pain is left behind...and within.

Chapter Twenty-Five

THE TRUTH ABOUT MY MOTHER

❧

I so wanted to help my mother, even while knowing I had no power over her or her addiction to alcohol. At one point, I got the notion that if she would just "see the light" on her own as I had done, she would see she had the ability to heal herself and to begin to have a happy existence. It seemed to me that the therapy she had tried over the last few years had not helped her change.

I decided that I wanted to get her into one of the self-growth weekend workshops I had highly prized in helping me shift my life, so I talked with her for some time, attempting to sway her into attending. She finally acquiesced and signed up for it. I was thrilled. I could see that the end of our suffering was at hand. From my perspective, this was the most potent road and the best I could offer to get her moving in the right direction.

We agreed that she would stay with Sean and me while she attended the workshop. This way, we could more easily support her if she needed it.

Two days before the seminar, we got a call from someone at the organization saying that in going through her paperwork, they noticed that she was in therapy but had not included a letter of permission from her psychiatrist to attend the workshop. As she relayed the story to Sean and me, she began to cave. Watching her, I could feel my hopes begin to wane and I started to panic. I said that she simply must do whatever it would take to get her in the workshop. We agreed that she would call her psychiatrist and ask him to write the note. She called and left him a message; it was the night before the workshop when he finally called her back. She had her lunch packed and was ready to go. When he learned what she was intending to do, he refused to write the letter. He had never experienced the workshop personally but felt she was not strong enough to be put through this type of thing. She pleaded with him, but he refused.

Although my mother appeared to be upset by what had happened, it seemed as if she also felt relieved by not having to attend the workshop. I was utterly devastated. The next day she packed her things and drove back home.

All my hopes of ever having a functional mother were gone, and I felt myself let go. Things began to deteriorate more rapidly for her after this.

One night within a year or so, I got a call from the emergency room. They told me my mother had attempted suicide and that they had just pumped her stomach. This was her second attempt, and like the first time—while Rick, her husband, was out of town —she took an overdose of Valium while drinking vodka, afterward calling the paramedics to rescue her. Her psychiatrist had stopped seeing her, so she was on her own. They told me that she was in their custody for seventy-two hours, and that if I wanted to have her transferred somewhere for help, this would be the time and I would not need her consent. I decided to have her sent to a care unit nearby that dealt with addictions. I knew they would at least dry her out and give her some therapy.

As difficult as it was, the period when my mother was in the care unit was a gift because it was the first time in my life that I witnessed her without alcohol for any length of time. I have vague snippets of memories of her—usually in the morning or early afternoon, before she began to drink—where I can recall her laughing without the encouragement of alcohol, or when she was being lighthearted and playful and singing for me with the quality of voice that let me know she could have been a torch singer.

Over her six-week stay, I got a glimpse into who she really was, mostly by coming to the family counseling nights. In group sessions, the patients and their families would sit in a circle, and one by one the patients would talk about how they were feeling. When she spoke, her voice trembled. She was so quiet that I doubt all could hear her. *I* heard her, though. For me her voice was a clear as a bell, exposing the enormous amount of pain that was in her heart. Although she was tentative, it appeared that she was at least somewhat willing to be in the process and to look at her life, and from my hopeful perspective, it seemed that perhaps she might embrace this new life. I found her to be funny, quite bright, deeply sensitive, and charming. I really liked this woman. I cherished the time I had with her and looked forward to our future. I began to open up my heart to her again, believing that perhaps her drying out was what she needed. I hoped she would see all that she had missed by being drunk, and that we (her children) were worth working to stay sober for.

Six weeks came and went quickly, and she planned a dinner to celebrate her return. With excitement in my heart, we drove to her house. I couldn't wait to see her sober in her own home and with us children together. I walked inside and could smell something delicious cooking in the kitchen. I made my way to my mother as she bustled away. I said hello, gave her a tight hug, and then it registered: on the counter next to where she was standing was a glass of wine. I gasped as I felt my heart sink. "Mom, I thought you weren't drinking anymore!"

In a lighthearted voice, she said, "Don't worry honey, it's just one glass of wine." I felt a weight hit hard in the room. I had done enough research over the years to know that an alcoholic doesn't just drink one glass of anything, and it wasn't possible that she would stop at a single glass of wine. Still, and probably so that I could make it through the night, I held to the empty hope that it would be just one.

As anticipated, my hope was dashed when within a short period of time she was back in full swing. Shortly after this, her marriage came to an end. Rick said that he had had enough.

Rick made a good living, and my mother had enjoyed a comfortable lifestyle. Now, however, she would have to downsize and find a place to live on her own. She wanted to live closer to her children, and so she moved into an apartment that was within fifteen minutes from where Sean and I lived. I had concerns about this because I didn't want her drinking to affect our lives more than it already had, but we also felt that having her close would be better if we needed to be of help. So while holding our collective breaths, we helped her move in.

Around that time, I attended a seminar for women only. Throughout the weekend we discussed many of the issues that we, as women, carried through life. I became disturbed in the seminar when one of the women talked about how great her mother was and how her mother was the best thing in her life. I had no such experience, although I wanted it more than I knew how to express. I had had moments of joy with my mother over the years, but they were always cut short when the liquor started to flow. I felt angry and wanted to express the pain I felt around this. I stood up and explained to the group that my mother only cared about herself, and that if she really cared for me, she would stop her drinking for good. I said I wished that she would just learn to cope with her pain so that she could be sober. I could not understand why this was so difficult for her. I sobbed as I heaved out my feelings. Then Diane, the seminar leader, said something that stopped me in my tracks. It was so simple and yet profoundly accurate. She said, "I disagree that your mother hasn't found a way to cope with her pain and suffering." She continued confidently, "Your mother's pain is so deep that talking about it just isn't an option. She obviously doesn't have the tools. Somewhere along the way she discovered that drinking helped her feel better (albeit by numbing). So, in fact, she's dealing with her pain and coping…the best and only way she knows how."

I remember clearly how her words penetrated me. Within seconds I broke down, unleashing the floodgates, as a powerful wave of compassion came rushing through me. I could see my mother's entire life and how she had lived by coping the best way she knew how. I could feel her profound pain, as well as her desire to have a life that had some semblance of joy in it.

My world and my ongoing experience of her was never the same after that. Although I still had to exert boundaries with her, it seemed less personal and was therefore less need for resentment.

PEBBLE

Humility is the pebble for this chapter.

My feelings of expectation, disappointment, sadness, and loss allowed me to live in anger with my mother. My arrogance prompted me to judge her. My love made me want to see her healed. My codependency prompted me to try to take her healing into my hands.

It was humility that shifted everything. It allowed me to see the truth about my mother, and in doing so to cultivate some peace with her and within myself. From this place, an inner strength began to grow in me, and with it, forgiveness and freedom from the blame that had been disintegrating my love for her.

Chapter Twenty-Six

THE HOUSEGUEST

∾

*A*nother part of the collage that was forming simultaneously with my mother's issues was that my father had become temporarily unable to support himself. He was still a land salesman, but his particular type of business was hit hard by the early-eighties recession. He became unemployed, and since he had no savings, he had nowhere to go.

He approached Sean and me and asked if he could live with us until he got on his feet again. It was early on in our marriage and I was not keen on the idea of supporting my father, but I could not turn him away. After some deliberation, Sean and I agreed that he could stay with us for a finite period of time. We lived in a two-bedroom home and figured we would let him use the second bedroom that was also our office.

It was challenging knowing that my father was so vulnerable. In the same way I hoped my mother would miraculously be healed, I hoped my father would become financially stable and emotionally dependable. I could feel that something was off with him, but I discounted my feeling and chalked it up to my just feeling uncomfortable with the situation. It was doubly difficult to have him living with me while my mother's world was crumbling during the process of her divorce. It felt like their worlds were collapsing onto mine, and this frightened me greatly. I had not yet learned to set boundaries with them, and I couldn't foresee a happy future with them in it. Thankfully, as far as my father being a houseguest, he was ideal. We hardly heard him or saw him. He was very respectful and considerate.

He lived with us for three months the first time and another several months a couple of years later when he became homeless again. In both cases, he left once he got another job. What I didn't know then was that it was just the beginning of him spinning out of control.

PEBBLE

In choosing which experiences to write about, I usually choose ones that had potent messages for me. The meaning in this story was a bit challenging to discover, however. At first it seemed that the pebble was simply that sometimes in life, one has to be of service to those right in front of you—that the overall picture of what is important in life boils down to the moment to moment personal choices we make. This is a valuable pebble to have collected for sure.

In hindsight, though, I also know that during this time I was intuiting something about my father that had not yet manifested—his general decline in health and well-being. Had I honored and expanded on my intuition, I don't know that I would have done anything differently in the situation described in this chapter, but I most likely would have been able to see more clearly what he was beginning to create in his life. Perhaps then I would have been able to center myself more, which would have been good for my well-being.

Chapter Twenty-Seven

GRACE TAKES HER HAND

❦

*M*y mother was settled into her apartment and we saw her periodically, always in the daytime while she still had her faculties about her.

Many nights over the next year or so, I got calls from her reaching out in her loneliness. While I talked with her some of these times, I realized that because she was usually inebriated when she called, none of what I said would stick, let alone be remembered the next day. I resorted to insisting that she not call me at night if she was going to call drunk. She tested me a few times, and when I could hear that she had been drinking, I reminded her that I wasn't going to talk to her. Then I told her that I was going to hang up and did. Although setting boundaries with her was very difficult to do, it gave me a feeling of strength and helped me maintain my sense of well-being. If I wanted to see her I would arrange to meet her early in the day.

In July of 1982, I got a call from a police officer. He told me that my mother had passed out while walking home from the store. (Evidently, when she awoke, the police asked her who could help her and she said that she had children but we would not come to her aid.) When he asked if I was going to be able to help her, I told him she had support around her and that I would be right there.

I took her to the emergency room at the local teaching hospital. They gave her an examination, and while she sat on the exam table I could see how distended her belly had become and how thin her legs had gotten. It broke my heart to see this. I had watched her body decline over the years, but it wasn't until she was sitting with only a gown on that I saw how frail she had become. I explained her history with alcoholism to the doctors, and they asked her if she had recently drunk. She said she had been drinking only very little. They weren't exactly sure why she fainted but told her that she absolutely must stop drinking and recommended that she go on a low-sodium diet. They hoped this would help with the terrible edema she was suffering from.

I left the hospital feeling like we had gotten no help at all, but I also felt that that was going to be as good as it was going to get. So on the way home, we went to the store and purchased several low-sodium items so that she could begin this new regime.

Two weeks later on a Saturday night, I received a disturbing call. My mother sounded very disoriented and said something about me doing something bad to her and her not being all right with it. I assumed that she was just drunk, and I assured her that I had done nothing. I then said that I would come over to check on her in the morning.

I called early the next day to see how she was and she still sounded odd, not drunk, but also not herself. She seemed disoriented and continued her accusations about me doing something to her. I felt that something was wrong, so Sean and I hurried to her apartment where we found her sitting on the couch with a strange look on her face. Blood was smeared on the wall behind her. I rushed over to her and asked if she was all right. Her eyes looked distant and not at all present. The back of her hair had blood all through it. We couldn't see a wound, but we figured there had to be one, so we immediately got her wrapped up, put her in the car, and drove her to the emergency room at the same hospital. They wheeled her in and sent us to the waiting room. We were there for some time before someone came out and told us that they had to run some tests on her and wanted to keep her at the hospital. They recommended we go home and that they would let me know as soon as they knew something. I felt utterly helpless but had some comfort that she was in good hands, so we drove home and spent the rest of the day waiting to hear. After no word by evening, we finally called to see how my mother was doing. They said that she was agitated and had been sedated. They still didn't know anything.

The next day was a workday, and as a way of keeping my mind occupied, I decided to go in to work. Some time midday I got a call from a doctor at the hospital. There was a grave tone in her voice that made no sense to me. When I asked how my mother was, the doctor informed me that she had a less than twenty percent chance of survival. "What do you mean?" I said. "She was there just two weeks ago and they told us she just needed to go home and stop eating salt." It was then I learned that my mother was now suffering from the toxins spilling out into her system. The doctor suggested that my brothers and me come to the hospital to get the total picture of what was happening.

I got off the phone, stunned by what I had just heard. The world I existed in usually felt quite large, but within the time span of that call, it went to feeling minute. There were no thoughts in my mind other than, *My mother is probably going to die? How could this be? This can't be. How could this have changed so drastically in two weeks?*

After getting someone to cover for me and calling Sean, my father, and my brothers, I hurried home so that Sean could drive me to the hospital. Stuart and Nate said they would meet us there as soon as they could.

We arrived first, and while we waited for the others, we went into my mother's room. The sight of her hooked up to IVs and monitors, and the smells that came from whatever medicines they were using, almost made me faint. I stood looking at her in shock. She was obviously agitated and disoriented and began to talk to me in hushed tones. She said I had no idea what they were doing to her in there and that I had to take her away immediately. I looked into her eyes and again saw the distant look. I realized that although she didn't like the tests they were doing on her, they weren't inappropriate. I also knew that what she was saying was based only in her reality. I tried to comfort her and let her know that whatever tests they were doing were necessary so that they could help her. She insisted that they were evil and doing terrible things to her. After a while, I felt that my being there was probably making her more agitated, so I told her that I needed to go but would be back.

I left the room and sobbed. Sean comforted me as best as he could, but this felt much bigger than anything I had ever dealt with and more immense than what could be comforted. All I could do was breathe and let Sean hold me.

Nate, Stuart, and Stuart's wife eventually arrived at the hospital, and while we were sitting in the family area, we updated them on what was happening. A couple of hours later two doctors came to us and gave us a clear picture of my mother's condition. She was in fact suffering from toxicity from her liver and kidneys being overloaded. They said that although they were not too hopeful it would work, they thought her only chance of survival was to surgically implant a shunt of some sort in her body. They hoped that diverting her blood would allow her to detoxify without causing her organs to shut down. They informed us that the decision would have to be made now because there wasn't much time. We quickly conceded.

Many of the details that happened over the next eight or so days are very fuzzy in my memory. What I do remember clearly, however, is that after the surgery my mother didn't regain consciousness. We waited and waited for a sign that she would come back; and in fact, one day it looked as if she just might pull through. One of the doctors expressed that they didn't want us to get our hopes up—they weren't sure if this was a true turn for the better, or if it was something that often occurs just before people let go. He said that if she did pull through, it would be a very long and difficult process of recovery. He was not sure how much permanent damage there was or how her quality of life would be. In any case, he suggested putting a photo or something she might like on the wall in the event she regained consciousness.

When I heard this news, I felt at once happy and like a heavy weight had just been left on my heart. I thought to myself, *Do I have anything left to give her?* All the pain I experienced throughout my life around her alcoholism seemed to flash in front of my eyes. I remember bowing my head and taking a very deep breath as I thought, *Oh, this would be a long road.* In that fraction of a moment, I felt a knowing within that I had to believe in her ability to heal. I then raised my head, and with the heaviness still in my heart I looked at her and thought, *Mom, if you want to live, then I will be here for you.* I looked at Sean and said, "Let's go get her something for the wall."

In the car, I began to run through all the different options of what would be best and decided that whatever it was, it should be large enough to be easily seen. Then it came to me. She had told me on many occasions that the favorite vacation of her life was when she and several of her friends went to Canada together. She was in her twenties at the time. She would show me the photos and reminisce that it was the most fun she had ever had and that the scenery was breathtaking. With this memory I informed Sean that I wanted to get the biggest poster of Canada I could find. Hours later we entered her room with a gorgeous poster of the Canadian Rockies. I felt that if anything would do the trick, this would. We lovingly taped the poster on the wall and waited for a sign. I prayed, *Just open your eyes, Mom. See what beauty there is in the world.*

She continued to stabilize that day and the doctors became somewhat confident that she would now be able to breathe on her own, so they took out the respirator. As I stood there, looking at her without the tube in her mouth, I had the strangest experience. It was as if she let me know what she was thinking. It went something like this: *I can't put you through this. I see that you will be here for me, but it will be too difficult on everyone.* I remember then thinking: *What a strange thought to have.* I chose to not tell anyone and kept it to myself. In fact, I have never told another soul about this until now.

The next day she took a turn for the worse, and they had to intubate her again. After the nurses had finished the procedure, I stood in the room looking at her and at the poster and thought about how we had tried.

At some point, either that day or the next, the doctors called us all into a room that had a blackboard. One doctor drew a picture describing what he thought would happen over the next few days. What he drew was a graph of her life from that day with a line traveling downwards until the time he anticipated she would die. He said that all of her organs were now ceasing to function and that her end was coming quickly, probably within a day or two; he was sorry, but they had done all that they could. He then said that he needed to know if we wanted them to perform CPR when her heart inevitably stopped. After recovering from the finality of what he said, we discussed it and came to the unanimous decision not to have them do so. It seemed clear it was her time to go.

At this point, I was not sure how to put one foot in front of the other. *How does one do this?* I thought. *How do I watch my mother die?* After some time it occurred to me that even though my mother wasn't religious or spiritual, I wanted to have Al, our beloved minister who had married Sean and me, come and perform a last rites ritual for her. I needed to feel Spirit strongly during this process, and I felt I needed support to do so.

That evening, Al came to the hospital. I asked that my brothers, my sister-in-law, and Sean all be there. Al was wonderful in the way he consoled us with his comforting words and empathetic presence. Brokenhearted, we all stood around my mother watching her as she lay there without any signs of life except the sound of her heartbeat from the monitor. We joined hands, and Al began to speak and to pray. I got very emotional and started to sob. I couldn't see or hear; I could hardly hold myself up. Then something happened that I would never forget. I was holding my mother's hand when all of the sudden a powerful thrust of energy moved from what in my mind's eye looked like beyond her body, then through her body, and then completely through my body. As the energy passed through me, I heard what seemed to be a message from beyond, my mother saying, *I love you Donna. Be at peace.* Then all at once, as if a spell had been broken, all the sadness left me. The crying stopped and I felt deep peace settle in. I stood there in wonder at what had just transpired, and I said a prayer of thanks. Shortly after Al completed his ritual, we all stood there hugging each other and looking at my mother. We knew her death would come soon.

During our drive home that evening, Sean asked me what had happened at the hospital. He had noticed the shift in me. I relayed to him my experience and he was affected by my story. He then said that he wanted to put some music together on a tape so that I could listen to it and feel comfort in the hours to come. I said that I would like that very much.

The next day we all waited at the hospital for my mother's passing. I hovered over her watching, waiting, and praying while we comforted each other. Late in the morning I had the feeling that I wanted to go outside and be in the sun for a short time. I asked Sean to come with me, and we strolled out to the front of the hospital. We found a large planter. Sean sat on it, and I lay down and rested my head on his lap. He put the headphones on me and turned the tape on. The music he chose flowed sweetly through my heart and mind as the sun warmed my face. I felt in a state of peace. It was during the gorgeous piece "Gynopedies," by French composer Erik Satie, that I felt my mother's spirit floating above me as if to say a final goodbye, and then it began to float away. Shortly afterward, I felt Sean's hand gently touch my shoulder. I opened my eyes to see my sister-in-law coming toward me and took off the headphones. Upon reaching me, she said that my mother had just passed away. I thanked her for coming to tell me and told Sean that I had felt my mother leave.

We walked upstairs to my mother's bed and looked at the frail body that no longer housed her spirit. I thought to myself, *There is nothing left. She now lives only in my heart and in my memory.*

After a time, the doctors approached us and said that because this was a teaching hospital, they would learn much from my mother's organs. They asked if they could perform an autopsy, and because we appreciated the care the hospital had given to my mother and to us, we decided to let them have her body. We hoped that their studies would help others, so we agreed and they thanked us.

Before leaving the hospital, I called Laura and another friend Cara (who I had gotten close to from my seminar days) and told them that it was over. They had been in contact with me throughout the last couple of weeks, and I promised to let them know when she was gone. As I was on the phone, I gazed toward the east and saw the afternoon sun begin to descend while scattered coastal clouds hovered. I felt the ocean call to me.

I asked Sean to drive me to the beach. We spent time by the water listening to the waves rustle up on the shore. It was the day before our anniversary, and we gave thanks that my mother left that day and not the next. The rest of the afternoon was spent in reflection. I was grateful that my mother's struggle and life of suffering was over. I felt deep love for her, and I knew that this feeling of love would remain with me always. I felt at peace with the knowledge that my life was now free of the constant pain of her struggle. And I felt deep sadness for the loss of her.

Beautiful flower arrangements began to arrive from friends and family. Each card that accompanied the flowers was heartfelt in its wishes. It was comforting to know that my friends were there to support me, and I loved receiving the flowers but also felt sadness that as beautiful as they were, that they too would come to an end. I recall wishing that their beauty could somehow last so that some semblance of the beauty of my mother would last.

My brothers and I had to discuss how we wanted to handle my mother's burial, and all of us agreed that we wanted to have a burial at sea. We contacted the Neptune Society and arranged to have a private burial.

A week or so after my mother's death, the family members who were available gathered to go out on the boat. It was a beautiful August morning. We powered out to sea and then stopped at the point where we wanted to have the service. Al performed a simple and beautiful ceremony, and we all listened while the water slapped up against the side of the boat and the warm sun shone upon us. My brothers and I took turns pouring our mother's ashes into the water. I watched the ocean receive her remains and carry them deep inside. My mother became the ocean and the ocean became my mother. Somehow, this was very soothing to me.

We came back to our home and Laura showed up at our doorstep with a huge cooked turkey and a delicious casserole to add to the smatterings of food that I had prepared. Although everyone's presence that day was appreciated, her gesture of love is the one I remember most. Because of my mother's cooking, I always associated food with nurturing. Laura knew this, and we all shared food as is traditional for these sorts of ceremonies. It meant the most to me, though. It felt like a perfect and poignant way to end my mother's life—all of us eating wonderful food together and loving the memory of the goodness within Betty.

∽

In Memoriam

Betty Irene
October 27, 1927—August 19, 1982
Beloved Mother

Your memory will always be cherished.
I send you warm cookies, baked with love.

∽

PEBBLE

In time, several pebbles appeared on my path from this experience.

I had known it was possible to witness miracles in life, but I didn't know that they could be witnessed in the dying process. By my surrendering to the situation and the inevitability of its outcome, as well as to the emotions that were present, I was able to experience the flow of Spirit—to its messages, to its love, and to its healing. I came away from my mother's death with the feeling that I had experienced something miraculous and supernatural.

And…as always, Grace was there to catch me, and recognizing this gave me the pebble of perspective. Within a three-month span of time before and after my mother's death, I was intricately involved in helping with and being in a close friend's wedding, and I was also present at the birth of Laura's beautiful son. The healing I experienced by the perspective I gained from these events and their close proximity to each other was potent and profound. I came out of this period knowing that death, although excruciatingly difficult to watch, was a fundamental aspect of life—as is love and birth. I moved forward feeling privileged to have experienced these elements of life on earth so intimately and to have the knowledge that one does not exist without the other. I found solace in this perspective.

Some time after my mother's death, I found a birthday card she had once given me. Its message read, "Daughter, You're more than just a breath of fresh air; you are more like a happiness tornado." I read it over a few times before something dawned on me. I was that for her—I had been one of the greatest sources of love and joy in her life. I once believed that her experience and expression of love for and from me was cancelled by her drinking, but in reading the card I understood that her love had prevailed through her despair, her suffering, her drinking, and even her death. Her drinking didn't impact her love for me—it only impacted my experience of love from her. This I could work with…and I did.

To this day, if I take a few moments and stop, I can feel what I perceive to be her love pressing into me.

Chapter Twenty-Eight

RELEASING GRIEF

⌘

*A*s one could expect, the months that followed were like riding an emotional roller coaster. At times I was at peace and at other times I felt intense grief from losing my mother, or more accurately, from not having a mother in my life. There were times when the grief was deep—like a part of my body was missing.

One night several months after her death, I was feeling the loss particularly intensely. Sean and I were at Cara and her husband's home for dinner, and I was very teary and not functioning well. Cara had experience in the self-help world and in working with people, and she suggested that I go into the bathroom and have a conversation with my mother. I thought it was a silly idea but was willing to try. Feeling self-conscious, I got up and walked into the bathroom. I looked at myself in the mirror and said, "Just close your eyes and talk to her." As I began to speak out loud I had a strange sensation that she, or someone, was listening to me. I continued to tell her how I felt and how much I missed having a mother, but in my mind I heard words that felt as if they didn't come from me. That voice explained that what kept me feeling connected to my mother was my grief, and as long as I kept feeling grief, I was feeling my mother. So, in essence, I had an attachment —or an investment—in staying in the state of grief. Once I recognized this, I understood that I had a choice of *how* to feel her in my life—either through my grief and loss, or through my enduring love. I decided to choose love. I walked out of the bathroom much improved and able to function and engage in life again.

PEBBLE

I will call this the processing pebble. Over the years, I had learned how to process—meaning that I gave deep thought to all sides of an issue in order to achieve a desired result, usually to gain a shift in perspective and/or to resolve or release a painful thought or feeling. I learned here that one could process and clear, not only with those present, but also with those we do not have physical access to. This essentially showed me that I could process about almost anyone and anything, given my depth of consciousness with regard to a given issue.

Chapter Twenty-Nine

TIRES TO THE ROAD

✍

$\mathcal{I}$ began to heal from my mother's death and stepped back into the happy life that Sean and I had together.

Around this time, Laura and her family moved back to Reno. Although I was deeply saddened by her move, and knew I would miss her terribly, I felt it was best for her. I knew our friendship would endure through time and distance, and I encouraged her to make herself happy. Knowing that she would be living in Reno and close to her parents gave me a strong sense of peace.

As I mentioned earlier on the path, Sean had taken on computer consulting to create a more substantial lifestyle for us. This was back in the day when computer programs were written out on what were called flow charts. I thoroughly enjoyed being around him while he worked, as well as helping him from time to time with the charting of the programs. We loved to travel, but we couldn't afford for him to take time off work for us to do so. Rather than have our lack of funds stop us, we took Sean's work on the road. We would pile his papers into our old Volkswagen van where he worked off and on during our journeys. He said that because we were together, it didn't feel like work. We would sleep in the van and every few days we would check into a motel and take a shower.

One of our road trips took over a month, driving from California to Oregon, through Washington, and high into the Canadian Rockies, then down into Montana, Idaho, Utah, Colorado, and Arizona. We saw some utterly breathtaking scenery as we wove our way through the states and Canada. We expected beauty and adventure, and we found it from one experience to the next.

While driving through Idaho one day, I was hungry for dinner and said to Sean, "What I really want is a great home-cooked meal in a place where the mom is the waitress, the dad is the cook, and the son washes the dishes. And I want a homemade dessert." He said, "Great, let's go for it," and there began our mission.

We followed our noses and pulled into the parking lot of a small diner that, from the outside, looked promising. We walked into the place and in the distance I could hear the sizzle of food being fried. It was hot inside, and there was a haze of smoke that made it difficult to breathe freely. I was then overcome with a smell like an over stimulated armpit. We looked around at the people inside, and people looked at us as if we were from another country. I looked at Sean and he looked back as if having the same visceral moment. "This definitely is not the place." I quickly agreed and we bolted out the door. We gasped for air as we laughed all the way back to the car.

We kidded that we were evidently not clear enough in asking for what we wanted, and we stated it again, this time adding the words *clean and hospitable* to the list. We got focused and began to look at the surrounding diners. Then one of us (I cannot remember which) saw a little place that looked cozy and said, "Let's try that place. It feels right." We parked the car and walked with hope in each step. As we stepped in, a rush of cool air passed around us and I noticed several large ceiling fans circulating air throughout the place. Standing just inside the door was a young woman with a pleasant smile. She welcomed us and promptly took us to a comfortable booth and handed us menus. We looked around, noting the place was spotless. "So far, so good," we whispered to each other. I then noticed a youngish boy collecting dishes from the tables and an older man in the kitchen. Within minutes another woman, probably in her late thirties, came over to our table with water, welcoming us with a smile. She asked if we wanted anything to drink and we ordered freshly squeezed lemonade. She informed us before she walked away that everything on the menu was home-cooked. Sean and I looked at each other and smiled. We looked down at our menus and our jaws dropped—everything one could imagine from a country diner was featured, including the unexpected surprise of homemade scones. When the waitress came back, we inquired about the place. She shared that she and her husband, the cook, owned it, and that their daughter was the hostess and their son was the busboy. Sean and I looked at each other victoriously and gave the woman our food order.

Our dinner was picture perfect and the service was impeccable. Of course, we couldn't leave without having a couple of their desserts, so we topped off our meal with scones, fresh out of the oven, with melted butter and a warm berry cobbler.

Another profound experience during the same trip came one day as we were driving through Wyoming, dazzled by the majestic, snow-capped mountain range off to our right. In the distance we could see a smallish building. It was out in the middle of nowhere and we wondered about its purpose. As we came upon it we saw a small steeple and realized it was a church. "Great location!" we said simultaneously. We parked and reverently walked inside. As we entered, I was overwhelmed by the sight of the mountains through a huge wall of glass with a large cross of rugged wood positioned up high and to the middle. Then I noticed the absence of sound and the silence that came over my mind. It was as if, for that moment, time had stopped. As I stood in awe of the view, I felt as if the building was saying, THIS, what you are looking at, THIS IS THE DIVINE. I felt humbled by the simplicity of it all. I looked around and saw no frills or ornate decorations, just a simple pulpit and several rows of pews for parishioners to sit in and commune. There was not even a floor; only earth was beneath our feet. We felt moved to stay for a time in the silence and continued to take it all in. I left there with a feeling that I had witnessed a holy place and that I was being given another example of how one could feel the holy just by being present in the moment and letting go.

Lastly, there was a day while traveling through the Canadian Rockies when we were stopped by a herd of sheep making their way from one side of the road to the other. There were hundreds of them. Assuming it would take a while for them to pass, and since we were in no hurry, we got out of the car to take a closer look. The man herding the sheep was kind and didn't seem to mind our presence. The sheep walked up to us as if we were long-lost friends and let us scratch their heads and pet them. More and more of them made their way to us, probably thinking we had food, but they didn't seem disappointed when they discovered that we didn't. In fact, they showed contentment just listening to me squeal with delight, petting as many of them as I could get to. I remember leaving there feeling that the joy I found in that experience was every bit as important as other moments in my life that may have been more obviously "meaningful." To me, feeling that kind of joy in living was feeling the presence and essence of Spirit, God, or the Divine.

PEBBLE

We had many journeys of this type throughout our marriage, and we knew we were blessed with each and every one—blessed that we lived on a continent where we could drive freely from one extraordinary sight to another; that there was such beauty in the world, that we had the eyes to see it; that we could laugh and enjoy each other the way we did, as best friends and as husband and wife; that we had the resources and good health to be able to take such trips; that we had a car to take us from place to place; and that these types of experiences brought a welcome equilibrium to my life.

Chapter Thirty

GIVING BACK

∽

*A*fter my mother's death, I began to come into my own.

Sean and I believed that the two of us together were bigger than each of us individually. We felt blessed, and we wanted to take the inspiration we found in each other and in our relationship and put it in service to others. We became great partners, and throughout our marriage we made music and produced and/or participated in many fundraising events. We knew that sharing ourselves was a way of connecting to our "higher purpose"—through our talents to spread love and goodness with those who came across our path.

We were fortunate to be able to ride on the gift of Sean's music. We toured together, and at times, when we had the group with us, I accompanied them on handheld percussion instruments. I had a strong sense of rhythm and was quite natural at performing. Sean and I, working together spreading his music, felt like a perfect union. He was prolific, and we made six albums together.

I remember feeling that each concert, no matter where we were, felt like inviting people into our living room. We always wanted our guests to feel welcome and to be part of a sphere of joy. At one concert in particular, where we wanted to show our gratitude to the two hundred or so fans who had bought tickets, we decided to have a reception afterward and invite everyone on stage to serve them wine and other drinks. But I wanted to do something even more special. *What could we do that would be the icing on the cake?* I wondered. Then I told Sean, "That's it! I'll bake cakes." After looking at me as if I had just said I would walk to the moon, he asked how many I would have to bake in order to serve everyone. I figured there would be two hundred people, not all of whom would eat. "Let's say one hundred and eighty people would want cake. One would serve about twelve, so I would have to bake fifteen cakes. No problem!" I said. We had two ovens in the house we were renting at the time, and after having baked dozens and dozens of cookies every holiday, this seemed like it would be a snap.

Sean played the concert and it turned out to be one of his best. It also happened to be one that was recorded and televised. The guests were delighted when Sean announced that there would be a reception on stage afterward. As people came up, many of whom I imagined had never been on a stage, they looked as if it were Christmas morning and Santa had just brought them something wonderful. The happiness in their faces was precious, and the joy in the room was palpable. As people waited their turn to meet Sean, I delighted at their bulging eyes at the array of cakes, smiling heartily as I served people and listened to their "Wows" and "Ahs." The evening must have been a smash, because the concert ran on the local TV station every year for the next several years.

An equally touching night occurred after another one of Sean's concerts. A couple approached us and said that they had taped some of Sean's music and played it during the birth of their child. They shared how the music greatly comforted the woman while in her birthing process, and they were happy that his music was the first thing their baby heard. I was deeply moved by their story, as well as by their sincerity and gratitude.

PEBBLE

We never truly know the reach of our actions and how they affect people known and unknown to us. These experiences were powerful learning moments for me.

I vaguely began to understand that all of our actions, whether positive or negative, spread out from us like a web or a wave touching all those in our path. In the years that followed, I became deeply immersed in the profound lessons to be learned from this principle.

Chapter Thirty-One

WHEN THE STUDENT IS READY

 confused

It was in meeting and working with four people, all of whom I met within a couple of years before and after my mother's death, that inspired me to take my life in a new direction. As you will see, they were all quite different in what they offered, yet each of them in very specific and complementary ways profoundly affected my existence and who I would become.

Shin Jyutsu®

A Japanese woman by the (married) name of Mary Burmeister brought Jin Shin Jyutsu®[1], an ancient Asian art of harmonizing the energy flows within the body, to America in the 1950s. Said to predate Buddha and Moses, this healing practice was rediscovered in the early 1900s by Master Jiro Murai, who, after recovery from a "terminal" illness, devoted himself to the revival of the art to help others.

Jin Shin Jyutsu is translated as "Know Myself It Is." A form of acupressure, the practice revolves around a person pressing their fingers on their own or another person's body in particular places and in an often complex order. Pressing these points frees up the energy current in the body and helps it flow in a more healthful way.

A close friend of mine who was having sessions with Glen, a man trained by Mary after he was healed from cancer, introduced me to this. She said that every time she had sessions with him, she felt very good afterward. With my sense that touch could heal or at least make people feel better, I scheduled a session with him to experience it myself.

I was utterly astonished by how I felt afterward. I was fortunate to be fairly healthy so I wasn't looking for big results, but an acute sense of well-being came over me during and after that session and all the ones that followed.

After having been so moved by the work, I decided that I wanted to learn how to work on people myself. I later took two seminars with Mary. She was a master at teaching, and although she offered a staggering amount of information, I thoroughly enjoyed learning from her.

After graduating from her classes, I worked with people off and on for years. Jin Shin Jyutsu became the inspiration for, and the beginning foundation of, a type of body/mind work I began to do later on down the path.

Clairvoyant Nutrition

The one area of my health where I needed help was with the way I ate. I was an intense *sugarholic* and had very little understanding about nutrition. I knew that when I ate certain foods, I could feel moderately sick but didn't know why. I also had regular bouts with a gastrointestinal issue throughout my life. The one doctor I consulted about this could not decipher the cause and simply suggested I take an antacid when the symptoms arose. After this I met Eileen Poole[2], a unique kind of nutritionist who showed me how to eat healthfully and taught me some basics about food combining.

There are a few ways to test for food allergies and intolerances —taking blood and scratching the skin are two methods— but Eileen tests by touching your hand and getting an intuitive impression. Henry Bieler, Eileen's mentor, called her clairvoyant. She, however, prefers to refer to herself simply as a nutritionist...

and she is great at it! Through my sessions with her, I learned that I was allergic to wheat (which explained why every time I ate wheat I needed to take a nap, got constipated, and had mucus in my eyes the next day) and soy. I also learned that I was lactose intolerant, which clarified the source of the innumerable horrendous stomachaches I had in my youth, as well as in my adult years after eating ice cream, which I did often. And I further discovered that I was intolerant of cane sugar (which explained Sean's statement, "You eat it now, I argue with it later."). My energy and emotions often felt like they were on a roller coaster.

When I stopped eating these foods, all of the symptoms ceased. I also found that eating the things that didn't work for my body caused me to carry extra weight I struggled to shed. This also weakened my immune system, which explained why I caught so many colds, flus, etc. As I mentioned previously, I had always thought of myself as being fairly healthy, but it was not until I stopped eating certain foods and began to eat more healthfully that I learned how much better I could feel. I saw how many of the uncomfortable symptoms I was putting up with, which I had thought were just part of my unique body function issues, were actually a result of poor eating.

My sessions with Eileen over the years truly changed the quality of my life.

Astrology

In the seventies, Chakrapani Ullal[3], an East Indian Vedic astrologer, was the private astrologer for the Swami Muktananda, a renowned Hindu guru (a religious teacher and spiritual guide). I had heard that astrology (a system of the influences of the stars' and planets' positions and aspects on human affairs and terrestrial events) was able to give people perspectives on their life paths— the twists and turns and ebbs and flows that we cycle through. I had understood qualities about myself up to a point, but it was not until I had my readings with Chakrapani, and later readings with an astrologer named P.J. Tyler[4], that I gained a much deeper understanding into myself. For instance, I learned that I am what is called a triple Pisces. There are twelve "signs" of the zodiac, of which Pisces is one. Each sign has specific emotional and mental attributes. On their good days, Pisces are kind, gentle, compassionate, giving, intuitive, and wise (they are the oldest of the signs). On their not-so-good days, they can be overly emotional, wishy-washy, moody, indecisive, and oversensitive. A triple anything is when someone's Sun (a person's center, their basic self), Moon (what gives a person their particular personality), and Rising (a person's awakening consciousness) signs are all in the same astrological sign when they are born, meaning they are expo-nentially *more* of all the attributes. The Sun is the overall sign that generally defines who we are and how we are seen. The Moon represents our emotions and how we feel. And the Rising represents how we present ourselves in the world. There are other signs that have to do with how we think, how we love, how we communicate, etc.

Those who are spiritually evolved will tell you that we can transcend our astrology. I have found that can be true to a certain extent, but there are specific qualities in our innate nature that, although they may shift or evolve, their essences still remain at the foundation of our being.

How I began to use astrology was to first discover who I had been; second, view more clearly who I currently was; third, consider who I could possibly become; and fourth, see the general direction that my life was heading. I found it immensely helpful having a context for some of the things that were part of my life, and this helped me in navigating more easily through it. I was fascinated by how I was able to gain more perspective into how, in a world that at times seemed so random and chaotic, there could be order and systems that pointed to a divine rightness.

Spiritual Guides

Ron Scolastico[5] is a transpersonal psychologist, author, artist, trance medium, and spiritual counselor. I had heard similar things about him that I had heard about Chakrapani, the difference between them being that instead of using a system to tell people things about themselves, Ron would go into an altered state of awareness and offer wisdom coming through him from his spiritual guides—souls who, because they have already mastered the human experience, no longer project themselves into physical form. I should note that he doesn't call himself a channel, in that no disincarnate entity takes over his body and speaks through him.

What further makes Ron unique is his excellent mainstream education—he has a dual Doctorate degree in Psychology and Human Communication Theory. In addition he has a well-rounded spiritual understanding; he reaches a deep state of meditation in his readings so that when he speaks, his conscious mind, ego, and mental process are not accessed much, if at all; he possesses a spiritual orientation in alignment with the past-life theory; and he never tells a person what he or she should do—his guides are advocates of the power of personal choice. In considering a given issue, they explain in great depth what emotional and mental processes are at play and/or give the history —this life or past—that is contributing to the issue. Once the scenario is fully explained, they usually suggest a few possible options. Either way, when one has a reading, he or she comes away with a very clear picture of what the real issue is and the energy behind it, which makes them better equipped to deal with it.

Several of the fundamental concepts that I adopted from The Guides are as follows:

1. *We can never be eternally damaged. We can feel intense emotional pain, but we are spiritual beings and our spirits live in the Divine.*

When this is understood, a great sense of relief and forgiveness can take over. One can then disengage from the habits of perfectionism and self-criticism. It is as if you can feel your Divine essence and your *true* perfection as you are working out your earthly foibles.

2. *The opposite of Love is fear; not anger or hatred.*

To clarify, this type of fear is not the intuitive fear that keeps us out of harm's way, but rather the emotional fear that holds people back from their potential. I have come to understand that at the core of most, if not all, emotional suffering—persistent, painful (what some call negative) human emotions such as hate, anger, envy, impatience, depression, disgust, shame, prejudice, criticism, and even grief—is fear. Fear has many faces: racism and discrimination (often caused by fear of what is not known or understood and fear of being hurt or of something being taken away); addictions; hostility and aggression; lying and deception; and self-destructive behaviors. And fear has many variations: the fear of separation, of being alone, of being bad or wrong, of being too fragile—or too strong, of being inadequate—or too much; fear of not being lovable, of feeling emotionally unsafe; fear of the past—or the future, of the abyss; fear of personal limitation, of humiliation, of annihilation, etc. If cultivated, fear can be quite powerful. As is evidenced by the state of the world today, if enough people are plagued with it, it can wreak havoc in large ways. What many don't understand is that most emotional fear (as opposed to instinctual fear that is intended to protect you) is what *A Course in Miracles*[6] calls **F**alse **E**vidence **A**ppearing **R**eal. We perceive, for instance, that we will be hurt or abandoned by the ones we care about most, or that someone will get to our destination first (our fortune, the closest parking space), and we are triggered into feeling fear. If we know how to recognize this fear, we can then approach aggression, apathy, withholding, blame, clinging, or pleading with the intention to overcome it.

As we work individually to understand and release our fear, we can begin to disengage from its grip, and approach our lives and others' with more compassion, understanding, and patience. This not only affects our inner circle, but the microcosm as well.

3. *The "evil" we see in the world is actually various levels and intensities of fear.*

    I wholeheartedly agree. With the work I have done on both myself and on others, I have seen that acts of unkindness and unethical behavior usually, if not always, stem from fear.

4. *Fear, negativity, and conflict exist only in the human experience, and not in the Divine realms.*

    It is challenging for some to accept that there is no devil coaxing us into "sin." The *evil* that some believe in is simply human fear incarnated into matter. Yes, our fear can be that powerful. The good news is that it's within our power to heal fear. The challenge is to take responsibility for our own healing.

5. *Love is always the answer, it is the only truth, and it is more powerful than fear.*

    This is one of their most potent messages for me, which affirmed my core truth.

6. *There is not just one, but there have been many saintly people, as well as groups, who have helped guide humanity to greater levels of consciousness.*

As a child in the churches we attended and in my father's family, I had been raised in the belief system that our Christian religion (which in their minds didn't include Catholicism) was the supreme religion and that all other religions were inferior, and in some cases just plain evil. This belief was the antithesis of my personal feeling. As I attended church after church, those with my family and those with friends, I found that some felt more authentic than others. But none, except one—a Methodist church in Irvine that had a brilliant pastor who got snapped up by the Brits and moved to London—matched what I felt true spirituality was. No one I knew honored any person in history, other than Jesus, who gave great spiritual contributions to the world.

I didn't speak about my feelings to people around me, though, because they seemed to operate from that narrow belief system in one way or the other. I simply disengaged myself quietly from any and all forms of religion and their teachings. After my work with the Guides, I became able to have a larger context in which to hold many concepts and ideas and to be at peace with what I believed to be true.

Because of my numerous personal readings with Ron and the occasional group workshops I attended, I felt my somewhat fragmented spirit begin to weave its way together into a glorious tapestry of vivid color and vibrant clarity.

PEBBLE

There are a multitude of pebbles here, a few of which I have already written about. My primary offering is that when a person is ready, the teacher—or in my case, teachers—appear. I knew when that would happen it meant my life was taking a drastic change in direction. As these people entered my world, I felt an even deeper resonance with Spirit and its guidance. I felt that I was being given some precious and powerful gifts and an even stronger foundation that would carry me through the end of my living days. This feeling still holds true thirty years later.

A note about "teachers": When there is something I need to learn, someone always shows up to be my teacher, or what I call my Buddha. Now, this doesn't mean that I always like the lesson…or the teacher. In fact, some of my teachers I got down right pissed off at, but the lessons were nonetheless profound. My mother was a perfect example. Many of the "lessons" I learned while she was alive were extremely painful, but they were also powerful, and they served to give me greater depth and compassion.

So please, do not shoot the Buddha! Whether they know it or not, they're only there to serve…

Chapter Thirty-Two

A DREAM FULFILLED

∽

$\mathcal{A}$s I began to discover deeper aspects of myself, I found that there were dreams I had yet to realize. The first was modeling. Because of my height, I had always been told that I should model. The notion that I could possibly receive money because of the way I looked intrigued me. I had been told I was beautiful, but I didn't believe it; I thought I was pretty at best. Then, one day, I saw an ad in the paper where a local modeling and talent agency promoted its ability to make a model out of anyone. I said to myself, *We'll see...* and called to schedule an appointment.

A week later I showed up for my interview, doing my best to look the part. I felt humbled as the well-poised and perfectly coiffed receptionist escorted me into the owner's dark and sultry office. He was a British fellow in his early forties, five foot six and rotund. After he gave me a brief explanation of what they did, I asked him if he thought I could make it as a model. It stunned me to hear him say yes. And after a bit more conversation, he directed me to sign on the dotted line.

Over the next several months, I underwent a major trans-formation of appearance. For the first time in my life, I learned to wear *serious* makeup. I exercised like a maniac and got down to a thin one-hundred-and-forty pound frame. (The ideal bodyweight for my height was one hundred and sixty pounds, but hey, thin is how we liked our models.) I polished my nails to make my hands look more like a real woman's, and I put blonde highlights in my hair. I rather liked all the attention I was giving to my appearance. I had never done that before and it was fun. But along with the novelty, something rather uncomfortable kept quietly gnawing at me. At times when I was being photographed, I noticed how shallow it all felt. I wasn't judging it as being beneath me; it just felt empty and void of meaning. I felt like an object and not the multi-faceted human being I hoped I was. I pushed those feelings aside, trying to convince myself that I would eventually get used to it. I also thought that if I didn't learn to love it, I could do it for just a short while and then move on to something else.

When my training was complete, I looked the part and had a portfolio and zed card to show it. (A zed card is a 5x7 card that shows several body and face shots along with the agency name and model's vital information—measurements, height, and hair color.) I was now ready to audition and to promote myself to the "big" agencies in Los Angeles.

As I began to figure out how to get interviewed in Los Angeles, I worked at getting modeling jobs in Orange County. The first professional job I booked was for a prominent jean company. They needed models to show their new line of pants and were paying five hundred dollars. *All right!* I thought. *I like this business.* I accepted their offer with glee.

A few days before the show, I got a call from my agency telling me that there had been a change of plans. The jean company was concerned that because of my height, I might not fit their pants quite right, and they wondered if I was willing to dress up in a costume for the show instead. The pay would be the same. I was disappointed for a moment but figured, "How bad could it be?" and said it would be fine.

I showed up for the show and saw that the entire room was decorated in red, white, and blue. I asked someone why that was, and they said that because it was an election year (1984), they had made it the theme of the show. I thought, *OK.* I then went to check in and find out what I was going to wear. The woman I asked looked at me and said, "Good. You're tall. Your costume will look good on you."

I thought, *Oh, this is going to be great. They'll probably have me in a beautiful southern belle kind of dress.* The woman walked me over to where the costumes were and pointed to mine. I did a double take and then looked back at her in amazement, "You want me to be a donkey?!" I asked.

"Yes." she said.

I laughed. "And I have to wear that donkey head, too?" She said yes.

"Oh." I replied.

"Didn't anyone tell you what you were dressing up as?"

"No," I answered.

"Are you all right with it?" she asked.

I replied that I didn't expect to be a donkey and have my head covered, but oh well, what the heck—I'll have fun. I then threw myself into being the best model/donkey I could be. And I did have fun even though it was hotter than heck in that suit!

It seemed that the pant company had a conscience because they booked me again for their next show, this time with no costume. They must have found some longer pants for me to wear.

I got a couple of other small jobs, but nothing to speak of. So I thought to myself, *It's time to get serious about L.A.!* I got the names of all the modeling agencies and visited each one with high hopes that they would scoop me up and turn me into a top model.

The reception I got was less than lukewarm. I heard things like: "Your legs are too long." "Your hips are too wide." "Your jaw is too narrow." "Your lips are too thin." Oh yes, and, "You're too old." Although very young looking, I was twenty-six and that was old in the business. With each interview, I became more and more disheartened until I realized it looked unlikely that I would ever become a successful L.A. model.

The next questions then became, do I want to go to New York and try it there? Do I want to go to Europe and try to break into runway? Do I want to continue to get small local jobs? The answer to all of these questions was no. In the process of the interviews, I noticed I didn't like my physicality being picked apart. I was too thin-skinned to subject myself to that kind of scrutiny. This, combined with my earlier ill feelings of being perceived as an object, led me to end my short-lived modeling career.

PEBBLE

The pebble here is an interesting one. I struggled with even including this story in the book because it seemed...shallow. But I kept getting the nudge to do so, and I listened.

In the few years before modeling, I had begun to see a depth and intelligence in myself that I respected and liked. When I was modeling, no one I worked with seemed to care about my inner world and I didn't like that. What was beautiful about this story, though, was that in living out this dream, I had found a new dream—I wanted to be loved and appreciated for talents that exhibited my inner wealth rather than for my appearance or outer beauty. It was a deepening of the insight I had when I was seventeen and first noticed by boys. This was an affirmation that youthful looks are transient, whereas depth and intelligence are precious and grow more effulgent with time. This concept became even more solidified over the years.

I will refer back to something Sean once said to me when it came to creating: When you're writing music, often a wrong chord is played. Now, sometimes a wrong chord is just a wrong chord, but many times what was wrong for one thing was right for something else...or...it can take you in a different direction to something new and, at times, better.

To me this supports the adage: There are no wrong paths.

Chapter Thirty-Three

TO BE OR NOT TO BE...
AN ACTRESS

∽

*A*nother dream I wanted to live out was becoming an actress. Since my class at Long Beach State, I had a feeling I might love it. I spoke to Sean, and we decided that I would go to Hollywood and find a class to take. Since I didn't plan to go back to college in the near future, we figured that classes in Hollywood would be more effective than those I would find in Orange County.

A friend of ours had a wife who was an aspiring actress, and I asked her if she could recommend someone. She told me about a man who helped her when she first started out. His name was Jack, and I don't recall him using a specific method of acting; mostly, I remember getting familiar with reading lines from TV shows. Jack said I had natural talent and recommended that I get an agent. He took me out one day and shot some nice photos of me so that I would have some head shots to send out. He then introduced me to a woman named Nancy, who had a small boutique agency. She liked my audition and said she would represent me. I was thrilled. I thought, *Fantastic! Right out the gate and I get an agent! This must be a good sign.*

She sent me on a few auditions for TV shows, and then I got my first audition for a movie. I remember it clearly. I was very nervous going there because it was my first time meeting with a Hollywood producer. I sat down with the man and we talked for a bit. Then nonchalantly he said to me, "I don't think you're right for the part, but can I see your breasts?" I was dumbstruck. I had no idea what was happening and fumbled my words, not knowing if I should show him my chest or walk out the door. I ended up leaving. When I got home and told Sean, he was furious and had me call Nancy to let her know what had happened. She apologized for him and gave some excuse that didn't appease me.

Some time later she called me and said that I had an offer for a job that involved some travel. They had seen my photo and were willing to hire me from that and her recommendation of me. I thought, "They really do that in Hollywood?" I asked her what the job was, and she informed me that it was to tour with a group of female mud wrestlers. I couldn't believe it—one, that women actually did that, and two, that my agent had no idea what I wanted. I told her thanks but no thanks.

After a couple months of classes with Jack, I stopped going. I went back to my friend's wife and asked if she had another recommendation—perhaps someone who was teaching actual working actors.

She highly recommended John. (I found out later that she had had an affair with him, so it was no wonder she spoke highly of him.) She told me he taught scene study classes and was teaching a couple of famous people. That was good enough for me. I signed up and began classes right away. I had been taking classes for a short time when one of the younger men in the class named Larry informed me that a writer/director at his agency was looking for someone to co-star in his film. They wanted someone tall, with blonde hair and blue eyes, but he thought that my light brown hair and green eyes might suffice. He said that if I wanted him to, he would recommend me for an audition. I asked him if he was sure that the film was legitimate, and he assured me it was. I said yes, and gave him my contact information.

A few days later I got a call from his agency, and they asked me to come in for an audition. They had a scene from the film that they wanted me to work from, and I was to get it from Larry. He brought it to the next class, and we read through it together. It was certainly an interesting role. For the audition, I was asked to do the scene as if I were in withdrawal from heroin. I read John the script, and asked him how to approach it. He asked me if I knew of anyone with an addiction to drugs. I said no, but I told him I had a mother who had a drinking issue. He said perfect, that I could use that as my frame of reference. I thought, *This is interesting. I never thought I could use my mom's illness in a positive way.* He asked me to remember specifics about my mother and to try to channel how she acted. It was easier to do than I thought it would be. We ran through the lines during class until I felt I knew what I had to do. Afterward, I went home and thought intently about my mother, allowing myself to feel her dysfunction inside me.

Before the audition, I was nervous about meeting the director. I spoke to John and he offered me something that had great value. He said that those people were no different from any of the music people I dealt with in Sean's world, that I operated at their level in some ways. That made sense to me. It felt right to see them as my peers, rather than people who were above me. He also told me that they genuinely wanted people to do well, that they weren't looking for failure. That was also quite helpful.

A few days later, I walked into Larry's agency with confidence and a smile. I met Ted, the director, and he seemed pleasant enough. He asked if I was ready for the audition; I said yes and sat down. I did what I had practiced and knew that I had done well. He seemed happy and said he would be in touch. He also had said that part of the film was shooting in Italy and wanted to know if I would be willing to go there. I left feeling excited and hopeful. I had never been to Europe and it was a thrilling prospect. It felt like my dream was about to be made into reality as I impatiently waited for the call.

A few days later I got a call from Ted saying that he was very sorry, but the producer of the film wanted another woman who had auditioned for the role—she fit the blonde-haired, blue-eyed character they had originally envisioned. He was not feeling good about the producer's choice, but they had already offered it to other woman. He apologized and said that if anything changed he would let me know. I hung up feeling quite sad that I hadn't been chosen, but I also felt happy that I had done so well at my first real movie audition.

A couple of days later, after I had let go of the movie, Ted called me again and said that he had been talking to the producer, and they were rethinking the offer they had made to the other woman. He said that his gut instinct was to choose me, and they wanted to know if I was still available. I said yes! He said that he would call me in a couple of days to let me know if they would be able to get out of the contract with the other actress.

I remember so clearly how I felt the day I was to hear the final word. It was June of 1985 during the NBA playoffs. Sean and I were huge Laker fans. This was back in the day of Worthy, Bird, Kareem, Parish, Magic, Thomas, and Dr. J., to name a few. The Lakers had lost the NBA championship to the Celtics the previous eight times they had played each other, and in 1984 they lost four games to three. They were fierce rivals, but Sean and I were certain that the Lakers would take home the trophy that year. As the end of the playoffs approached, The Lakers had won three games and lost two. The day I was to hear about my film was the day they were playing the game that could bring them the championship. And to make matters tougher, they were playing on the Celtics court. The game was so intense. With the excitement of the game and waiting to hear if I got the film, I couldn't talk. I was a mess. As the game progressed and I still hadn't heard, I felt more and more like I might explode into a million pieces. Finally, late in the third quarter, I got the call. I ran into my bedroom so that I could hear Ted clearly. He said that he fought for me, and in the end they retracted the offer they made to the other woman, choosing me to play the part. I just about fainted I was so happy. Trying to keep my cool, I thanked him and made arrangements to finalize the specifics.

I got off the phone screaming wildly to Sean, telling him that I got the part. We hugged, kissed, hopped, and jumped, celebrating my win. We then calmed down and focused on bringing the Lakers to their victory. Beating the Celtics 111-110, they were the first team ever to beat the Celtics in a championship game on their home court. Even now, as I recreate that day, the excitement is still invigorating.

PEBBLE

Many pebbles were accumulated from this experience. The first was allowing my mother's illness to actually help me live out a dream. It was so poignant to willingly bring her inside me and to feel her pain living through me. It felt very healing. Earlier in Sean's and my relationship, when I was upset about something and expressed myself in a way that reminded him of my mother, he reflected back to me in words what he was seeing. When I heard this, it stopped me in my tracks. However, it also prompted me to do some work on myself to find out what negative aspects of my mother were still living in me. I believe it was this work that helped me separate what was inherent in me and what behavior I had learned from others. When I was able to see it, without blame or judgment, I was able to heal it more effectively.

While studying my character before I made the movie, I arranged to spend time with a woman who was withdrawing from heroin. The woman actually allowed me to talk with her while she was delusional. It was tragic and immensely powerful to be with this woman as she courageously fought to leave that part of her life behind her. I later visited her, and she was surprised and happy to discover that I had been real and not a delusion. It did my heart good to see her doing well in her process. This was the second pebble I received from this experience. I am deeply grateful to this woman who allowed me to speak with her, and I hope with all my heart that her life turned out happily.

My third pebble was seeing the result of not putting another person of perhaps more influential or powerful position above me, even if they signed my paycheck. This allowed me to be more at ease, which helped me be more myself, which helped me more fully access my creative juices during the audition. Knowing that Ted truly wanted me to do well was a profound insight, and it helped me in future auditions and in other similar situations where I could have otherwise shut down.

Lastly, being chosen for something I intensely wanted and because of my own internal resources was very affirming to me. And as one could imagine, this boosted my personal confidence and belief in my creative talent and what came uniquely through me.

The name of the film? Well, that will have to remain a secret. I will say this; it was a wonderful experience—filming in Rome, traveling to Florence on my days off, and eating my way through both cities. The filming itself was quite comical, though. It wasn't exactly a high-budget film, and the director was a "you're on your own" kind of guy. For someone like me, who up until then had a fairly small number of acting classes under my belt, it was definitely a learning experience! I have a few copies of the film that only a select few have seen... those who I know will laugh with me.

Oh, and did I mention the food...and the gelato? Every morning I had croissants and cappuccino on the rooftop of my hotel overlooking Saint Peters Basilica. Every lunch and dinner was like an adventure in flavor and aroma, from topini de patate (potato gnocchi) with roasted vegetables to pollo farcito (stuffed chicken) with sauces of fresh, ripe tomatoes or cream. Then there was Scrigno alla Cecilia, the most delectable pasta dish I have ever had, at the Ristorante Cecilia Metella, a historical restaurant right on the Appian Way— the cobblestone road that runs from Rome to Brindisi Apulia—in southeast Italy. The restaurant was built atop the tomb of Cecilia Metella, who died at twenty years old and was the daughter of Metellus, the conqueror of Crete. Then, there were lunches from the "lunch truck" on the set: fresh mozzarella with basil, tomatoes, and light but fragrant extra virgin olive oil; or a fettucini with a light cream sauce. Then, after each of my meals, I would find the nearest gelato stand and indulge. This alone was worth the price of admission. Until you've tasted the likes of chocolate hazelnut, maple walnut, mango coconut, melon, Zabaione Marsala, and of course Espresso Bean gelato, with their delicate, creamy textures and sublime flavors, you simply have not had ice cream.

Chapter Thirty-Four

WINDS OF CHANGE

∽

*W*e must again take a non-linear path, for so much of what occurred in the next couple of years happened seemingly simultaneously.

You may have noticed earlier when I spoke about the authentic communication Sean and I had that I said we practiced it "for most of our relationship." This next leg of the journey is when we…or, more accurately, I…didn't, and as a result the unraveling of our marriage began.

We were now almost eight years into our relationship, and although on many levels we had a tremendous marriage, I had started having uncomfortable feelings that I didn't understand. I loved Sean immensely, and I could not decipher where these unwanted feelings were coming from. They scared me at such a deep level that I didn't know how to speak to Sean about them, nor could I even imagine *saying* that I didn't know how to talk about them. I just kept them inside.

I imagine you, the reader, will notice that some of the things I will write about seem rather contradictory…and they are. Herein lies the challenge and the difficulty I had in finding a resolution to my dilemma.

These issues are in no particular order; they seemed to surface around the same time, each building on the other and adding strength and magnitude to my fear.

I was still afraid of the dark and of being alone, and these fears immobilized me in many ways. I wanted to be free of them, but I was too afraid to approach it. I desperately wanted to know that I was capable of being alone, but I had no idea where to begin, or that I even could. As a result, I felt trapped and dispirited.

Around this time, I had two intensely powerful dreams that when I awoke from them, I felt it was vital to pay close attention to their meaning. In the first one, I was in a large dark room with probably fifty people. There were two lines: one with those who were alive and present for a reason I could not surmise, and a line who were going to die. I was in the one with those who were slated to die.

At the head of this line, there was a being of sorts. I perceived it to be a male who accepted each person as they met him. I saw no fear in the two lines of people, just a knowing of what was to occur. One by one, the people before me walked forward and vanished. As I was in line watching everything, I began to feel uncomfortable with my fate. When I got to the front of the line, and in close proximity to the being, I began to cry uncontrollably. I realized at that moment that I was not finished with my life on Earth. I then began to grieve and gasp at the thought of not being able to complete what was left for me to do. I insisted that I wasn't finished. The enormity of my grief seemed to match the work I had yet to complete, although I didn't see what it was I was supposed to do. I continued to writhe in my anguish, wishing that I could have a second chance. While in this state, I awoke crying intensely. Once I realized that I hadn't died and was still alive, I gave sincere and deep thanks for the gift of the reprieve I had been given.

After I fully wakened and recovered, I took several minutes to reflect on what had just transpired and what it meant to me. I got out of bed and began my day knowing that my life was about to change in a profound way and that there were some large and important things I had yet to accomplish. Even though I had no idea what they were, I was grateful for the opportunity to live to see them.

After the second dream, however, I wasn't as fortunate. I don't recall the details of the dream, but what I do remember is that I saw myself standing next to a cliff at one moment, and the next I watched in horror as I fell from the cliff. I can still see my face realizing that "this is it." I awoke from this dream understanding that even though I believed I was going to live a long life, in truth, we don't know how long we have. With this, I had a strange sense of foretelling that some kind of change was coming.

Although I had never expressed it to anyone, I had always wanted to be a mother—throughout my childhood and young adulthood it was one of the things I most looked forward to. I assumed this would be part of the marriage package, and so I never thought to speak about it with Sean beforehand. Then, about two years into our relationship, I discovered that he was quite adamant about not having children. Even though I was using a diaphragm, I thought at one point that I was pregnant. When we found out I wasn't, I told him that I would like to some day have children, wondering when he might be ready. He responded that he didn't think he ever wanted children. I was surprised and disappointed, and after a few days of going back and forth about the issue, he said something that I took to mean that if having children was something I had to do, that we would probably not make it.

This profoundly saddened me, and I remember feeling my heart pull back when we reached what I perceived as a non-negotiable stalemate. I never spoke with him about it again.

From my observations and several conversations Sean and I had early on, I knew that his parents and grandmother weren't my biggest fans. They tolerated me, but I never got the sense that they liked me much. I didn't have a college degree (his parents both attended Stanford and were well read), and their predetermined opinion of me was evidenced—albeit subtly—in the condescension I sometimes heard when they addressed me. Consequently, I felt they never truly accepted me into their family.

I remember clearly, one evening during the holidays, having a conversation with one of Sean's brothers—the first we had ever had of any depth. While talking, he looked at me with a rather startled expression. "You *are* intelligent." This comment let me know he had been under the impression that I was not.

I came to understand that my lack of education, coupled with the fact that I didn't come from "good stock," enabled Sean's family to merely tolerate me. Over the years, with the ongoing judgment filtering from his parents through Sean and down to me, I begrudgingly withdrew myself, which was difficult because I desperately wanted a solid family and to be accepted by them.

I further recall a pivotal moment when, at some point after my mother's death, I was standing in my bedroom, looking at an abstract multi-colored art piece hanging on the wall, feeling joy at how stunning the piece was. That feeling of witnessing beauty reminded me of how beautiful I thought my mother was when she was younger. An unwelcome wave of grief overtook me and I tried to push it away because it hurt too much. But the feeling wouldn't leave and I couldn't take it anymore, so in an attempt to make it stop I declared to myself, *I don't ever want to love anyone that deeply again. It's too painful.* It was such a powerful moment, I actually felt myself immediately begin to pull back from love. Though I didn't take the declaration I had made seriously, I was nonetheless grateful for the momentary relief. I had no idea that I had actually put something into motion.

Sean was in some ways a "typical guy" in that he would constantly check out women—their breasts and their behinds—when something good passed by. This was not only disrespectful, but it irritated me, too. It also scared me. I knew that a part of my feelings about his gawking stemmed from an irrational fear that he might find a woman with a sexier body than mine and want to leave me. My father had had affairs while he was with my mother, and even cheated on his wife before my mother, so I didn't totally trust men. Because I didn't know how to deal with my fear, I wanted him to stop looking so that I would not feel threatened.

We did talk about this often. We also tried different processes to both disengage my feelings about his looking and to help him see the shortcoming of his habit, but the processes didn't really work. We never got down to the bottom of it nor found a place where we both felt resolved. As time went on, I became more fearful and resentful of his looking.

I discovered over time that I had a tremendous amount of sexual energy that I didn't know how to express. At some point I began to feel that if I expressed the true magnitude of my sexual self, I would overpower Sean. I felt that I was "too large" for him, not in the way my father had said, but in an energetic sense. I believed he couldn't meet me on the same level, nor could he help bring it out of me. As good as our sex was, I sensed there was something more to it than what we had experienced, and even though I didn't know what it was, I yearned for it.

For reasons I didn't understand, I had begun to resist making love with Sean. At some point on our journey of sexual intimacy, I had stopped opening myself sexually with him and began to shut down. As a result it became challenging for me to get interested in sex with him. It would take quite a bit of coaxing on Sean's part to get me there. When I was in this state, he would lightheartedly refer to me as a mackerel, and then lovingly try to get me going.

Eventually there were long periods of time when I would not make love with him at all, because during sex I had begun to experience the same feelings and emotions that I did when I was molested as a child—intense anxiety, violation, and a strong desire to make the violator go away—although I couldn't name them as such. I could not comprehend why I was having those feelings or where they were coming from, and that deeply disturbed me. Now, it's important to note that although I knew as a child I had been touched in ways I didn't like, I didn't understand that those experiences were molestations, so I had no context for the feelings I was currently having. Sean was a sensitive and attentive lover, so my feelings made no sense to me. All I knew was that I had lost interest in and felt threatened by sex with him. It also became more and more difficult to reach orgasm.

Sean was my best friend and partner first, my lover second. Other than in the beginning of our relationship when I was first discovering orgasm, I don't recall feeling a strong sexual magnetism with him. When I was twenty, the most important elements in love were to have good communication, feel safe, and have a best friend and companion. As I matured, I noticed that I also needed to feel a spark and fire between my beloved and me. I didn't feel that with Sean, nor did I understand why it wasn't there or how to get it in our relationship.

I also became aware at some point that I was noticing other men in ways I had not before. I even felt drawn to some of them. I wondered why this was, because I was very certain that I was in love with Sean. I didn't feel good about noticing men, especially knowing how I felt when Sean stared at women's body parts, and yet there was a feeling of excitement in it. My excitement became disturbing to me, and I wondered why I didn't feel that way about Sean. Deep love, yes, but not excitement. It became even more disturbing when I realized that I hadn't felt that way about him for quite some time, if ever.

Over time this feeling intensified, and as it did, I began to believe that something was wrong with me. I didn't know how to even begin to speak about it—there was so much shame and guilt (as anyone who has survived molestation will tell you). In ways I didn't understand, the idea of being in control of my sexuality seemed less threatening, so I began to flirt with men. In doing so, I noticed I was able to prolong that feeling of stimulation and that this made things with Sean more exciting. In my ignorance, I eventually convinced myself that what I needed was to ignite the passion inside of me, after which I could bring that passion back to my marriage. Although I felt doing this would hurt Sean if he ever knew, I would do anything to bring passion into my relationship with him. So, I made a pact with myself to fix my problem on my own and to never tell him.

Then it happened. I met Morgan on a commercial. He was tall and handsome and he flirted back with me. He rode a motorcycle and was a gritty man. I found myself very attracted to him. At the end of the shoot he recommended an acting teacher that he was studying with, and I decided to give this man's class a try.

During this period, I was staying in Los Angeles two nights a week so that I could take acting classes. Morgan and I had gotten to know each other a bit over the month or so of classes when one night he invited me to come over to his apartment. After I arrived, we relaxed for a short while until it became apparent we both had something else in mind. I felt nervous and shy, but I also was aware of why I was there and what I wanted to accomplish, so I tried to get my mind and body into what was happening. We started kissing, but it felt awkward because kissing is very intimate—an expression of love. I didn't love Morgan; I didn't even know him. I decided to avoid kissing and override my discomfort by going at it from a different vantage point—lust. Clothes started coming off and our bodies began to touch. At one moment I thought, *What am I doing?!* and a sadness came over me. I couldn't breathe but quickly shut down my emotions so that I wouldn't cry. I then went through the motions, and an hour or so later I lay next to him wishing I were home with Sean. I got up out of bed and said that I had to leave; Morgan knew I was married, and didn't protest.

The next day, when I returned home and held Sean, I didn't want to let him go. I wondered, though, why I didn't feel like I thought I would—excited and fired up to have sex with him. After much thought, I realized that I had not been fully present in the experience with Morgan. I had checked out. I was mad at myself because I hadn't done what I set out to do, so when he asked me again the next week to come over, I did. I decided before leaving that I was going to stay present and fully experience what I was doing.

Well, that time I did stay present, immersing myself into having sex with Morgan. When we finished I lay next to him feeling that I had accomplished what I had set out to do. I also noticed something this time that I hadn't noticed before. Morgan had folded my clothes and set them on a couch so that they weren't lying on the floor. I thought, *That was a nice thing for him to do.* I realized then that he actually cared for me and that I would not be with him again. Shortly afterward, I got my things together and said goodnight. The next time he asked me to come over, I declined, explaining to him that I couldn't continue to do what we had done. He wasn't happy, but he accepted it.

My experiment seemed to work. For a short period of time I felt sexually fulfilled with Sean and we had more spark than ever in our relationship. I felt guilt for having had sex with another man, but my relief that I appeared to feel passion for Sean again outweighed my guilt.

But as one can imagine, it eventually wore off and I found myself again trying to bring passion into our lovemaking by being with other men. I had three other affairs. The first was a singer I had met dancing, and the other two were actors—one of whom was married. His name was Dan, and we were in the same acting class in Sherman Oaks. I had seen an article in our local acting magazine where Dan was being interviewed. He spoke about the theater class he was involved in and how great it was. After reading the article, I decided I would check out the class.

When I arrived, Dan wasn't there; he was away shooting a television series. But I liked the class and the teacher and decided to stay. A few months later, Dan came back. I remember seeing him walk in with his chiseled six-foot-four Adonis-like body and dashing smile. I thought to myself, *I want him.* He noticed me and evidently felt the same way I did because he immediately asked me to do a scene with him.

Seeming to both want the same thing, we looked for as much excitement as we could. We would tempt fate and have sex in the most risky places—under the theater seats during class, in the back of the theater, in restaurants, outdoors, etc. This went on for a month or two. It was thrilling to be so free with sex. It was the first time in my life that I felt I was experiencing the magnitude of my sexual energy, as well as the polarity I had sensed was possible between a man and a woman.

I got a rude awakening, however, when a woman with whom he had previously had a fling came back from filming. I saw the look they gave each other the night she came back to class, and shortly after that he stopped calling me. I felt jealous, not because I loved him, but because my ego had been bruised. But I didn't mourn for long.

Soon after that Rick, Dan's best friend, asked me to do a scene with him. When we met to run the lines, he told me that he was interested in the same sort of scene work I had done with Dan. This infuriated me. I told him I wanted nothing to do with him and I left. I then called Dan and pressed him to tell me what he had told Rick about me. Though he didn't confess at the time, I later found out that he had told Rick I was up for grabs and that I was a good lay. I told him that he was an ass and never spoke with him again. Even though I was incredibly angry with Rick and Dan, I felt in my heart that I deserved everything that was happening to me.

I had my final affair another seven months later with an actor I knew from the same acting class. He was directing a play I was in, and we had flirted throughout the rehearsals and during the four-week run of the play. On the night of our final performance, we had sex after the show. Afterward, I sincerely wished I hadn't done it. We actually liked each other as friends, and having sex ruined our friendship. We could never go back to being just friends—not if I was to stay married, which I planned to do.

As one would expect to happen, the temporary relief I felt was no longer outweighing the guilt I felt, and I began to feel I would implode. I retreated further and further from Sean sexually to where I could not have sex with him at all. When he would talk to me and try to find out what was wrong, I couldn't explain it. I saw the hurt in his eyes and that made me want to beat myself. I desperately wanted to make my relationship with Sean right, but I had no idea how to do it.

PEBBLE

All in all, this chapter is a perfect example of what not to do in a basically good relationship—not to fail to communicate about the things that are most important, and not to refuse to consult someone if the feelings seem bigger than you're able to handle on your own, therefore enabling you to do something stupid and/or hurtful. I knew how important it was to be truthful and authentic. Why did I not speak to Sean or a therapist about what I was feeling? Simple. I had too much fear of losing love and losing Sean. I was convinced that all of the issues I mentioned were monumental and insurmountable. I know now that they weren't. The pebble here—the more fear, hurt, or anger involved, the more important it is to talk—no matter what. I know there would have been quite a different outcome had I addressed my issues and underlying feelings. This is not to say that there hasn't been a positive outcome (more on this later on the path), but I don't know if we would have stayed together if we had talked. What I do know is that by not talking and by taking matters into my own hands, I hurt the one I loved the most.

As I began to come to terms with what I had done, I resolved to heal myself so that I would not repeat this story ever again.

ADDENDUM

With the more recent years of my work in the arena of conscious loving and sexuality, and in the re-telling of these events, I received two very important pebbles with regard to my sexuality and the ability to love.

First, it has taken me twenty years of looking and prodding and apology and sitting with what I did, as well as being willing to speak of these things authentically, to understand where a large part of my actions originated from. At some point, probably starting when I was molested the first few times, I learned to separate my heart from my body, more specifically from my genitals. The closer Sean and I felt in our hearts and sexually, the more my heart and body wanted to reconnect the two, but because I hadn't healed from being molested, I couldn't. It was absolutely terrifying to feel connected and to feel pleasure with him. Sex and feeling sexual pleasure had always brought me shame. This largely explains the disturbing feelings I had during our lovemaking. Our sex was good, which made it bad. The deeper our intimacy, the more threatening our sex became.

As women, our hearts and genitals are naturally connected, and if all goes well, they stay connected. Men's hearts and genitals, by and large, are not. They learn at a very young age, in America anyway, that women are objects to get them off, whereas women, generally speaking, have sex as a means of opening their hearts more deeply. These are broad generalizations, but they are also fair assessments. The point I'm making is that it wasn't natural for me to have this disconnection, but I grabbed for it to keep me feeling safe. I had learned that in adopting a more masculine way of being sexual, I felt I had more control over my body and my life.

I also learned (more recently) that by having sex outside of my relationship, I was able to stay in my comfort zone. Although feeling guilt and shame were not easy, sadly they were familiar and more comfortable than feelings of pleasure or ecstasy, which was very threatening. To feel ecstasy, one needs to surrender and not be in control. Control in my mind was my protection.

Second, although my grief around my mother's death was much diminished by earlier insights, it wasn't until years after these events that I discovered I had been unaware of how deeply they had affected me. I also came to see that my declaration of not wanting to feel that kind of devastation again had a profound impact on me. With this unprocessed and therefore unresolved pain, and wanting desperately not to feel anything resembling it again, I had silently put protective barriers around my heart that affected my ability not only to love, but also to allow love in, even from Sean.

The moral of these stories? If there is an issue to be healed, keep working with it and pressing through it, even when it seems an impossible feat. Healing happens in layers, so one must be patient and brave. Resolving an issue can take an instant, or it can take the better part of a lifetime.

Chapter Thirty-Five

THE TOWER

✍

his is a chapter of the dissolving of structures and of releasing the illusion of security. To illustrate this leg of my journey, I will draw upon the Tarot, the method of divination (an act or practice that seeks to foresee or foretell future events or a means to discover hidden knowledge or meaning) that I was introduced to by my childhood mystical friend, Kim. The card I have chosen is the Tower. Its picture and meaning exemplifies how life, as I knew it, was over. Along with it went outdated concepts of who I was and what life was about. Through this, my path shifted directions in a profoundly surprising and unforeseeable way.

The Tarot is a set of seventy-eight cards, each of which tell a story by their allegoric pictures. The reader shuffles the cards with a question in mind. Then, when he or she feels the cards are in their correct place in the deck, the reader lays down the top-most cards, facing up, in one of one hundred or so possible patterns. The reader then translates the message he or she sees in the cards. The Tarot is used for a variety of reasons including practical problem solving, as a tool of understanding, and for divination and fortune telling.

The Tower Card

The picture (depending on the deck)—You see a tower on a rocky outcropping, a powerful bolt of lightning, one or two figures falling from the tower, and sometimes waves crashing below.

The story—As the Fool (the oblivious traveler) leaves the throne of God, he comes upon a Tower: fantastic, magnificent, and familiar. In fact, The Fool himself helped build this Tower back when the most important thing to him was making his mark on the world and proving himself to be better than other men. Inside the Tower, at the top, arrogant men still live, convinced of their rightness. Seeing the Tower again, the Fool feels as if lightning has just flashed across his mind; he thought he'd left that old self behind when he started on this spiritual journey. But he realizes now that he hasn't. He's been seeing himself, like the Tower, like the men inside, as alone and singular and superior, when in fact, he is no such thing. So captured is he by the shock of this insight that he opens his mouth and releases a shout. And to his astonishment and terror, as if the shout has taken form, a bolt of actual lightning slashes down from the heavens, striking the Tower and sending its residents leaping into the waters below.

In a moment, it is over. The Tower is rubble, only rocks remaining. Stunned and shaken to the core, the Fool experiences grief, profound fear, and disbelief, but also a strange clarity of vision, as if his inner eye has finally opened. He tears down his resistance to change and sacrifice, and then breaks free of his fear and preconceptions of death; he dissolves his belief that opposites cannot be merged and shatters the chains of ambition and desire. But here and now, he has done what was hardest: destroyed the lies he believed about himself. What's left is the bare, absolute truth. On this he can rebuild his soul.[1]

After my final affair, I found it increasingly difficult to keep my indiscretions secret from Sean; I wanted to tell him everything. I knew that he highly revered me, and with all I had done, I knew I didn't deserve his respect and trust. Another part of me didn't want to tell him, but rather to protect him from the pain I knew my telling would cause. I wondered if perhaps I could just put it all out of my mind and move past it, having learned from the experiences. But I could feel the secrets eating away at me and our relationship like a cancer. There was a saying from our self-growth group that one cannot build where perpetrations are present—they compromise the strength and integrity of the structure. I knew that these significantly large ones would eventually destroy our relationship if I didn't come clean. So with the hope of healing myself and of saving our marriage, I decided that I would tell him.

I asked Sean if we could take a drive and spend the day together. I told him I had something very important to talk with him about and that I didn't know how to go about it. Being the caring partner he was, he agreed, and we drove up into the nearby mountains. Over and over again, I started in my mind to tell him, but each time the words never made it to my lips. I began to feel nausea, as if I was trying to hold back what naturally needed to spew out of me. Finally, after we returned home hours later, I sat him down on the couch and began my confession. I kept away from as many intimate details as possible but also let him know I would reveal whatever he needed to know. I told him about each man I had been with—where I had met him and how long the affair lasted. I watched Sean's pained expression as each scenario struck his heart, each new blow hitting harder than the one before. It was excruciating as I watched the man I loved so dearly experience this depth of pain.

After my confession was complete, I apologized over and over and told him how I never meant to hurt him. Although I didn't yet understand why I had done what I did, I was clear that it had nothing to do with my love for him, and I reiterated this over and over, hoping he would not take what I had done as a message that there was something wrong with him. At the end of my stream of apologies, and with the clarity of mind that can only come from truth, I promised, "I will *never* do this again. I don't understand how I could dishonor you like this, but I *will* find out why, and I *will* heal myself."

Sean, as always, surprised me with his compassion and depth of love. After letting everything sink in for a few moments, he said he figured it was going to be something like what I had told him. Although he was profoundly hurt by what I did, he didn't waver in his love for me. He told me that what was hardest for him was watching *me* be in so much pain, and this was perhaps the most painful statement of all, because I didn't feel that I deserved his compassion. I fully expected that he would punish me for what I had done. (I think being punished might have made me feel better, like I had gotten what I deserved, in return.) But he didn't. He expressed that he was hurt, but didn't once say anything punishing or degrading.

Then he asked me the question that was most important to him: Did I want to stay in our marriage? I was surprised and thrown off balance by this. I thought for sure he wouldn't want to forgive me and not want me to stay. I was not prepared for him to so easily accept my deceptions and be willing for us to move forward together. I answered yes. He then added that if I was to stay, I could not continue on as I had, and I agreed. So many thoughts were whirling through my head that I couldn't articulate the feelings that were bubbling up inside me as we spoke. I told him that I loved him so very much and wanted to stay, but even as I made that statement, something tugged at my heart.

Over the next several days, I did my best to sort through everything that had transpired. And although I was grateful that I had come clean with Sean, I continued to feel incredibly guilty for what I had done. I also knew that I was not at the bottom of what caused me to have the affairs in the first place. I had an uneasy feeling there was something more that needed to be done.

One thing I had contemplated earlier was moving out on my own. I felt that in many ways I didn't really know myself—or, perhaps more accurately, didn't know who I was separate from Sean. In many ways, I had functioned very well as Sean's partner, as Sean's wife, as Sean's support, as the one Sean provided for, but for some time I had felt that, left to my own resources, I would not be able to survive in the world. This belief about myself had become hard to live with. From time to time, I wondered if living on my own for a period might enable me to find my inner strength and help me to discover who I was as an individual, but given my intense fear of the dark and of being alone, I had not allowed myself to entertain this idea. These thoughts haunted me while I labored over what I needed to do, and finally it came to me;

regardless of my fear, I simply had to move out. I knew I would not be a complete person until I proved to myself that I could make it on my own.

Soon after this realization, and full of sorrow, I let Sean know what I needed to do, and as I explained my reasoning, we both wept. I told him that my intention was to find my way back to him, and that we should consider this as a sort of sabbatical. I hoped that once I found out what I was made of, I would be a better partner and wife.

Again, Sean supported me. It seemed as if he knew that this was what I truly needed to do. I had heard that if you really love someone you must do what is best for him or her, even if it means letting him or her go. Sean exemplified this with great courage and beauty.

I don't have much detailed memory from the time I told Sean I had to move out to the day I packed up and drove away. The two things I remember clearly is how gentle he was with me and how he loved me through his pain, and how he helped me create a plan.

Carrie, his aunt who I was very close to, lived in Marina del Rey, a beach community in Los Angeles. When I spoke to her of my choice to move out, I asked if it would be possible to stay with her for a while. Graciously, she said yes, and in the spring of 1987, I began my proceedings to move.

I did my best to give meaning and intention to all of my preparations. If I was going to do this, I wanted to be successful. I was unwilling to go haphazardly forward without direction and not accomplish what I so deeply wanted.

When the day came that the car was packed and ready to venture north, Sean and I stood facing each other as I apologized once more for what I had done and the pain I had caused him. I told him I loved him deeply and I thanked him for his love. We kissed and I sobbed as I slowly got in the car, grieving while knowing that I was both leaving behind unconditional love and security, and going into a great and petrifying unknown.

PEBBLE

This is an example that shows how taking actions that are out of alignment with one's sense of integrity and honoring often, if not always, lead to the undermining of love, creating heartbreak and damage to all parties involved.

Even knowing the events leading up to my leaving Sean, some who watched me leave called me brave. They knew that many would not have left as I had, unless they were to leap into another's arms or had a financial cushion to soften their landing. I jumped into the abyss alone, without a known or even semi-certain outcome. Regardless, I just knew I had to go. It was a calling, and I had to heed it. I was not willing to go back into a relationship with Sean until I learned to know and trust myself. Of course it would have been more constructive and honorable if I had been able to arrive at this conclusion without having the affairs. A previous pebble that speaks to this—and it is an important one—is that we all are doing the best we can, given our level of consciousness and understanding. If we could do better, we would. Coming to this understanding helped me live through the guilt I felt and guided me to a place of healing. Some may think I should have been punished, or punished myself for my indiscretion, especially after also having affairs when I was with Daniel. Believe me, self-flagellation would have been a relief for the guilt I felt. But I wasn't interested in feeling relief for my guilt. There were reasons I acted out in the ways I did, and I wanted to know what they were. I wanted to heal myself, and anyone who has punished themselves for wrong actions knows that punishment does not heal. It's intended to train—you do something wrong, you get punished; there's no inner reflection involved. And although it may be effective with animals, it is mostly ineffective with humans. Look at our prison system. It is no coincidence that close to seventy percent of inmates released are re-arrested for a felony or serious misdemeanor within three years of their initial release[2].

Of all the events I have relived and written thus far, these past few chapters have been the most challenging, more so even than my mother's death. Several of the stories I have written about were seemingly out of my control, whereas here, I was responsible for Sean's immense pain and for our separation. I believe it is only in the extraordinary experiences that I lived, and lessons that were taken to heart subsequent to my separation, that I have gained enough compassion for the person I was back then to write about it now.

∽

When I reflect back through my life on who most taught me about the foundation of relational love, it is Sean who stands out. He loved me in his joy, and he loved me in his grief. He loved me when I was with him, and he loved me enough to let me go. He loved me when it was easy, as well as when it was extremely challenging. He wanted what was best for me, even though it caused him great pain. He loved me through it all, and for that I am eternally and utterly grateful. I know Sean's love for me shaped my definition of love.

Sean and his love are the diamonds for this chapter, and they are some of my most cherished pebbles then, now, and always.

Chapter Thirty-Six

WOBBLY LEGS

∽

*C*arrie lived in a spacious two-bedroom apartment within a ten-minute walk to the beach. I moved into her spare bedroom and stayed with her for three months. In many ways, it was a wonderful time. Although my grief in leaving Sean was often heavy on my heart, I also felt a glimmer of lightness beginning to grow within. I thoroughly enjoyed my time with Carrie; we had always had deep and meaningful conversations as well as a lot of laughs. She was a great source of comfort and support while I sorted things through and looked for a place to live.

Shortly after I moved to Marina del Rey, Cara, who had moved there a few months before I did, introduced me to Marin, a writer, whom she had hired to do some editing. It happened that Marin needed some part-time help in her office, and I needed some money, so I began working for her. The job didn't pay a lot, but it was a good place to start.

A close friend of Marin's was Kay Baxter, one of the original competitive female bodybuilders in the country. She needed some help organizing and responding to her fan mail. As payment, she offered to train me at a local and very private gym. It was expensive because many celebrities worked out there, and that was the gym's way of keeping out the general public. But the owners of the gym knew Kay well, and for a time they offered me a reduced price.

Here began my second round with bodybuilding. (The first was about six years into my marriage, when I wanted to get my body in shape for my acting. For about six months, I trained with a man at five a.m., five days a week, and loved it.) Kay was a wild and wonderful woman—eccentric and adventurous, compassionate and wickedly funny. I would work out with Marin five mornings a week, two or three of which Kay would work with us. The workouts were both grueling and exhilarating. I recall one day after our workout, my arms were so tired that I couldn't lift one of them to put the key in the lock to open the garage. Then there were days when all I could do was hobble. But I knew that with each day I was getting stronger and healthier. I was focused solely on building my body, and as my body began to strengthen, so followed my mind and heart.

While I worked out at this gym, several other experiences contributed to shifting my life in interesting ways. Two of them, in particular, are worthy of mentioning.

To tell this first story I must travel backwards. It was about 1983 when I first heard Lewis sing. He was a top pop artist and budding soap opera actor. Every time I heard his voice on the radio I would get a feeling of familiarity in my body. Eventually, I purchased a couple of his albums to hear more of his music and appease my curiosity. When I got the albums home, I looked at his photos and was immediately drawn into his eyes. As I continued to gaze, I felt a strange sensation. It didn't make sense as we had never met, but still I felt as if I knew him well, even at his core.

Then one day several months later, I was looking through the paper and saw that Lewis was coming to town for a concert. Something inside me said, "Yes! I must go to this show." I told Sean that I wanted to go and asked if he wanted to go with me. Since he had no desire to see him, I asked a girlfriend to go with me. I called for tickets and two great seats were still available—third row back, in the center. I was thrilled and snatched them up.

About two months later, my friend and I sat in an audience made up of mostly women. The excitement around me was palpable. I, however, noticed that I felt more nervous than excited, like what one might feel when they're going to a high school reunion or to visit a long-lost friend. Suffice to say, I was not prepared for what would happen over the next couple of hours.

As Lewis came on stage I became overwhelmed with feeling— not like a teenager with a crush on a big star, but like seeing someone I knew and adored do what he loved most. I felt happy and proud of him. I didn't feel like I was a spectator; I felt like I was up on stage with him. Every move he made, I felt like I made it with him. There was nothing for me to do with what I was feeling, so I just sent him appreciation from my seat. About a half an hour into the show he gave me a puzzled look as if to say, "Do I know you?" Obviously I couldn't respond, so I smiled and he briefly smiled back. This interaction happened a few more times. When he left the stage at the end of the show, I felt both happy and relieved; happy that I had been able to "meet" him and relieved that it was over. I knew there was nothing to do, so I said to myself: *I don't understand this connection, but it's time to let it go. Blessed be.*

Back to 1987. One day that summer, I casually walked into the gym and who was standing facing the door as I walked in? Lewis! My knees weakened and halted, and I practically tripped and fell through the door. I didn't know what to do, so I just forced my legs to move, gave him an embarrassed smile, and walked past him. I flashed on the synchronicity that would cause this to happen, and I wondered if there was some order and meaning to it. I saw Marin and practically yanked her into the bathroom and quickly relayed the whole story. We both marveled at the coincidence and wondered what, if anything, I should do. Over the next month or so I saw him often. Each time he was around I felt the same feeling as when I first saw his photos on those album covers years earlier, but I wouldn't approach him as I felt it would disturb his peace and privacy. Marin said that he often stared at me when I was lifting or not facing him. From time to time he would give me a wonderful smile as we passed each other, and each time he did this, it felt oddly familiar.

For several years, I had been having semi-regular sessions with Ron Scolastico, and it was time to have another. I decided I would ask a question about Lewis to see if I could gain any insight to this seeming connection. I explained my feelings of depth and my curiosity about how I could feel such things for someone I didn't know. I asked the Guides if they could give me any insight into my spiritual connection with him so that I could come to a place of peace with what I was feeling. In my session, they explained that in a former life he and I were spiritual teachers (both male) in Asia. They described our relationship as being one of profound respect and honor. They mentioned how we loved each other deeply as brothers and knew each other at our cores. In essence, they described exactly what I had been feeling. They said that we taught together for many years, and for various reasons I had carried some of those feelings for him into this lifetime. In hearing this, I felt a resonance within. The Guides went on to say that they didn't feel this was a connection that would necessarily bring about a male/female relationship in this lifetime; they suggested that I just continue as I had been doing and send him blessings.

That night I went into meditation, and I brought Lewis into my awareness. I imagined us devotedly teaching together, and while in this process I sent him love and gratitude. As I did this, I noticed that my body and heart felt as if they were opening very wide and deep. Eventually his body left my meditation, and I began to float. I continued to open, and as I did, I felt a presence above me. I looked up (in my mind's eye) and saw a very large obelisk slowly descending toward me. It was immense and dense and it felt inviting and quite loving. I realized that it was the soul, or higher spirit, of Lewis. The closer to me the obelisk got, the more open and moved I became. Down it continued, and then as it reached my body, it didn't stop. It merged with my body and soul and as it did, I felt a profound sense of love and of completion. After a few minutes, a thought entered my mind that this was a promise we had made to each other, to meet in this lifetime and bless each other.

After coming out of this meditation, I had a sense that now that this promise had been fulfilled, Lewis would soon leave my life. The next time I saw him we gave each other gentle smiles and I sent him a silent blessing. A short time after this, he went on tour and I never saw him again.

The second story from the gym happened some months after Lewis left. Either before or after our workouts, I would do some work for either Marin, Kay, or both, and we often had dinner together afterward. Kay would tell crazy stories about all of her adventures and we would talk about mysticism. It was a glorious time. They also introduced me to Wicca. Simply put, it's a Goddess-oriented "religion" that focuses on coming into harmony and balance with oneself and the nature surrounding her; learning and growing through self reflection; and attaining knowledge in directing one's power in positive ways and using the natural elements in a ritualistic manner to materialize what is desired. One can only practice Wicca if committed to harming no one and serving the greater good. Kay reminded me somewhat of Kim, the woman who introduced me to mysticism. Marin had studied Wicca for years and knew a lot about it. We spent hours and hours discussing it and its practices. It was fun and exciting to learn about something that felt very natural and in alignment with being a woman.

I experimented a bit with some of the rituals Marin had taught me, and one of the resulting experiences was particularly powerful. As previously mentioned, many well-known people were members of the gym. One man who worked out there daily was a world-renowned actor. He was very handsome, cocky, and full of himself, but he was also funny, generous, and had a huge heart. I'll call him Edmond. Although he didn't remember me, I had met him about three years prior when one of his bodyguards, who I was in an acting class with, invited me to Edmond's birthday party. The bodyguard had invited me to mingle and network with all the high-powered industry people we expected would be there. I can still recall the excitement I felt walking onto the yacht and seeing several actors and actresses I had seen on screen and TV. It was a fascinating experience, and although no one could have cared less who I was, I was glad to be there. Interestingly, I came away from that experience with a strong feeling that I would meet Edmond again some day.

Anyway, back to the gym. Edmond and I talked often. He was married, and Sean was still in my heart, so I maintained a friendly distance. Unlike many of the women who paraded around him, I was genuinely interested in *who* he was—apart from his profession —and I think he sensed this. He seemed to relax when I was around. The more we talked, the more I sensed that he wasn't happy in his marriage. When his wife showed up at the gym one day, I watched them together, finding it obvious that they were on two different plains. He looked relieved after she left.

Over time, I looked forward to seeing him, and he appeared to feel the same about me. Then one day he surprised me when he asked if I would like to meet him at an event he was attending. He said I could bring a friend so I wouldn't be alone, so I asked Marin to go with me. I was a bit uncomfortable with the notion of being in public with Edmond because he attracted a lot of attention wherever he went and was still married. I didn't want anyone to make anything out of my being at the event, so I convinced myself that since we didn't go there in the same car, it was harmless.

When Marin and I got there, Edmond invited us to sit behind him and his brother. His bodyguards sat on either side of us. He wanted to make sure that Marin and I were taken care of, and the bodyguards were given the job of getting us whatever we wanted. One of them even went and fed my parking meter when I realized the time would soon run out. Although it was decadent, it also felt quite sweet. Marin and I carried on about the event between the two of us, and from time to time, Edmond would turn around and talk to me. As the evening went on, though, he seemed to feel more comfortable, and he talked a bit more openly and animatedly with me.

At the end of the event, we stood up and spoke briefly about what we had just seen, then Edmond turned to be close to me. I looked at him and he looked into my eyes and smiled. I felt like we were swimming in a fish bowl as people gawked at him—and at us, I suppose—from all directions. I felt self-conscious and I think he sensed this. The next minute he took his hand and placed it on the small of my back, pulling me in close to him. He gave me a big smile, and kissed me slowly on the lips. I was surprised that he would do that as I hadn't really understood until that moment he actually liked me in that way. I felt excited and quite embarrassed. I must have turned scarlet because he smiled bigger. Then he asked if I wanted to go out to a bar and have a drink. When he asked me this, two things struck me: one, I felt excited by his offer and his interest in me, and two; I didn't like the thought of watching him drown his woes about his wife. Not feeling my feet touching the ground while at the same time not being comfortable with the scene, I felt my heart begin to shut down. There was no part of me that wanted to go to a bar and drink with him, so I declined the invitation. He looked disappointed and asked me if I was sure, and I said yes. I smiled at him and assured him that I would see him at the gym the next day.

On the way home, Marin and I talked about my not knowing if I was ready to date. If I was ready, I knew I would not date a married man—I wouldn't go down that road again. I debated aloud, if Edmond wasn't married, could I date a man who was that famous? I expressed that I was just starting to get to know myself, and I feared that if I dated him for any length of time, I might then become "the woman who is with Edmond" and lose my individuality and myself. With the hopes of gaining clarity in the matter, I decided to do a ritual that Marin had taught me.

When I got home, I took a shower and focused on my question: "What is the highest possibility for Edmond and me?" I then asked the heavens to please show me the pathway to this outcome without harm or ill will to anyone. I prepared all the elements for my ritual, and then I stood in front of my altar. I focused hard and stated my requests and declarations and lit my candle. As I did this, I felt like something moved. It's difficult to explain the feeling, but it was as if something clicked—or perhaps shifted—into place. The feeling was sensory, yet also oddly physical. I was convinced that *something* had happened. After I finished my ritual, I released my request to the ethers and gave thanks. I then surrendered myself to the will of the Universe, went to bed, and fell asleep.

I awoke the next morning, wondering if things would be different with Edmond. After I got some work done in the morning, I got on my gym clothes and went to meet Marin. As I entered, I felt an air of electricity in the room. I saw Edmond and smiled. He returned my smile with an inviting grin, and I went over to say hello. He had a funny look on his face, like he was a cat trying to hide the feathers hanging out of his mouth. He seemed excited about something, though he didn't say what. Marin caught my attention and excitedly gestured for me to follow her into the ladies' dressing area. I asked Edmond to excuse me for a few minutes. As we entered, Marin turned quickly to face me, hardly able to contain herself and asked, "Have you heard the news?"

"No." I answered, wanting to know more.

"Then, you haven't heard?"

"No," I answered emphatically..

"Oh my God. So you don't know!"

"Know what?!" I insisted, starting to feel uneasy.

"Edmond announced that he's divorcing his wife! It was on this morning's news!"

My knees buckled. Luckily, something caught my dazed fall. "What?!" I said incredulously.

"It's true! I can't believe you didn't hear."

I felt waves of exhilaration and fear, like I had just heard the best and worst news all at once. "What do I do? What should I do?!" After a few minutes, I decided I should go over and tell him that I heard about his news and that I felt for him.

I composed myself and walked out of the dressing room. Edmond was in the same place he had been when I left him. He looked at me eagerly, and I made my way back over. Shyly, I communicated what I wanted to, telling him that I was there if he wanted to talk. He said thank you, and I lingered momentarily as we smiled at each other before I rejoined Marin to begin our workout. A bit later he approached me and mentioned he was going away for the weekend and asked if I wanted to go with him. That was too much. I wasn't prepared emotionally for the speed at which everything was happening. I stuttered and thanked him, apologizing as I said I wasn't available. He looked disappointed and said, "Ah, come on." I apologized again and told him to have a good weekend.

Over the next couple of days, I took some time to think about what I wanted with Edmond. While I liked many qualities about him and his life, there were several things that troubled me. Besides my concern about keeping on my path of self-growth and individuality, I had two other chief concerns. One, I wondered if I would be able to have a real relationship with Edmond. He was kind to me, but I questioned his ability to be deep with a woman. I supposed he might have opened in time, but there was another part of me that thought he likely would not. Two, I was worried for my family and their anonymity. My father had some troubled people in his family, and I didn't want their lives to become public. I realized that the media might not care about my little life, but I didn't want to take a chance. For these reasons, I decided that even though I liked Edmond very much, I just could not imagine a relationship with him.

Things changed drastically after his weekend away. Although we continued to talk, women seemed to come out of the woodwork. His announcement gave the impression that he was now fair game, and the gym became a circus. I wasn't comfortable with the ensuing frenzy and began to retreat from him. Besides, I had heard that his next film was about to begin production, and I expected he would leave for the Middle East soon.

One day he came up to me as I was working out with Marin and we began to talk. I told him that I knew he was leaving, and that I hoped his filming would go well. He confirmed his departure and then looked straight into my eyes and asked if I wanted go with him. I kidded him: "Why would you ask me when you have countless other women who would jump at the chance.?" He looked at me in a way that made me understand he was sincere, so I apologized and explained that I couldn't go with him because my life was in Los Angeles. I went on to say that it was not the right timing for me. Although he looked disappointed, he said he understood. I wished him well, and he hesitated momentarily before walking away. Between that moment and the weeks before his departure, I watched him playfully acknowledge women's advances and the somersaults they did to get his attention.

Edmond was gone on location for some time, and while he was away, I decided to stop going to that gym.

I saw him a year or so later at the Rainbow Bar and Grill on Sunset Blvd. He was sitting in a booth with a couple of cute blonds, Greg—his primary bodyguard, and several other people. Greg saw me and got up to give me a hug. He asked how I was and if I wanted to go say hello to Edmond, but I declined. I asked him to tell Edmond hello for me, and I left. There was a bittersweet pang in my heart.

PEBBLE

The pebbles from my experiences with Edmond: Be careful what you ask for! I was definitely reckless in asking for the opportunity to see what was possible with him when I wasn't really prepared to follow through. In all fairness to myself, I don't think I imagined that something with Edmond was truly possible, and it was not until the opportunity was upon me that I realized I didn't want it.

Also, although I don't believe that my ritual caused him to do something he would not have done otherwise, I also don't believe it was a coincidence. He wasn't happy with his wife, and they would have split sooner or later. I hold that his announcement was a response both to my call and to my opening to him. I was deeply affected by the results of the experience, and since it happened, I have only done a manifestation ritual a few other times and never involving matters of the heart. I prefer instead to get clear on my desires, work toward them as intelligently as I can, trusting that the Universe will present me with what it deems best for my well-being…even if it's different from or contrary to what I had envisioned.

A noteworthy result from this experience is that after seeing what kind of attention the famous get, and from knowing how challenging the acting industry can be on the soul, I decided to stop my progress toward an acting career, at least while I was single. I loved acting, but I was not willing to lose myself, and I felt I would have if I had continued. What was more appealing and inspiring was to have stability in my life. I figured if I really missed acting, I could always join a community playhouse.

I still see Lewis's face from time to time, and whenever I do, I send him a silent blessing. One of the pebbles from this experience is that even though I cannot prove that what the Guides said was true or accurate, I honor that it felt true to me. In essence, when it comes to more esoteric matters—mystical, spiritual, and unknowable truths—what feels right to us is truth. Though it is subjective, we know these truths by what our body feels when we hear them; it doesn't matter if they jibe with anyone else's. We can feel it in our gut, in our skin, or in our hearts. These truths cannot be argued, only honored.

Another pebble I was fortunate to witness again is how the Universe works in mysterious and purposeful ways. I saw, very tangibly, that I can trust there is an order in how the Universe operates, and the best I can do is regard what comes my way, even when—and probably especially when—I don't understand it.

And another: Although there is nothing "physical" that I gained from my experience with Lewis—he and I didn't become friends or lovers, for instance— I came away with an affinity for him that I believe I will carry always. I imagine it can only be good to have an anonymous person holding you in high esteem and praying for your well-being.

Through these experiences, I became even more aware of how the Universe constantly presents me with powerful opportunities for growth, understanding and deeper levels of living.

Chapter Thirty-Seven

NEED VS. DESIRE

∽

*C*arrie (Sean's aunt) was working in the film industry as an assistant to a producer, who at the time was doing a film for Lionsgate. She was very well-connected and heard that Donald Simpson and Jerry Bruckheimer were looking for an assistant. She described the qualifications and asked if I was interested. Two benefits immediately came to mind: 1) It would be a stable job with a good income, and 2) I could make money doing something I would enjoy. I said yes, and she set up an interview for me.

A couple of days later I was on my way to their offices at Paramount Studios. I was excited by the possibility of working for such successful people—they were at the top of their game, and it all seemed so inviting.

I walked into their lush office and was struck by what their level of success looked like. They welcomed me to sit and then joined me. It all felt very comfortable; they were personable, and we chatted for some time about my background and experience. I told them I had been a record producer and co-producer of a label for eight years, and when they described what they were looking for, it sounded very doable to me. It would be very long hours, but I didn't care, since there would be no one waiting at home for me. It felt like the interview was going well. Then Jerry asked me what I was looking for in a job and why I wanted this one in particular. I answered the first question well and then said, "I want this job because it would be a great job for me, and I need the work. I've just separated from my husband, and I want a stable job."

He asked me a couple of other questions that I don't remember and then said, "Well Donna, it's been a real pleasure meeting you. I think in many ways you might do well in this position, but we are not going to hire you. Would you like to know why?"

My heart sank, but I appreciated his candor. "Yes, please."

"Your need for this job is what's most important to you. We want someone who wants this job because they love it so much that they have to have it. I appreciate the situation you're in, and I wish you well. I hope you can find something you love to do." And with that, the interview was over. I thanked them for their time, and feeling both appreciative and humbled, I left the office.

PEBBLE

Jerry was right, and I knew it. Wanting something from a place of need was based in fear and from a small place within. It was a need to be taken care of rather than the desire to be an integral partner. They wanted someone who was confident and capable. At that point, I was not capable of jumping into that kind of large and complex life. It was more appropriate for me to take smaller steps. It would have been very difficult to go from not knowing how to take care of myself to working with men of such caliber.

Although I was somewhat disappointed at not being hired, after some thought, I was mostly grateful. Jerry's candor served me greatly. From it, I learned that I would find more success and fulfillment in going for what inspires me and what feels "right" than in going for "being taken care of" to fulfill a need. I wanted to live a larger life, and from this, I understood more clearly my path.

Chapter Thirty-Eight

FEAR REVEALED

∽

*C*arrie had decided to move to Colorado, and so I had a month to find a new place to live. I put the word out to everyone I knew in L.A., and shortly afterward, I got a call from Susan, Ron Scolastico's wife, who told me about a small guesthouse on the property where they lived. It was very tiny, but they thought I might like to live there. I saw the place and loved it. They approached the landlord, and he agreed to my moving in.

There was some lag time between when Carrie needed to be out of her apartment and when my place would be ready, so I was concerned about where I would live for ten days. It so happened that Ron and Susan would be on vacation during this time and asked if I would be willing to stay at their house to keep an eye on one of Susan's daughters. *Thank you, Universe. Perfect timing*, I said to myself, and agreed.

Although I was happy to be moving into my first home, I still had a fair amount of anxiety about living on my own. I wasn't sure how I was going to do it, but knowing I had friends close by helped me grope forward.

The first night I slept in Ron and Susan's home, I had a night terror that awoke me. I dreamt a very scary being wanted to hurt me and was inches away from my face. I woke in a panic, panting heavily. I shook from fear as I went to get the phone to call Sean, but then I hesitated as I realized it was hours after midnight. I didn't want wake him, but I knew no other way to calm myself. My fear won over and I grabbed the phone. As I began to dial I heard a voice—loud, yet very soothing—speak to me in my mind. It was commanding, and I stopped and listened. It said, *What you are feeling is not your fear, it is your resistance to* feeling *your fear.* It went on to say, *Allow yourself to feel your fear.* Only briefly did I wonder where the voice was coming from. It didn't matter; I felt the words resonate through my body and *knew* I was hearing truth. The voice ceased, and I paused to concur that yes, I was terrified of feeling fear. I had spent my entire life feeling frightened and trying to avoid feeling it. I put the phone down and willingly brought my dream back up into my consciousness. I then allowed myself to fully feel how afraid I was, and the next moment, as if by some magical force, my fear vanished…utterly and completely. After a lifetime of agonizing over my fear, it was *gone*, and all it took was my willingness to feel it.

PEBBLE

Healing fear is not optional. It is a key practice for a fulfilling life. There's a great saying that goes, "What we resist, persists." Being willing to feel emotions and release them are key pebbles for working through fear and emotional suffering. This practice freed me twenty years ago, and it continues to be an important part of my daily growth. Nowadays, when I feel fear about something, I gently ask myself, "What are you afraid of?" Once I name it, it usually vanishes—simple and yet profoundly powerful.

Sometimes, if the feeling is particularly intense, and I cannot easily release it, I allow myself to imagine the worst possible projected scenario for a short period of time, maybe five minutes or so. This is different than allowing old tapes that run in my head to keep playing. Instead, I ask myself, "What am I most afraid of happening in this situation?" and then allow myself to see the answer. In giving myself permission to imagine my worst fear, I'm telling my subconscious that I'm strong enough to live through it. Once this is established, the emotion releases its hold. When the emotion is released, a kind of peace sets in. This is a breeding ground for positive things to occur. From this peaceful place, one is able to be in a mindset of creation and new possibility.

To illustrate the negative result of not working through emotions, I'm recalling a cartoon where a character sees water leaking from a hole in a dam. He puts a finger in the hole to keep it from leaking more, but when he sees the pressure building and more leaks appearing, he realizes the danger he is in and becomes frightened of being swept away. In an attempt to protect himself, he pushes his fingers and toes in as many holes as possible. Eventually, of course, the pressure of the water bursts the dam anyway, and the flood takes him with it. From this illustration, I see that if I don't deal with an emotion in time and the dam does break, I can at least be a witness to it, instead of being at the mercy of it. The good news is that a little water never hurt anybody!

Another way of looking at this is exemplified in the Law of Attraction— what we focus and pray on, we attract to us. Applied to the emotion of fear, it would appear then that 'feeling fear is praying for what we don't want.' I was focusing on not wanting to feel my fear. So guess what? That is all I could feel. Once I allowed myself to feel the fear, I realized there was nothing to be frightened of. I turned on the light in the very scary room and realized that the thing I was so frightened of was really this small, helpless thing that only wanted my love and attention.

Chapter Thirty-Nine

DOLL HOUSE

∽

*A*fter Ron and Susan returned from their vacation, I moved into my first home. I loved it. It had much of what a normal home has —kitchen, eating area, bathroom, closet, dressing area, living room and bedroom—it was just about an one-eighth of the size. The largest room was the kitchen, which I was grateful for. The larger the kitchen the better, I always say. The bedroom was just (and I mean just) large enough to fit my queen-size bed and a couch table to set things on. There was no walking space around the bed, so to get into it I had to leap from the doorway!

The best part of the house was that it was smack dab in Santa Monica Canyon, and the back deck overlooked it. At night I would marvel at the sounds of wildlife. Late one afternoon as I was trying to nap, I heard several little feet running around on my roof. I slowly walked out onto my deck and looked up. Just as I did, two little black and white raccoon faces careened over the edge to look at me. "What are you doing up there?" I said. "I'm trying to take a nap. Can you please keep it down?" With that I walked back inside, giggling to myself. For a short time afterward they played what seemed like a game of hockey and then scampered off for the evening. I fell into a deep and happy sleep.

For the first time in my life I was on my own, in my own home, in a beautiful location, and feeling strong and content.

Then one day Sean said he wanted to come up and have a date. I felt nervous to see him. I had been on my own for several months now, and I had begun to relish the transformation I was putting myself through. Part of me wanted to go back home to him and feel safe and nurtured again, but another part of me knew it would not be what was best. Still, I loved him and agreed to see him.

It was a lovely evening. We had dinner and a heartfelt conversation. During dinner, he gave me a song he had written that spoke of me being on my way to something new and grand. When we got back to my home, he brought out his guitar and sang the song for me. As always, his music brought me into my heart and broke it open. It was beautiful, and painful. The song openly moved me, and Sean took this as an invitation. He wanted to make love, but I knew I couldn't. I felt that making love with him would have been a statement that I wanted to get back together, and I knew I wasn't ready to do that. Hurt by my rejection, he asked if I thought I would ever want to be with him again. I told him I loved him very much but that I wasn't ready, and I wasn't sure when I would be. I could see that what I said landed hard, and I was sorry for it, but I had to tell him the truth. He deserved it and the opportunity to move forward with his life. Our parting that night was bittersweet. Our love and connection were strong, yet it could not change my mission.

Understandably, Sean was upset by my choice. Shortly afterward he explained that he needed to not talk to me—for how long, he wasn't sure. He said that he was going to allow himself to just be mad at me. I understood and told him he should do whatever he needed to do for his heart.

As it turns out, this didn't last for long. Our desire for the other's well being outweighed the temporary pain we felt. Within a few weeks we were back in communication, speaking from time to time. Although we were parted, our connection remained strong.

One morning, I was driving to work on the freeway when I looked over to my left, and who was in the lane next to me? Sean! He was sixty miles from his home on his way to who knows where, and we just "happened" to find each other on the freeway! We waved at each other, and again it was affirmed in my heart that we would always remain close, in one way or another.

PEBBLE

Ever hear the phrase, "Love brings up all things unlike itself"? Here is my version, and it is the pebble for this chapter: "Love heals all things unlike itself."

Some of the things "unlike love" that Sean and I could have gotten trapped in were fear (of being alone, of not being enough, etc.), anger, spite, victimhood, the list could go on and on. Because of our commitment to love, in time we were able to transcend the pain and fear we both experienced. We were willing, and therefore able, to release our suffering. We trusted that our love, even if it had a different form, was what was most important.

Although this may sound idealistic and perhaps impossible, it isn't. Sean proved that he was more interested in loving and growing than in resenting and stagnating. I, too, was more interested in loving and in my own growth. I was committed to healing at my core so that I could love better, no matter how scared, uncertain, or lonely I felt. I preferred this to deflecting responsibility and burying my head in fear, self-criticism, or wallowing. The choices I had begun to make were out of love—for all concerned.

Chapter Forty

TIME TO MOVE ON

I knew that my job with Marin wasn't going to last much longer, so I began to look for other work. Cara had recently divorced and was seeing a man named Joe, who was a marketing whiz and president of his company. He was managing the marketing for a gourmet bakery that had two shops: one in Beverly Hills and one in the San Fernando Valley. Both also carried impressive gifts and dinnerware, and their main location was looking for a store manager—someone who could run the store and manage the employees as well as the gift operations during the holidays. Joe arranged an interview and I landed the job. I worked there for about a year and a half, and for the first time in my life, I felt real pride in the work I did and the responsibilities I had. The holiday hours were grueling and the pressure was intense, but I enjoyed the job and the people I worked with.

One day I was in the back when one of the employees came to me. "There's a sheriff out front looking for you."

Curious, I walked out into the store. "Are you Donna Thomas?" he asked. I said yes.

"Would you please sign for these papers?"

"Sure," I said. I signed for them, thanked him, and returned to the back. I opened the envelope to find divorce papers, signed by Sean. A wave of grief came over me. I was hoping to have more time to work things out. I had no right to be upset, but I was.

Customers were waiting for my help, so I pulled my emotions together, put the papers in my purse, and went back to work.

That evening, with the deck door open and an ocean breeze filling the air, I sat on my little couch in my miniature living room, gazing out into the canyon as the sun began to set. *It's time*, I heard myself say. I looked down at the papers in my lap, took a deep breath, and watched the ink meet paper as I signed my name. It was done.

PEBBLE
IN MEMORIAM

Ending our marriage remains one of the most painful and regretful experiences of my life. Not because of any bitterness or anger directed at me by Sean, but because I loved him, and I knew I caused him great pain. This is also not to say that when all is said and done, ending our relationship didn't ultimately have positive rewards, because it did (as you will see). There are just experiences in life that remain in one's heart as deep love and deep loss. This is one of those.

Grace is a pebble I have already acknowledged, but I cannot exclude it from the pebbles of my relationship with Sean. Grace brought him to me, and Grace is what guided us both onto our new paths.

Another pebble—and this is the pebble of all pebbles—is love and the strength inherent in it. Love and our dedication to it is what kept us together for almost ten years in marriage, and it's what keeps us the best of friends another twenty years later.

Last but not least would be Gratitude, for I am certain that I'm a better person for having had Sean as my partner and husband.

Chapter Forty-One

FLYING FREE

∽

I began to get restless at my job. Although I loved my work, it took all of my focus and attention. I missed my own creativity, and I missed baking. The second Christmas I worked at the bakery, I was so yearning for creativity that I baked twenty-five fruit loaves and seventy-five dozen cookies and sold them to people I knew. I also made fifty pounds of toffee—meticulously wrapping half-pound portions of it in gift tissue and placing each into one hundred gift bags—for a close friend who was having a large office party. Then, I decorated twelve miniature trees for centerpieces that were to be raffled off at the party. All this about did me in while working full time, but it was also an absolute gas.

I also missed music and performing, although I missed music with Sean more than music in and of itself. I missed it so much that I had to be involved in it in some way, so I began looking for bands I could play with. I found a local one that was performing around town, playing mostly original songs, which I liked, and they were looking for another back up singer who could play light percussion. They weren't great, at least by the standards I'd become accustomed to, but it was music. I rehearsed with them a couple of times, and then we began playing in nightclubs. Eventually, we recorded a demo.

I couldn't play music and keep the schedule I had at the bakery, so I gave them notice. After a fair amount of research, I decided that the best job to support me while performing was being an airport shuttle driver. I was a good driver, having learned in the mountains, and I loved it, so even though I didn't know my way around L.A., it felt like a natural fit. I applied with an airport shuttle company and got the job as one of only a few women hired. During the year I worked there, I was one of their top drivers (thanks to *Thomas Guide*). I made huge tips, especially on Halloween when I dressed up as a belly dancer, met all sorts of interesting people, and had the time of my life.

The more I came into my own, the more I saw my personal power and my ability to touch others. From the beginning of my stint as a driver, my intention was that I would give every person who rode with me a dose of love, genuine caring, and positivity, whether it was from a simple smile or by the care with which I drove the van. I even sang to my passengers when they asked. I always carried my tape recorder in the van because I practiced singing when I was alone. So, when the question came up, "What else do you do besides drive?" I could show as well as tell.

The hours were grueling (up at twelve a.m., to work by two a.m. off at two p.m.), but because of the tips, I only had to work four days a week, which was great for my music schedule. I remember more than once driving home from work and being so happily used up and deliriously tired that I pulled off the road, got out of the car, walked onto the beach, and collapsed on the warm sand to nap.

After living in the Palisades for about a year, the owner of the property the Scolasticos and I lived on decided he wanted to re-inhabit the houses, and we were given notice to move. Marin lived in Topanga Canyon and suggested I look there for apartments. It seemed that for the time being it was as close to the mountains as I was going to get.

Soon after, a friend told me about a small apartment owned by a family of actor/performers that was available. Even though it was more expensive than I could easily afford, the grounds were beautiful, and so I took it. What also swayed me was that walking twenty-five feet out my front door landed me in the state park. I was thrilled that I would be able to power walk up in the hills.

Topanga Canyon has passes from two directions: the ocean side and the valley side. One day when I was driving home from the valley side, the sun was beginning to set behind the hills, casting long and peaceful shadows. I looked out over the rolling hills and it registered that years earlier, when driving back to Orange County from an acting class, I had said to myself that I wanted to move there. I didn't even know where I was back then; I was just moved by the scenery. Realizing this made my heart feel warm and aware of the magic of how things sometimes happen.

PEBBLE

The pebble here is the joy one can find just by following one's nose and heart. Although, in some ways, I was doing at age thirty what most people do in their twenties—going to college and getting out on their own, it was also a time of beginning to manifest my own heart print onto the world around me. I was listening to what interested and inspired me and acting on it. I was beginning to understand what Joseph Campbell called "following your bliss"—which, by the way, I highly recommend.

Chapter Forty-Two

STANDING TALL

✍

I cherished my time in Topanga. I hiked up into the hills almost daily, and as I did, I reestablished my connection with nature and worked through concerns that weighed on me. I would massage deep thoughts I had and solve many of the world's problems up there. Unfortunately, there was no one in the hills listening!

Living there was also greatly transformative. I continued to learn about personal power and how, with grace, people co-create their own reality according to their personal beliefs. In addition to this, several major events occurred. The next few chapters will describe these events, and how they created change in my life.

My father, who at the time was selling timeshares for a living, had been struggling to make enough money to stay afloat. From what I understood, he was also going through one of his binges of taking Valium and drinking, and while working in Arizona, he got himself in trouble. He came back to California after another stint in jail (his third) and lived with his mother for a time.

One day, I got a call from him telling me that a "big deal" was about to go through, but he needed a car in order to make it happen. Evidently, he had somehow lost his car in Arizona— probably to repossession. He promised that if I rented a car for him, he would use it for three days—just enough time to handle the deal. My instinct told me not to do it, but as usual, my instincts gave way to others' needs and I rented him the car. Two days came and went as I felt I was sitting on pins and needles. The third day came and went with no word, so I called my father to see when he was going to return the car. He said that he was still wheeling and dealing and couldn't yet return it.

I said to him, "Dad, you promised you would return the car in three days. Please return it now."

"I can't," he said. "This deal's about to go through. I'm going to keep it a while longer."

"Longer? You can't! I can't afford this right now. Dad, please!" He refused and I hung up the phone. I felt hurt and betrayed, and I didn't know what to do.

The next day I called again, and he refused to return the car. I felt something snap. Anger rose up toward him that I had never felt before. "Dad, return the car." Again, he said he wouldn't. Years of pent up hurt and resentment seemed to bubble up inside me. "Fine. If you don't return it, I'll tell the police you stole the car."

"You can't. You rented it for me to drive."

"Watch me!" I said.

I was furious that my father would take advantage of me so blatantly. After a good sob, and working with my heart and head on what to do, I decided to go to the police. While I dressed I felt as if I were in slow motion, contemplating what I was about to do.

I drove to the local police station, and as I got out of my car, I paused briefly and looked at the building. *Dad, I love you but you've brought me here. You can't take advantage of me anymore.* Conscious of my shallow breath and pounding heart, I walked into the station and explained to an officer that my father had stolen the car I had rented, and that I wanted to press charges against him. After giving the officer the details, I told him where I thought my father was.

I left there with the solid realization that my hopes were permanently shattered of ever having the kind of father I could count on.

It took the police a few days to find my father. They caught up with him when he evidently tried to pass off a bad check to pay for a sunroof he wanted installed in the rental car. He tried to outrun the police and got into a high-speed pursuit with them on the freeway. I watched it on the news. They finally cut him off, he crashed the car, and they captured him, breaking his thumbs in the process. They carted him off to jail, where he stayed for several months.

When speaking to my grandmother about what happened, I told her I didn't want him to call me when he got out of jail and that until he learned how to treat me with respect, he didn't deserve to have me in his life. She tried to convince me that he just needed help. I explained that I had had enough of helping him and being taken advantage of. I hung up the phone feeling a combination of relief, strength, guilt, and pain from what felt like a gaping hole in my heart.

PEBBLE

First of all, this was a great example of a previous pebble—allowing emotions to propel someone into creating positive change. Until the car rental incident, I had never allowed myself to get truly angry with my father, or to set strong boundaries with him. It took an incident of this magnitude to allow my anger to surface enough to move me into taking action that I would not normally take. Yes, it would have been optimal to stand up to him earlier, before things had snowballed, but my childhood taught me to have a high threshold for pain. I still have a high threshold, although nowadays I speak up before things get unwieldy.

As painful as it was to file charges against my father, it was also liberating. By standing up to him in this way, it felt as if I had finally ended the cycle of abuse of trust. This act was a statement that I would no longer allow him to control or take advantage of me, and that whatever approval I used to look for from him no longer mattered. I had finally taken a stand that if he was ever to be in my life again, it would be on the condition that he treat me with respect.

In writing about this experience, I realize that I had wanted to be treated with respect throughout my life, but at the same time thought I didn't deserve it. If I had believed otherwise, my father and others would have treated me differently. It took some time to work this out, but in more recent years I've come to understand that we innately deserve to be respected. Those of us who are not treated with respect grow to disrespect others and ourselves in various ways. In realizing this, I was inspired to appreciate who I was and what was good about me. Once I saw and embraced what was good about me, respect was no longer an issue.

ADDENDUM

The rental car company billed me a few thousand dollars for the extra rental days and the damage done to the car when my father crashed it. Because I couldn't pay for all of it at once, I arranged for them to bill me a small amount monthly. It was years before my debt with them would be clear. But through some miracle, after several months, the rental car company stopped billing me and I never heard from them again. I had told a few friends my story, and I have a feeling that someone cleared my debt, but I will never know who.

Many, many blessings go out to whomever helped me. He or she eased my emotional and financial burden considerably.

Chapter Forty-Three

GRACE TAKES
ANOTHER HAND

∾

*W*hen Sean and I were married, our close friends Will and Maura asked us to be the godparents of their first child. We had known Will for years from the personal-growth group in which we were involved. He was creative, handsome, and witty. He had strong ethics and we adored him.

Late in his twenties, he married Maura—an extraordinary, intelligent, passionate woman with a wicked sense of humor— whom he met while she was on staff with our personal-growth group. She matched him in many ways, and we thought they made a wonderful couple. The four of us were of like mind, and we were all very close.

For about a year, shortly after the birth of the first of their two sons, Will worked for Sean booking radio interviews and promoting his new albums. Later, he landed a job at a prominent movie production company. It seemed he had the world in his hands. He had a fabulous job working for a top producer, an incredible wife, and two amazing and gifted children. I recall thinking I had never met such intelligent, vibrant, and loving children. I couldn't get enough of them. I remember the first time their eldest son hugged me. It felt as if love itself had swallowed me whole in a wave of bliss.

Like many of us in the personal-growth movement, though, Will was drawn to it because of his painful youth. He had an alcoholic and abusive father who beat him. His inner demons had been tamed somewhat by the inner work he had done, but it was revealed later that they were still strong enough to give him bouts of depression. As far as I know, he was never treated for his depression, nor did he ever take meds.

Sean's and my divorce upset Will greatly. He thought that we, of all people, would stay together. In the months that followed our divorce, I recall thinking he seemed more affected by it than I would have imagined, and I began to see sadness in him that I had never seen before.

For my thirty-second birthday (about a year after Sean's and my divorce), Will and Maura invited me to their home for a small birthday party with their kids. We had a lovely dinner together and finished off my celebration with the traditional cake and ice cream. Will's only vice that I knew of was ice cream. He was crazy for it, and it was a joke amongst those of us who loved him. That night, I assumed he would fill himself with the usual mound of cold sweet concoction, but he served himself only a smallish portion, ate some, and then shifted the remaining cream back and forth in the bowl. He kept gazing into the bowl as if looking for answers to some questions that eluded him. He was not himself that night. He seemed preoccupied and low, and when I asked if he was all right, he feigned a convincing expression and said he was fine. I brushed it off as a bad mood, although my instincts told me something was really wrong.

The next evening, in my peaceful Topanga home, with the fire lit in my pot-bellied stove, I got a frantic call from Maura. I could hardly hear her words. "Donna, Will committed suicide!" she sobbed. I felt the world get very still and dark.

"What?" I cried. "How?!"

"They think he drank strychnine. Oh, Donna what am I going to do?" She went on to tell me that they found his dead body, with poison in his hand, in his car parked in the hospital lot overlooking the wing where his children were born. As I took in Maura's words and heard her sobs, I went numb. I couldn't feel or think as she told me what she knew. Though I asked her what she needed, there was nothing I could do at that point, and we arranged to see each other the next day. I hung up the phone in a daze. *Why would he? How could he? Why? Why? Why?*

Will had evidently planned his death for some time. No one knows for certain what the final straw was that caused him to take his life. His job was going well. Maura said things seemed to be fine at home. Will left a note for Maura, but it revealed nothing. Everyone was left to develop their own assumptions and theories as to why he had killed himself, as well as their own ways of coping with his death. For self-preservation, some idealized it, particularly at his service. To preserve Will's memory, many attendees focused on what was phenomenal about Will and how heroic he was. No one seemed to want to speak about the pain he must have been in, and this bothered me. I wanted to say to them, *Yes, Will was an absolutely amazing human being, and we all loved him and will miss him terribly. But can we also grieve and pray for the part of him that felt tortured and that suffered in a way we cannot even imagine? Together, can't we embrace his tragic end and not pretend that destroying his life was his only option?* I didn't say this, though. I kept these thoughts to myself; I imagine others did the same.

When I finally allowed myself to feel again, I still found it difficult to completely let in what had happened. By this I mean that there was a part of me that didn't want to feel the *pain* of his death, because in order to do that I would have to let in the *reality* of his death. I would have to feel the tragedy of it and acknowledge his pain. I would have to bear the fact that I would never again see him laugh or cry. This part of me just wanted to skip over it like a rock skimming water. I had no experience with the depth of pain that would lead someone to take his or her own life. When I tried to enter into this quagmire of feeling, I still could not comprehend leaving behind all those I loved in that way. I was both angry with him and sad for him. I was deeply empathetic for his grieving family, and I was sad for myself for having lost one of my favorite people in the world.

Since I was having such a hard time understanding why Will had made the choice he had, it began to feel important for me to spend some time with my feelings—not so much to try to figure them out because I knew I couldn't, but to find the place in myself that could access that kind of depth of despair. It felt important that I have compassion for him, and in order to do so, I had to embrace it as best I could.

I spent time with this in my meditations. I asked to understand his suffering and what lesson there was for me to learn from this experience. What came out of these explorations was the sense of hopelessness that many people endure. I saw that prolonged hopelessness—tragically, yet understandably—could feed into a desire to be taken away, at any cost, from the pain and agony associated with it. This was immense to grasp.

One day, while driving past our local veterans' cemetery, I replayed some of the romanticized conversations I had heard about how Will's death was somehow a heroic action. I understood that in idealizing his death, people were able to keep alive a larger, brighter picture of him. I realized then that suicide had never before been a reality for me. Although I knew it was something real, it had seemed more like a fairy tale or something that happened in another world. I realized at that moment how this kind of despair might lead someone to think that suicide was the only way out. As I drove past the cemetery, I imagined how one could adopt this kind of thinking, and how—if ever I was to fall into deep hopelessness—I could see this as a way out. I looked out over the sea of tombstones when I heard a voice say very loudly and very clearly in my head, *No! Do not idealize this. With this death, all possibility is gone! Nothing remains but the ache of loss.* Hearing this shocked me. It was as if some higher part of me wanted to make perfectly clear that no matter how hard it might get for me in life, this could not be an option. The feeling, which felt more like a message, seemed to be telling me to cultivate the strength to stay among the living, and to live in peace with the pain that befalls us all at some point in this human existence; and that my work was to learn to transcend pain through love. But to do this, I had to live!

I drove down the street feeling Will, sending him thoughts of love and compassion for whatever journey of reckoning he had become a part of.

PEBBLE
IN MEMORIAM

In life there will always be unsolvable mysteries. Sometimes the only thing we can do is embrace the fact that these mysteries exist and then meet them with as much patience and compassion as we are capable of, for it is likely that these will not be solved until we are hovering over this tragic, beautiful place. Until then...

"Be patient toward all that is unsolved in your heart and try to love the questions themselves, like locked rooms and like books that are now written in a very foreign tongue. Do not now seek the answers, which cannot be given you because you would not be able to live them. And the point is, to live everything. Live the questions now. Perhaps you will then gradually, without noticing it, live along some distant day into the answer."

~ Maria Rilke, Letter Three (23 April 1903)

Your Spirit remains forever in my heart, Will.

Chapter Forty-Four

ANSWERS TO
LIFE'S RIDDLES

∽

$\mathcal{W}$ill's death, and the helplessness I felt at not being able to see his depression, or to help him, prompted me to go deeper into my quest to understand the human condition. I felt if I could understand and heal my own fears and pain, then perhaps I could help others. As previously mentioned, I thoroughly enjoyed and was fairly adept at psychology when I was in college, and at some point I seriously considered going on to study it further, but it no longer felt like a good fit. I wanted to be in a field that felt more akin to my nature—more intuitive, subtler, dealing with the sub-conscious. Not that I didn't want to use my mind, but when it came to looking more deeply into the nature of things, I felt that my mind had limitations and was often not as reliable as my intuition, so I decided to study divination. I knew that certain forms had been used for hundreds of years, and with their deep, rich histories, I felt confident that there would be something there for me.

The first method I briefly considered studying was astrology. I had continued to have annual readings from P.J. and found its general guidance and insight to be beneficial. I pumped P.J. for information on where and how to study astrology. She relayed her experience in mastering it, and when I combined her information with my own research, I discovered that it was very complex, more like a science actually, and one of the most left-brained and linear forms of divination. After much thought, I felt that people like P.J.

and Chakrapani were already so good at what they did that I could not add anything unique. With this, I decided to look at other options.

The first method I began working with was dream journaling. I had been told that many of the great *intuitives* and best psychologists used this method to understand the subtleties of the mind, our subconscious and emotions.

Each morning before getting out of bed, I would roll over, pick up my pen, and diligently journal what I had dreamt the night before. My practice was to first write exactly what happened in the dream, including the emotions I experienced, and then write what I thought and felt the dream meant. As I wrote, I often received an "Aha!" type insight and then understood the dream's meaning more deeply than I had initially thought. With the regular practice of trying to discover my dreams' meanings, my connection to the part of me that seemed to know more than my conscious mind was strengthened. The more I practiced this, the more my dreams seemed to speak as if to guide me. In time I got to know my dreams like a new language or a new acquaintance. The better I got to know them, the more clearly I understood their subtleties and how they uniquely spoke to me. I cannot recall any of my dreams from that period, but I do know that it was a time of revelation of many things, and with these revelations came insight, and with these insights came the opportunity to be more cognizant in my living and to make more conscious choices.

As my dream journal practice continued, something seemed to organically bubble up to the surface. "The Voice"—which I call the part of me that seemed to know more than my conscious mind could easily grasp—gained volume as I listened to it more intently. With this came a new feeling that there was something inside me I could access when I wanted further insight or guidance. From time to time I would sit quietly, close my eyes, and ask this voice what it wanted to tell me. I could feel energy move through the top of my head and though my arm and with my eyes still closed, move the pen in my hand to write a message in response. The messages were very loving, and I always felt good after one "came through," but there was a part of me that wondered if the messages came from something larger than myself or if they were simply from me, just writing what I wanted to hear. Their syntax though was much different than the way I spoke, and this made me wonder. I continued to write in this manner, though, if for no other reason than to connect to a place that felt very loving.

Then there was the Ouija Board[1]. I remember a party I attended back when I was married to Sean. Someone brought out a Ouija Board for fun. I had played with one while in my teens and recalled the feeling that I could sense energies outside myself while using it. People at that party had put their hands on the device intended to spell out words, and it didn't move, so I offered myself as a conduit. I stepped forward, sat down, and placed my hands on the device, joining one other person who remained. I closed my eyes and asked him to do the same. I wanted to see what would happen if I were to rely solely on my intuition, guidance, or the forces outside myself. Before I started though, I said a quick prayer and stated that only goodness and love were welcome. As I took a deep breath, I immediately felt a strong energy moving through me. The device started to move seemingly on its own, and the group excitedly started asking simple questions. "Who are you? Where are you from? What do you want to tell us?"

Two things from this experience stayed with me as confirmation that I could indeed sense subtle energies. First, when the group asked the "entity" (for lack of understanding of what it truly was) Claude (as he identified himself) to tell us about himself, he said he was an *octoroon*. I had never heard the term and thought we had just spelled out gibberish, but Sean's sister-in-law, a lawyer, promptly stated that an octoroon is a person of one-eighth black ancestry. With this I felt confirmation that something outside me was communicating to us, and it felt very comfortable. We stayed engaged with Claude for about twenty minutes asking him questions and receiving answers. He even responded jokingly when we kept mispronouncing his name. "You don't speak French, do you?" he asked us.

The group was so fascinated by this process that after our communication with Claude was complete, they wanted to continue. I agreed, and again closed my eyes. I sent Claude a blessing as I said goodbye. I opened myself again and felt a new energy begin to come through. It felt quite different though—heavier than the previous one. As before, the group asked questions and my partner and I began spelling out answers. Something didn't feel right though. The heaviness started to feel dark and I began to feel uncomfortable with the process. I took my hands off the device, opened my eyes and explained what I was feeling. I felt that something about this new entity didn't feel happy or good and that I thought it was best to stop. The group agreed and a few of the people even said that they felt the energy shift as well. I released my connection to the entity and also sent it a blessing. I left the party feeling deeply stirred by what had transpired.

I was interested later to find out that Ouija boards had been around since the mid-nineteenth century. The first use of "talking boards," as they were called, came with the Modern Spiritualist Movement in the United States at that time. This method of divination used various ways to spell out messages, including swinging a pendulum over a plate that had letters around the edge.[2]

I was fascinated by the possibility of both "speaking" to non-physical beings, as well as the notion of helping others by being a conduit for benevolent energies or spirits to speak through, and I wanted to connect to these energies myself. I intuited that if they were to pass through me, I might somehow be better able to access answers to life's questions.

I considered trying a Ouija board again as a means of connecting to my intuition and the unseen realms, but because of my experience at the party, I had the feeling that this method would connect me to energies too close to earth and to the fear and unrest that are inherent here. The guidance I wanted to access for myself was from a source transcendent of the earth and firmly rooted in the realms of goodness and grace. I had a strong sense that I could access these realms myself; I just needed to find the most direct route.

Then I met Lauren, a woman who read and taught Tarot cards. Because of the positive experiences with my childhood friend Kim and her readings for me, I welcomed the opportunity to work with Lauren. I immersed myself in her classes and in learning how to let the cards speak to me.

I knew that Tarot readings were originally done with traditional card decks—in fact, the word Tarot (French) is taken from the European card game "Tarrock" (German) or 'Tarrochi" (Italian)— but I was fascinated to learn that the Tarot had been around for over five centuries. It appears that the first Tarot decks were created in Italy between 1410 and 1430, when "trump cards" with allegorical illustrations were added to the more common four-suit decks that already existed. These new decks were originally called "carte da trionfi," or "triumph cards." The first literary evidence of the existence of Carte da trionfi is in a written statement in court records in Ferrara, in 1442.

Over time, passion for using the Tarot grew while powerful religions, wanting to keep control over their followers by inflicting fear, condemned the use of the cards claiming them to be Black Magic and the work of the occult, or the devil.

Then, in the nineteenth century, the famous occultist Eliphas Lévi discovered a correlation between the Tarot and the Kabbalah, the Hebrew system of mysticism. This fueled a new belief that the Tarot may have originated in Israel and contained the wisdom of the Tree of Life. The new theory brought all seventy-eight cards together as keys to the mysteries of life.

It is also fascinating to note that psychologist Carl Jung supposedly subscribed to Tarot beliefs. He attached symbolic importance to the Tarot cards, attributing them with inkblot-type properties. These enabled the psychologist to form evaluative inferences about an individual's archetypal characteristics. The cards helped identify those that represent the subconscious symbolic and pre-symbolic attributes that affect how people view themselves, others, and their environments.[3]

I worked with the Tarot and a few other oracle decks and discovered how, through my intuition, I was able to see deeper into an issue, and at times even get a glimpse into someone's future opportunities. I enjoyed using myself in this way and felt my intuitive muscles being further strengthened.

Then I learned to cast the Rune stones, a Scandinavian form of divination dating back to 600 A.D. I found their perspective insightful, as well as spiritually and emotionally uplifting. It was during this exploration that I came to understand and begin adopting the ways of the Spiritual Warrior. By this I mean one who is willing to fight against darkness (fear, whether one's own or another's) and to bring about light (truth and deeper realizations of love).

Following are two of my favorite quotes from *The Book of Runes*. They give a flavor of the insights and messages that can be gleaned from this divination.

Looking Forward

I no longer try to change outer things. They are simply a reflection. I change my inner perception and the outer reveals the beauty so long obscured by my own attitude. I concentrate on my inner vision and find my outer view transformed. I find myself attuned to the grandeur of life and in unison within the perfect order of the universe.[4]

Then, from the sacred Hindu test, *The Bhagavad Gita*, chapter six, verse five:

> *Lift up the (smaller, ego driven) self by the (higher) Self*
> *And do not let the self droop down,*
> *For the Self is the self's only friend*
> *And the self is the Self's only foe.*[5]

Whereas I used the Tarot primarily for insight into situations, the Runes were used as means of self-reflection.

Next, with an introduction by my adopted "fairy godmother," Kenrooding, I learned to cast I Ching coins.

Kenrooding and I met through her son, Mick. We had become close while we both worked at the shuttle company, and he thought I would like his mother so we planned a weekend in San Diego where she lived. The first night in San Diego, Mick and I went out to dinner with Kenrooding and Mick's stepfather, and as she and I began to talk, it was as if the men faded away. We talked non-stop for an hour. She and I seemed to lock into each other like mutual tractor beams. We had similar philosophies and outlooks on life. She also happened to be a Gemini, which was my favorite sign for female friends. Most of my best friends were Gemini—something about their intelligence, quick wit, humor, and playfulness disarmed me.

Kenrooding and I continued to get on well and she became like a second mother to me. She affectionately began calling herself my fairy godmother. I spent long weekends at her beautiful garden home or at her friend's cozy desert cottage outside Joshua Tree, talking late into the night about philosophy, mysticism, and spiritualism. We drank tea, laughed, and communed in the aura of friendship. It was during one of my visits with Kenrooding that she introduced me to the I Ching, an oracle she had used for many years. I would do Tarot readings for her and she would do I Ching readings for me. For one of my birthdays, she lovingly gave me my own book and set of coins.

Kenrooding taught me that the I Ching is the oldest known form of divination. It originated in China some 3,000 years ago, supposedly by Confucius, and was used by Carl Jung, one of her favorite thinkers. In the foreword of *The Book of Changes*[6], Mr. Jung wrote, "Since I am not a Sinologue, a foreword to *The Book of Changes* from my hand must be a testimonial of my individual experience with this great and singular book...For more than thirty years I have interested myself in this oracle technique, or method of exploring the unconscious, for it has seemed to me of uncommon significance." I so respected Mr. Jung's work, I felt that if he saw value in this divination, then so might I.

I Ching, I discovered, is an intricate and comprehensive form of guidance. The word "I" (or yi) has three meanings: ease/ simplicity, change/transformation, and invariability. The original meaning of "Ching" (or jing) is regularity or persistency, implying that the text describes the way (or path) that will not change throughout the flow of time. According to Manual B. By, Jr. in *The Chinese View of Time: A Passage to Eternity*[7], it is a "reflection of the universe in miniature." Thus the three principals underlying the I Ching are the following:

1. *Simplicity* – the root of the substance.

   The fundamental law underlying everything in the universe is utterly plain and simple, no matter how abstruse or complex some things may appear to be.

2. *Variability* – the use of substance.

   Everything in the universe is continually changing. By comprehending this, one may realize the importance of flexibility in life and may thus cultivate the proper attitude for dealing with a multiplicity of diverse situations.

3. *Persistency* – the essence of the substance.

   While everything in the universe seems to be changing, among the changing tides there is a persistent principle, a central rule that does not vary with space and time.

The way it works is you toss three coins on a surface, as you might do to get heads or tails, or in this case yin (feminine) or yang (masculine). Depending on which sides of the coins are facing up, you draw a trigram—three stacked horizontal lines either broken (representing the yin) or solid (the yang). These trigrams form eight possible combinations. Then you toss the coins again to get another trigram. The two trigrams are then combined into one of sixty-four possible hexagrams. As with the cards of the Tarot and the Rune stones, each hexagram offers a different allegorical insight.

I enjoyed the way the I Ching wove together a tapestry showing what was going on underneath the surface of the question being asked. I also agreed with its basic principles. In the end, I used the I Ching in conjunction with the Tarot when I wanted a more comprehensive, or merely another, perspective. I also incorporated astrology for a more multi-dimensional picture.

I felt my consciousness expanding with the many ways one can receive guidance, and with these new ways of connecting to deeper levels of awareness, I felt a true sense of fulfillment, adventure, and celebration. For years after learning these methods, I gave readings of some sort to any friend who asked, and with the readings there were often conversations that went on for hours about the nature of our existence, what purpose drives our lives, the loving force that animates all things, and how to personally access this force.

PEBBLES
lots of them…

A note about divinations: Although I cannot prove whether by using these divinations I was simply tapping into my own intuition, or connecting to higher aspects of myself, or tapping into the so-called Collective Unconscious, or if I was accessing some aspect or representative of the Divine, or if all of these things are actually the same, I do know that after my readings, I was always left with a stronger feeling of happiness and contentment and a deeper resonance of love that pervaded my mind and heart. I often noticed having the thought that I was "living in the answer," as if life's questions were the wind passing lightly through my hair. What started to take form was an intrinsic awareness that the Universe (what I sometimes call the unseen forces that surround and keep us and could just as well be called the God-force, Life-force, Spirit, or All That Is) —was always conspiring for my and others' highest good (pebble number one).

I may not have understood why certain things occurred in my life, but I trusted that while I was going through difficult times, there was always immense love surrounding me, benevolent meaning to be derived from the experiences, and profound growth offered as recompense.

As for other pebbles that lay on my path from this time and from this chapter, putting them on paper was much more difficult then I expected. The path of beginning to listen to Spirit was vast and all encompassing, indescribable and subtle, at times in my face and always in motion; constant, non-linear, and chaotic, yet ultimately in a peaceful order. Attempting to relay how this path began to take form feels like trying to trap air, or collect water without a container. To expand my awareness so as to embrace communication with and guidance from another plain or reality, I had to release my need for solidity and absolutes. In my writing of this I had to do seemingly the reverse. This was tricky business. What I eventually did was write whatever I intuited was important to relay, in whatever order it came, and then pieced it together like a puzzle.

This is not unlike how this experience worked on me, and herein lies the next pebble. I opened myself to it, not knowing what "it" was. I just kept opening to what felt like a yes and what felt good and right and loving. I had no clue at the time that opening in this way would change my world. It isn't until now, as I look back and write about it, that I realize what huge changes took place at that time. In certain ways my life turned from black and white to Technicolor. As I was honoring myself—doing what I loved, doing what pulled me forward, what drew me into feeling more loving toward myself and others and what inspired me—Spirit changed me like weather carved out the Grand Canyon from flat rock. I was still made from the same material, but my structure was different. Little did I know that this structure would become the foundation for the next twenty plus years of my life.

Another important pebble: In working with these divinations, I began to honor the part of myself that I accessed in order to translate what was being presented in my writing, the cards, the stones and the hexagrams. I realized that a significant part of my makeup was innate impulses, intuition, and insights, but because they had not been acknowledged as such while I was growing up, and were in some cases ignored or invalidated (as in the case when I shared with my father my vision of the importance of Love in the world), I had not honored them for the gift that they were and didn't develop them. By not honoring them, I dishonored and invalidated a large part of who I was. This of course worked to undermine my general self-esteem and self-confidence. Thank the heavens above these "powers" didn't abandon me. They were there as they always had been, and I suspect always will be, awaiting my trust and my permission to be accessed more fully, and with this they welcomed me wholeheartedly.

As previously mentioned, I cannot prove what it is I accessed in these divination practices, but my understanding is that the forces, or energies, that enabled me to sense the subtle realities are of the same forces that sustain life. I realize that this is a very big statement. Given my early childhood experiences of expansion and unity, and my understanding that love is the essence of all things, and with the revelations and freedom I experienced as I accessed these realities, I found myself pressed into the awareness that I was tapping into what felt like an underlying and all-pervasive force. This force felt infinite in its ability to create change, promote healing, and to sustain love and happiness, and the more I accessed these forces, the more I seemed to take them in. The more I invited them in, the more they began to live and breathe in me as part of my own framework. This is not to say that I believe I became something other than myself, but I do believe that through this work I re-discovered and began to consciously embody love, and this is one of the most precious and important pebbles of all I have laid on my path.

Chapter Forty-Five

LOVE LIVES AGAIN

✌

I had dated a bit, but still I would not allow myself to get involved with anyone for two reasons. First, I knew I was not done
grieving my failed marriage, and two, because I wanted to wait to
involve myself at that level until Sean was in love with someone
else. I couldn't bear the thought of entering into love with a new
man and leaving Sean with even more pain to deal with. My
friends thought this was a huge noble gesture on my part, but I
don't think it was at all. It felt like the only choice to make; the
most loving thing to do.

Sean had been dating, too. The two women I met seemed nice
enough, although I couldn't see Sean with either one of them for
the long term. I met them when I would visit Sean, or when I
attended one of his Christmas carol parties.

As time went on, Sean's and my pain lessened and we became
better and better friends. I even entertained the thought for a short
time that perhaps I had done enough growing on my own and that
maybe, just maybe, we could...

Then something happened; something wonderful. Sean fell in
love again. When he told me of his newfound love, I let go of all
thoughts of getting back with him and gave way to his new
happiness. He so deserved it.

We had both stayed close to Maura after Will's death, and at
some point the two of them felt something growing between them.

Eventually they fell in love, and several months later they decided to get married.

I could not dream of a better woman for Sean, nor could I think of a better man for Maura. I was so utterly happy for the two of them. I knew in my heart that they would have a strong and lasting relationship.

To make matters even better, when they were planning their wedding, Sean called and asked that in lieu of a best man, I would be his Best Woman. I said there was nothing I would rather do more and gave him a resounding yes. On the day of their wedding, with family and guests gathered in their beautiful garden, and Maura's sons (Sean's and my godchildren) giggling joyously in the background, I stood alongside him...but this time to his right... as he recited his vows.

PEBBLE

Life is so interesting when it comes full-circle, or in this case from one side to the other. I cannot express on paper the magnitude of gratitude that I feel for the lessons of love and forgiveness that my relationship with Sean offered. It would seem that the pebble for this chapter is that in challenge there are always potent opportunities. If we continue to meet challenges—pain, anger, loss, suffering and such with love, we will inevitably find love—perhaps not in the form we expected, but is anything of value in life exactly how we expect it will be?

Chapter Forty-Six

FOIBLES AND ALL

⌒

S ometime around then, when I was sitting in my small Topanga Canyon hideaway overlooking the sunset as it lingered behind the trees, the sun's dimming rays were backlighting the canyon in such a way that one could easily imagine a unicorn or fairies frolicking through the trees. It was so utterly beautiful, and in my stillness I was completely at peace. I took a deep breath as I felt gratitude rest in my heart and on my contented smile. At that moment it was as if all the beauty in the world had resided outside my window, presenting itself for my pleasure.

Then, a thought passed through which filled me with such awe that I burst into tears. I realized, at that moment, that I loved myself. I had never thought about loving myself before. Mostly I had seen my mistakes, what I had not accomplished, and what I had done to hurt those I loved. But in that moment, I saw only that I loved myself, without reservation and without a thread of condition. I realized that I had surpassed the person I was afraid I was and had become the person I always wanted to be. There was nothing about myself that I could not accept or love. All foibles were simply part of my humanness; all mistakes were part of my growth and learning. In that precious, private moment I had fallen in love with myself like no one ever had, like I never had, and I knew from that point on that I would always be with me—that I would be my best friend, confidant, cheerleader, mother, and sister.

I could rely on me, in any weather, and at any time. I had finally met the love of my life.

PEBBLE

This may be a no-brainer for you, but it wasn't until I began to love myself that my life started to transform into one of true fulfillment.

From what I see in the work I currently do with people, many think (as I did) that they need to heal and/or fix something inside before they can completely love and honor themselves. The dichotomy is that the process of healing and self-realization (the fulfillment of one's own abilities or potential) involves cultivating unconditional empathy and acceptance from within—through your past and current imperfections and shortcomings, pain and suffering, anger and fear, projections and implosions, underachievement and overachievement, wrongdoing and mistakes, and for all that you have been (and been through). With this work, a real and lasting love relationship with yourself cannot help but ensue.

Chapter Forty-Seven

AN UNLIKELY
SPIRITUAL PRACTICE

∞

*N*ow, to bring other facets of this story up to date.
After almost getting hit by a bus as I was getting out of my shuttle at the airport, I felt it was time to leave my job as a driver. I was offered a part-time job with Cara and Joe, who by this time had gotten married. I would help them with their work in marketing, advertising, and PR. The biggest drawback was that although I could type a bit, I was fairly inept with a computer, or what I then called a "confuser." They were willing to train me on the computer and so began a long and mutually fruitful relationship.

Joe was the president, account supervisor, and creative director. Cara was the vice-president, account executive, and office manager. I started off as Cara's assistant and eventually took over as an account executive. The work was interesting—our clients were the gourmet bakery I had worked for previously and a gourmet coffee company. But the real gem of the situation was that I had landed work where I was being paid for doing something I enjoyed, in addition to working with people I loved and admired. Like me, they had a deep spiritual practice and had done years of self-growth and communication work themselves. So going to work each day felt more like going home. They were immensely and intensely intelligent and had a strong work ethic, but they were also wise and compassionate. This is not to say that issues and discomfort didn't arise, because they did, but the uniqueness of this situation was that each of us had the ultimate goal of working together while honoring each other's (and our clients') needs and preferences. When an issue arose, we dealt with it in ways that allowed all of us, in the end, to feel satisfied and content. Joe's philosophy was that our clients and vendors were our Buddhas (teachers). I agreed with this and adopted it as my personal creed.

Interestingly, when I began working for Cara and Joe, I was in what is referred to in astrology as a "marriage cycle." Those who know astrology will tell you that marriage cycles, or any of the cycles they refer to, are at times literal but often metaphorical. The "marriage" I was entering into was a committed relationship of a different sort. To work well, I had to make use of the practices I used when I was in a committed love relationship (conscious communication, wanting for the other's well being, respect, compassion—all of which I consider spiritual practices), only without the most intimate and sexual aspects. It is interesting to note that in doing my work, I could consciously feel my love and devotion for Joe and Cara motivating me. They felt it, and with their appreciation in return, more and more fulfillment was generated all around. In addition, the relationships I formed with people in the media were created with the desire to serve the highest good for all parties concerned. My contacts felt this as well, and so they often offered our clients special opportunities that they didn't necessarily offer to others. (By the way, this is an example of my earlier pebble of how our actions are far-reaching. It is applicable in work as well!)

PEBBLE

The first pebble—that my spiritual practice could not only be deepened through my day-to-day living, but also in my work—was very valuable. It proved even further that life in its totality, each and every moment, is an opportunity to evolve.

As our long-term work/personal relationship has morphed into different forms, my time with Joe and Cara continues to be one of the most profound blessings and teaching grounds of my life. If only the management and company heads operated in a way where the well-being of their employees was at least as important as making money, business as we know it, I am certain, would be revolutionized. What many of them don't realize is that happy, appreciated and fulfilled employees make better, more productive, and more inspired employees.

The next pebble is the importance of acknowledging that I co-created this work situation. In the fine print of the metaphysical principle that we co-create our own reality, I am certain it applies across the board, even in employment. I was grateful that Grace guided me to such a wonderful place to work, but had I not done my inner work, I doubt I could have attracted this nurturing work environment to me. Certainly, I could not have sustained it. Acknowledging one's co-creations can empower them and increase their confidence to create more. This is an important aspect of personal power. This is by far preferable to believing that most things occur by happenstance or by accident, and that we have no control over what opportunities (and painful situations) come into our lives.

Chapter Forty-Eight

MAKING AMENDS

ॐ

*T*hrough my brothers, I found out that my father was being released from jail. I asked his mother (my grandmother) to relay to him that I didn't want him to be in contact, at least until he was willing to treat me with respect. I didn't hear from him for some time. Then, at the wedding reception of a family member, my younger brother Nate told me he was there. I looked around and saw him standing in the shadows at the back of the room. Stunned, I turned back around and thought to myself, *What am I going to do?* My first thought was to just keep facing the other way, but then Nate said, "Donna, he wants to talk with you." I looked back again and saw the wanting in his face. My heart broke seeing him again. I looked at Nate and said, "Okay. Give me a minute." I took some breaths, told my date I would be back in a few minutes, and slowly made my way back to him.

His eyes looked sad and worn. He hugged me and said, "I've missed you."

"I know, Dad."

"I'd like to meet with you and talk about some things. I'm staying at (my) Mother's. Can we meet?"

Hesitantly, and not totally convinced I said, "Yes." Then square in his face I added, "Dad, I can't do this unless things are going to be different. I just can't."

He looked at me, his face full of regret, and said, "I know. I just want to talk." I nodded and said, "Okay."

We set a time and place to meet the following week, and I said good night and returned to my date. A few minutes later I looked back again to where he had been standing, and he was gone.

We were to meet at San Pedro Harbor, where there were shops and a few restaurants. As I drove into the parking lot I noticed that my heart was beating hard. I was nervous. *Nervous about what?* I asked myself. I was nervous that reconnecting with him would start the pain and difficulties all over again. I promised myself that if I didn't feel his sincerity and willingness to create a different relationship, I didn't have to continue the reconnection further. I also promised myself that I would be authentic and truthful.

He was waiting for me at the spot where he suggested we meet. He had been late for just about every commitment and appointment I had ever seen him make. I noted that today he was early. He greeted me again with a hug and we began to talk. Much of the beginning of the conversation was me expressing my disappointment in his actions, both recently and in the past. He responded with apologies and admissions that he had in fact been careless and hurtful. He also revealed that he had had an issue combining alcohol and Valium, and that this contributed to his undoing. He explained how the recent recession had hurt his real estate business, and that this pressure was difficult for him to manage.

I wanted to keep my promise to myself, and so I decided it was time to reveal to him some things about my life of which he was unaware. I wanted to tell him these things not to hurt him, but to allow him to know me better. I also wanted to see if he could be present with me in my telling of the stories. I told him some of the reasons that Sean and I split, about being molested as a child and about being coerced into having sex as a teen. I could see that the stories affected him. He said he was very sorry that those things happened and sincerely relayed how he wished he had been there for me.

I then spoke to him in a way that I never thought I could. Calmly, yet with confident strength, I said that although I would always love him, my relationship with him was forever altered. If he was going to come back into my life as my father, he could not treat me with disrespect again. He would have to be truthful and stay off the drinking and drugs. He assured me that he had no intention of going back to his old ways. He seemed sincere, and I accepted his apology and received his promises.

We stayed together for about two hours. When we each said everything we came to say and it felt complete, we hugged and said goodbye. Before he let me go though, he pulled back and said, "I love you, Princess, and I'm very sorry for hurting you."

"I know, Dad." I said, hugging him again.

As I walked away, I realized that this was the most honest, clear and deep conversation we had ever had. It felt good that we were able to go to that place together. It felt as if our relationship had, perhaps, finally transformed into one of mutual respect.

PEBBLE

For the first pebbles of this chapter I will recycle a couple of earlier ones— authenticity and honesty. My willingness to no longer settle for being treated disrespectfully by my father brought about the possibility of creating a new and potentially satisfying relationship. My authenticity and honesty showed him the boundaries and framework in which I expected him to function.

Of course he had to do his part and actually honor my request, but our relationship could not have been altered had I not honored myself by being honest. It was interesting to discover that the word honest comes from the ancient Latin word honor. I find that being honest is an act of honoring oneself, which is the second pebble. When we honor our needs and ourselves, the Universe and our closest circle of friends then know how to provide support for us.

I must also say that it took a great deal of courage for my father to meet me and to present himself in the way he did. He had no agenda other than to admit to and apologize for the things he did, and to make amends. I have to add these pebbles to my path—admit wrongdoing and make amends. Although his apology didn't erase all his shortcomings over the years, it allowed me to love him more easily and to start on my own journey on the path of forgiveness. His courage also allowed him to feel better about himself, which he needed to do in order to heal, and I was glad for him.

Chapter Forty-Nine

ANOTHER BRUSH
WITH PROVIDENCE

✑

I want to take a quick detour to tell another story of how Grace continued to look out for my highest good.

During this time I had been doing quite a bit of physical cleansing. Given my dedication to cleansing my body, mind, and spirit of old and counterproductive qualities, and because of my history of gastrointestinal issues, I thought it would be wise to do another ten-day cleanse. These entailed fasting, taking herbs, and having colonics. It is known that when one starts to fast, after about three days or so, toxins begin to be released and one may not feel well for a day.

Mark, an acquaintance of mine, was a long-time friend of John F. Kennedy, Jr. One day when we were chatting, he said he thought that John and I should meet. John was in between women, and Mark intimated that we might get on well with each other. A group of John's friends were going to be playing soccer at a local park, and Mark told me to show up so that he could introduce John and me to each other.

I had already prepared to do my cleanse and I didn't want to alter my plans just because I was going to meet "the most eligible bachelor in the world," so I planned the fast so that my third day would come a few days before my meeting with John.

The third and fourth days came and went without incident. This is to say that I had very few symptoms, and I was energized and excited, ready to tackle the fifth day.

The fifth day, however, I awoke feeling like a truck had hit me. I tried several times to get out of bed and put on my clothes, but with each attempt I fell back into bed, lightheaded and nauseated. *Interesting*, I thought. I had never had such strong symptoms prior to this. After several more attempts, I lay back and wondered if I should quit trying and just let it go. A few minutes passed when it occurred to me that perhaps I had some underlying resistance to meeting John, so I convinced myself to go anyway. But this time when I tried to stand, I got a very strong message that said, "No!" and I fell back into bed again. I was struck by the potency of the message. As I lay there, I realized that my meeting John wasn't going to happen. This would be our one and only chance, and somehow it was appropriate or best that we not meet.

The day his plane went down, I was shocked and saddened like the rest of the nation, but I also had a strange feeling that this was why I couldn't meet him on that fateful day—that it could have been me in that airplane. I'm not suggesting that John and I would have married, but had we hit it off, who knows what would have transpired. Either way, my sense was that I had been kept from meeting him for good reason, and as a means of protection.

PEBBLE

Sometimes it isn't until much later, and with hindsight, that we can understand events, chance meetings, or unexpected detours that life throws our way. This was one of several experiences I had where I said to myself afterward, "Oh, now I see! This is why that happened."

I interpret this experience as another example of the Universe looking out for my highest good.

Chapter Fifty

WITHOUT CONSENT

∾

*A*long with the magnificent experience of falling in love with myself came the assumption—or illusion—that any man I loved would love me back just as deeply as I loved him. How could he not? I had discovered that everything about me was worthy of love.

This is Chance's story.

While in Topanga Canyon, I lived in a studio apartment below the owner's family home. The mother had an older son who periodically came by to visit. One day I happened to be upstairs visiting when I saw Chance ride up on his sexy sport bike. I watched as his six-foot lanky frame, covered in leather, sauntered through the front door. He had blond, wavy hair and a cool grin. His mother introduced us, and with mutual smiles, my hand momentarily slipped into his as we greeted one another. I noticed his deep resonant voice and then felt my knees wobble as we locked eyes, his Persian blue to my green. *Oh boy*, I thought to myself. I'm sure I blushed, and I'm even surer that he noticed. I felt him look right inside me as I made my way to the door. I clumsily muttered that I hoped to see him again and then hightailed it downstairs to safety.

I began to listen for the hum of his bike arriving at his mother's. Whenever I could think of a good excuse to go upstairs while he was visiting, I used it. In a very short period of time, it was obvious that we had crushes on each other.

Even though, or perhaps because, my brother and a cousin were killed on motorcycles, I had an intense fascination for them. There was something utterly sensual about them—riding on a machine that vibrated underneath you while the wind stimulated every pore on your body. During one of our *flirtfest*s I asked Chance if he would give me a ride on his bike. He happily agreed, and we arranged the ride for later in the day after I was to see my father in San Pedro. It felt auspicious, or at least meaningful, to be seeing my father after a year on the same day that I would be going on a first "date" with Chance.

Upon my return from San Pedro, I changed my clothes and dashed up the stairs, filled with electricity on seeing Chance. He smiled when he saw me and asked if I was ready to go. Again blushing, I gushed out a "Yes." I climbed onto the back of his bike and proceeded to have two blissful, sensuous hours riding in and out of the Malibu canyons and up Mulholland Highway. Wrapping my arms around him felt so natural, and when I would squeeze him tighter, he rested one of his large leathered hands onto mine. It was a perfect moment in time.

We returned exhilarated and windblown. Not quite sure what was to come next, I looked at him shyly with a question on my face. He must have seen it, because he wrapped his arm around my waist and said, "Come in." His mother wasn't home, so we went into the den and he shut the door. I settled down into the large pile of pillows lying on the floor. He lay down next to me and we chatted for a few minutes about how nice the day had been. He must have seen the invitation in my eyes because he began to gently press his lips against mine. His lips were soft and...man oh man... no man had ever kissed me so lusciously. He was perfectly attuned to me, without any requests or coaching. I surrendered, white flag and all, and we spent the next three hours kissing, licking, grazing, exploring, sucking, and gnawing on each other's lips and tongues. Eventually my chin got so raw from his stubble that it looked like I had fallen down and skinned it. Mother Father God, it was spectacular kissing and being kissed, and I didn't want to stop...

ever! His sisters started to descend upon us though, so we pulled away and set another date. I floated down the stairs feeling the fountain that had perforated my panties and an intense but welcome stinging as the breeze met my chin.

We had not seen each other again, but had spent some time on the phone, when one afternoon he said he needed to talk to me. He sounded distant and disturbed, and I said, "Of course,"telling him to come right over. When he arrived, he looked sad and beaten. I invited him in, and we sat on my sofa. He proceeded to tell me that he was in the midst of splitting up with a woman, and that he didn't feel he was able to start a new relationship. He wanted to, he said, but didn't feel he could. He apologized, and then went on to confess that he had begun to start something with me before he had actually broken it off with her. As a result, their relationship ended badly, and she felt deeply hurt by him. I watched his face as his guilt took him in and out of being on the verge of tears. I saw his pain, and my heart opened to him. *He's such a good man to tell me this*, I thought. "Take whatever time you need," I said. He seemed surprised at my lack of resistance and the conversation evolved into a deep and revealing one. At one point I looked at him and thought to myself, *I have never seen a more beautiful man. Even with all his troubles, I absolutely love him.* In that moment, I jumped head over heels in love with this man, without consent or invitation, and within a month he was living with me.

I won't go into the gory details of our troubled and tumultuous yearlong relationship. Suffice to say that in that very full year I experienced everything from deep love to unbridled and desperate passion; endless exhaustive attempts to open him to love to profound disappointment and loneliness; drained finances (mine) to deception and liaison with another (his); prolonged pain and suffering to severe weight loss; and finally utter devastation and hopelessness. Like a street urchin, I begged him to love me, hoping dejectedly that his sporadic pennies of love would some day turn into a pot of gold.

Toward the end of our relationship, the body where my vibrant spirit once lived was exhausted and weak. I knew that if I didn't do something for myself that I would end up sick or deadened, or both. Maura cried on the phone as she heard the pain and sobbing in my voice. "I've tried everything and he won't open to me. He allows me close enough to keep me wanting, but holds me far enough away to keep me in agony."

"Donna, it kills me to keep seeing you like this," she said. She then begged me to get some outside support. I told her I wanted to but didn't know where to begin. I wanted to regain my sense of self but had fallen so far out of balance that I could not remember how to get back. Maura suggested that I re-attend the personal development seminar that had changed my life. Desperate for my life and my livelihood, I signed up.

A few weeks later I told Chance I was going to attend the seminar and that I hoped it would help me feel myself again. He asked how long I would be gone and seemed happy when he heard it would be the entire weekend. A surge of fear ran through me and I felt a tug not to go. I was afraid of something, what I didn't know. But as my fear began to take hold, I felt a stronger and wiser part of me take over. Its strong hands took me by the shoulders, lifted me up, looked me in the heart, and said, *NO MORE!* I knew then that I was done giving myself away to this man who didn't know what to do with me. A feeling of strength emerged, and as it did I realized that this seminar was my chance at getting myself back. I awoke the next morning, said goodbye to Chance, and showed up at the seminar ready to be brought back to life.

As I walked in my door that night it became apparent why Chance had been happy to see me go. All of his things were gone. He had moved out, without a word or a note. He was gone for good and I knew it. I broke down. It was done. There was no hiding from the inevitable any longer, and I stood there alone in the center of my apartment, sobbing and wondering what to do with my feelings of loss and immense grief. Then, from the back of my mind and through my storm of tears, I heard a quieting voice say, *You are not without a net. You are loved and you have a place to go tomorrow. You are going to be all right.* As I felt the words enter me, I was grateful to know I still had access to that place and that voice, and I felt comforted. Still, I wondered how I would get through the night. *I'm so tired,* I thought. *But how am I going to sleep?* I was wired, and at the same time, emotionally exhausted. In my medicine cabinet there were Chinese herbs that I had been taking to help me sleep. But one of the agreements participants make in the seminar is to not take any sort of drug or alcohol for the duration. I knew I would not sleep without help, so I made a huge plate of pasta for myself and loaded it with an emotionally comforting rich cheese and butter sauce. One of my negative reactions to wheat was that it would make me fall asleep. I trusted that my body would have the same reaction that night, and I ate to my heart's content. Within an hour I had cried myself into a deep, self-induced sleep.

I awoke the next day groggy and congested, but all things considered, reasonably well-rested. I was held throughout the weekend by the blessing of self-discovery, and as the seminar had done before, it reminded me of my strength and of what I was capable. I reflected on how I rushed into the relationship and projected onto him all sorts of wonderful but inaccurate qualities, and how I allowed this relationship to wear me down. I showed up at the seminar with my passion and pain, taking responsibility for my part in it, and in doing so, got through the first weekend of the rest of my life without Chance.

Even with my inner discoveries, the pain was not quick to pass. I recall driving to work one morning feeling like my heart had been ripped out of my chest and wailing, "This hurts. Oh my God, this hurts! How do I get through this pain?" *One minute at a time,* the voice said. *One minute at a time.*

Before we leave this chapter, there is one more piece of the story that should be told. A few months after Chance's leaving, he began to visit his mother again while I was home. I was certain we wouldn't get back together, but I did want closure. To help me with this process, I wanted to hear what had happened from his perspective.

I got his new phone number from his mother and called one day to ask if we could talk. I assured him that I wasn't trying to get back with him, and that I only wanted to have more clarity about what happened so that I could move on. He agreed, and we set up a time for him to come over.

Chance walked into my home that evening as he had done a year and a half before, and he was just as beautiful. He sat down on my couch, and with regret in his eyes proceeded to explain that he hadn't been able to find the strength to tell me he didn't know if he loved me. He wanted to move out on his own so that he could find out who he was and what he was made of (he had not yet lived completely on his own), but he didn't know how to tell me. He also said he had met another woman.

Our relationship had ended how it began, with him jumping into the arms and lips of another before having ended his previous relationship. I asked him how that relationship was going. "Not so well. Kind of off and on," he said. When I asked if she had known about me when they started out, he said yes.

Because I wanted to end things in a more loving fashion, and because I wanted to be authentic with him, I told him that even though our relationship was over, I would love him forever. As I said this, I felt the flash of chemistry between us that had always been so strong.

Maybe because I still loved him or wanted to feel some sort of recompense for the way he left me, or maybe because I wanted to feel that I had some control over my life or a bit of all of the above, within minutes our clothes were off. I made love to Chance with all of the love I had ever had for him. This time when he left me, he did so with a bittersweet kiss. And with it, I felt resolved. I knew I still loved him, and probably always would, and I knew I could and needed to live without him.

Within a couple months I moved out of my Topanga studio, away from Chance, and into an apartment in a dingy and inexpensive area of West Los Angeles.

PEBBLE

The months of mourning my relationship with Chance were slow moving but ultimately beneficial in that I learned firsthand the strength, heart, and intelligence it takes to rebuild oneself after having been emotionally and physically depleted.

The primary pebble for this chapter of my life I owe to the 19th century German philosopher Friedrich Nietzsche. One of his many insightful aphorisms states, "What doesn't kill us makes us stronger." And as a young, hip, socially savvy friend of mine says, "'Nuf said."

One might ask, if I loved myself so completely, why then did I get so deeply immersed in a dysfunctional and emotionally unfulfilling relationship? Remember the alternate subtitle of this book? Love didn't make me brilliant. I had not yet learned how to pick a man who was in alignment with my highest ideals. Love did, however, make me strong enough to begin my healing process and to remain open so I could keep following what I yearned for, and to keep on keeping on.

Chapter Fifty-One

LIGHTNING STRIKES

∞

*K*arma: Through the law of karma, all actions continuously create present and future experiences, making one responsible for one's own life and the pain and joy it brings to themselves and others.

A few months before my move, I had an annual reading by my astrologer, P.J. Among the jewels of information she imparted was that sometime in June or July of that year, something powerful would happen that would feel like lightning had struck. She didn't know what it would be, but she said it would change my life. I had had enough readings to know to pay attention to this.

Fast forward to June. I assumed that my last encounter with Chance, and my move out of Topanga, must have been what she had spoken of. I moved in with Anna, the daughter of a friend, on a weekend in mid-June of 1992.

The pressure of moving into a new neighborhood that was loud and dirty, combined with the emotional stress of walking away from Chance for good, had me feeling like I was dangling by a thread. The Monday following my move I awoke to a sweltering heat wave, and as I got ready for work, an ominous feeling began to arise in me. I do not do well in the heat, and it seemed to add weight to the heavy-hearted state I was in. I was angry and mournful. I also felt stress at not knowing how long it would take to get to the office from my new apartment, and I was running late. I assumed that the ominous feeling was due to the many factors present that morning.

I rushed out the door, not accounting for traffic when planning my route, and as I was waiting to get on the freeway behind at least twenty cars, I felt my stress level dramatically increase. Finally it was my turn, and I sped up to match the speed of traffic. I turned on my signal to merge and saw a car in my way. I waited for it to pass so that I could get onto the freeway, but it didn't budge. I thought, *Doesn't this person see my signal? Geez!* Then, *Okay, I need to speed up or slow down to get by.* I looked behind them, and there was another car close behind. At that moment I realized I had run out of space to merge and I had to act quickly. At that moment, something snapped inside. I became enraged at the apparent lack of consideration of this driver and that it had now put me in danger of having to drive off the road. I sped up to get around the car, and as my car quickly merged into the lane, I felt my car weave from my tires hitting the gutter off the road. Once in the lane, I looked in the review mirror and noticed the car move from behind me to the next lane over. Reaching my boiling point, I glanced over to spot the car, which made me swerve into her lane, so I corrected, but much slower than I could have. My anger and personal turmoil seemed to culminate as the car steadily pulled up alongside of me, and with my energy blasting I flipped the twenty-something woman my middle finger. I felt momentarily avenged in expressing my anger, although I felt a twinge guilty for doing so. After my release, I returned my attention to the road.

Out of the corner of my eye, I noticed that her car was still alongside me, and as I looked over at her, it registered that she was Black. She was obviously angry, making some kind of hand motions at me. Feeling as if her anger wasn't justified, I just smiled at her, and then turned to face the road. She then sped up, pulled in front of me, slowed down, and motioned as if to tell me to get off the freeway. I had no time to talk about what had happened, nor did I wish to engage with her—at that point I was ready to let it go. So I moved into the next lane over and sped up, and as I did,

I could see in my peripheral vision that she was still gesturing at me. I then looked over at her and shook my head to say, "No more." I brought my attention forward again and noticed that my offramp was coming, so I sped up and changed lanes so that I could exit. As I did, I noticed in my rearview mirror that she was following me. When I stopped at the traffic light, I saw her get out of her car and start to walk toward mine. *Amazing!* I thought. *She wants to talk to me after SHE wouldn't let me in the lane!* I felt my heart pound hard as I got out of my car. She didn't meet me with words, though. Her tall, hefty frame met me with her fists as she began to beat my body. I hadn't hit anyone since I was a child and knew nothing about self-defense. I felt the pain of each blow as she continued to pound my head and face over and over again. I heard my dress tear and felt her nails dig into my chest and then felt another blow to my head. I recall it all being very loud. She was yelling at me, but I couldn't decipher what she was saying. When she was through, she turned around, walked away, and got back in her car.

I stood there dazed, with my dress hanging off one of my shoulders. I looked around and saw several stunned people inside their cars staring at me. Not thinking well, I didn't know what to do next. So I got in my car, shut the door, and started to slowly drive forward. As I turned to get onto Sunset Blvd., a man in the car behind me honked his horn. I pulled off the road to let him go around me. As I stopped I noticed that the man had gotten out of his car and was walking up to mine. He looked very concerned, and I opened my window.

"Are you all right?" he asked.

"I don't know. I, I think so."

"Did you get her license plate number?"

"No."

He then gave me the piece of paper on which he had written her license number. He said he was sorry for what had happened and then walked back to his car.

I didn't know what to do next, so I drove to my office. When my Cara and Joe saw me, they immediately called 911. The paramedics loaded me into the back of the truck to transport me to the hospital. Cara followed me in her car. On the way to the hospital, the paramedic lectured me about not using their services unless there was an emergency. I assured him that I didn't call 911 and that I was sorry for inconveniencing them. I lay on the gurney, now feeling guilty as well as beaten.

Cara had also called the police, and they met us at the hospital to ask me questions. Still dazed, I relayed my story in as much detail as I could. When Cara asked if I should press charges against the woman, the police said that because I provoked the incident by flipping her off, it probably wouldn't stick. They went on to say that things were still tense in Los Angeles since the riots (they had happened just two months prior), and that this happened most likely because she was Black and I was White. The officer told me I was lucky she didn't have a gun, or I might have been shot. "People are still very angry," he said. I then felt even worse about my actions.

They informed me that if I decided to press charges, I should know that someone might try to attack me again. They counseled me to walk away, but they also said that I should do whatever felt right to me.

There were several golf ball sized knots on my head, so the hospital wanted to do a scan to be sure my skull wasn't fractured. Luckily it wasn't. My lip was broken open but didn't warrant stitches, and I had a black eye, but luckily, no broken nose. Because the woman dug her nails into my skin, they recommended I get a tetanus shot, which caused the most lasting pain of all my injuries. All in all, I was very lucky.

I decided not to press charges against the woman, and not because I feared further attack by her or someone else. My reasons were two-fold. First, I felt that anyone who knew how to hit that well must be familiar with violence and/or must have a large amount of anger inside her, and this made me feel sad for her. I believed a more compassionate choice would be to let her have her own course of karma—meaning I trusted that just as I had experienced instant karma from acting in anger, she would eventually get her lesson as well. My pressing charges would perhaps make her feel punished by the judicial system, but I believed that the deeper lesson for both of us would occur in living our lives.

Second, I felt that my part in this was the most important thing for me to focus on. No, I didn't deserve to be beaten. But I did take part in the event. I knew better than to act in anger against another. I could have just said, "They must be running late, or they're having a hard day or a tough life to not let me in the lane." But because I was off center, I responded in a reactive way, and in doing so I stepped onto a "lower road." This was my responsibility and my lesson, and these had nothing to do with her. Her acting out was a reflection of my state of consciousness. She was being my Buddha.

Upon further reflection, I sent her a prayer of love and compassion. I prayed that she forgive me, and I forgave her. I prayed that her anger would be transformed into something good and positive, and that her lessons be as gentle as they could possibly be. I didn't wish her harm, only peace and healing.

PEBBLE

Telling this story has been a humbling experience; for other than my affairs, this was one of the most regrettable things I have taken part in. I didn't want to re-experience it again, nor did I particularly want to reveal such a thickheaded action on my part. It was important, however, to include this story because of the potency of its pebbles.

It should be noted that these pebbles were not immediate. They came after months of reflection and a fair amount of emotional and physical healing.

You might be asking yourself (and you would be justified in doing so), "Given her path, how could she have done this?" Herein lies the first pebble.

When one chooses a path such as mine, everything that is hindering one from becoming conscious will be brought front and center to be cleared. I had a very "hot button" for people doing unfair and disrespectful things that hurt me. I am certain that this stems back from my childhood experiences and was triggered by what I had experienced more recently with Chance. Because I had not cleared this hot button, when the woman did what she did, I ceased being in the present moment, and was launched into my unconscious past. This moment of unconsciousness allowed me to forget my humanity and the larger aspect of who I was, and react as an injured child would: "You did that to me, so I'm going to this to you." At some point in our lives, most of us become unconscious and reactive, and it is not pretty or elegant when it happens.

The second pebble is related to an earlier one: We never know the far-reaching effects of our actions, whether positive or negative. A blessing (and a curse) of self-growth and personal awareness is the quickening of feedback, or what I call the Law of Instant Karma. As we begin to attain new levels of awareness, there comes a natural ebb and flow of actions and opportunities to learn and self-correct. When one is centered, one is able to make adjustments in an effortless and gentle manner. When one is out of balance, the lessons become as forceful as they need to be. On either path, the lessons are always quick. Before this experience, I had a vague sense of how it worked. After this experience, it was emblazoned on my forehead. This pebble could also be explained with one of Newton's Laws of Motion: "Every action has an equal or opposite reaction." Just take this law, add the word instant to it, and you've got it. Speaking of the Laws of Motion, I might as well mention the other two laws because they apply here as well: "A physical body will remain at rest, or continue to move at a constant velocity, unless a net force acts upon it." (There is no escaping that I was moving with an unconscious energetic velocity until the woman stopped me in my tracks.) And, "The net force of a body is equal to its mass multiplied by its acceleration." (I certainly felt this law in effect with each blow.) You just cannot escape those laws of physics!

Another pebble: I stayed in a relationship that didn't serve me and was hurtful. The level of anger and disappointment that had built up was extraordinary, though not expressed. In an effort to keep my relationship together, I had abandoned the part of me that needed care the most. When we abandon ourselves, when we don't express our emotions by suppressing them and holding them hostage, and when we don't honor our needs and disappointments enough to allow them to be acknowledged and worked through, then guess what? The emotions get expressed whether through us or through another person, usually someone closest to us. I knew this principle but had not plugged it into this situation. Now that I have the insight, I can see that this entire incident was a reflection of the anger inside me.

The final pebble is my gratitude for the solid example of the metaphysical principle that we are simply and utterly reflections of one another. This woman's anger was not separate from mine. The anger that passed through her, and the anger that is expressed in the world at large, is the same anger that passed through me. I used to think that the anger and violence I saw in riots, terrorist acts, wars, violent acts against children, or domestic violence was somehow different than the anger that flowed through me. Anger is anger, and it flows through all humans at various levels and in multiple ways, and although it may have varying degrees of experience and expression, it is the same energy. It's important to house this knowledge in one's being so as not to create separatism or feelings of superiority. No matter what one's status of power, leadership, or teaching status, anger flows through all humans at times. It is part of a "collective" anger (which comes from the collective fear) that holds most humans in bondage. For those of us who feel anger, it is important to cultivate compassion, both for others and for ourselves. This will enable us to find equanimity so that when anger surfaces, it becomes a temperature gauge—a means for reflecting that changes needs to occur—instead of a state of being.

In the final moments of this chapter, I would like to reflect on how this beating brought both lightning and lightening into my life, and with it, the opportunity for the next level of my personal growth. This experience broadened my awareness of how my discomfort and impatience is never all that there is— there will always be someone with more grief, more anger, and more suffering. In this realization, my compassion was exponentially deepened, and for this I am sincerely grateful.

Chapter Fifty-Two

MAKING CONTACT

 confusion

*A*fter a year of repeated immunity-busting turmoil, the stress of moving, and the emotional and physical affects of the beating, my health plummeted. I got severe Candida (when fungus accumulates in the body from an immune deficiency), and was often in a state of ill health with various colds, infections, lung issues, and influenza. My weight dropped to one hundred and thirty-five pounds. With my six-foot-one frame, there was very little of me left, but with help from alternative medicine, I slowly and methodically began to rebuild myself. I lived from day to day, sometimes walking, sometimes crawling (metaphorically speaking), while looking for ways to bring happiness back into my life.

Then, on a cold November evening of the same year, I was housesitting for Cara and Joe. Tired from an arduous week, I was grateful to spend some quiet time. As I lay alone in the semi-darkness, I gazed up through the skylights and into the starlit sky. On the couch, feeling the peaceful warmth of the lit fireplace, I began to connect again to the depth and endlessness of the wounds in my heart. The agony of losing Chance hit me like a tsunami. When the regret I felt over my interaction with the woman in the car added its final blow, it was all I could do to hold on and not be swept away into endless darkness. I began to weep deeply, wondering if I would ever stop.

As I lay on the couch, loving myself as best as I knew how, I felt a strong urge to get up and open the sliding door so I could feel the fresh winter air and have the garden in full view. As I stood there, a presence—a sublime and magnificent, supremely loving, ultimately benevolent and munificent force/energy—emerged and completely enveloped me. It came from behind as it wrapped its cloak (or arms, or wings) around my entire body. I could see nothing, but it was without question that something, or someone, was present. It held me with a strong yet tender intensity, beckoning me to release into it…and I did. After a time, it would ease its grip for a moment and rock me gently back and forth, as if giving me a short reprieve, then come close again with all its power. Each time it tightened its hold, I sobbed as if purging, from dark recesses within, unconscious and inaccessible memories of past pain and grief. I didn't know what times, places or lifetimes the memories surfaced from. I could not think, nor did I want to. All that mattered was to feel this love and magnificence around me and to surrender to it. At one point, when I felt cold from the winter air, the presence turned me toward the couch, and I walked over to it and got my sleeping bag. I wrapped it around me, walked back to the window, and the process continued. After ten minutes… thirty minutes… an hour of being moved through several dimensions of release, it let me know through whatever the equivalent is of the mind's eye for the heart —intuition maybe—that it would be with me for the rest of my life. I didn't know what it meant, but I trusted its message and accepted it as I would a precious gift.

The intensity of the presence gradually dissipated, and I stood there for another few moments feeling the magnificence of grace, love, and the God-force around me as I looked out again toward the garden and up to the heavens. I knew I had just experienced something that would change me. I offered up a prayer of profound thanks, shut the sliding glass door, and lay back down on the couch. After reflecting for some time on the phenomenon that had just happened, I fell into a deep and peaceful sleep.

I awoke the next day feeling light and much relieved of the sadness that had plagued me for so long. It felt like a door had opened to a renewed sense of hope and love. With this came an internal glow of awareness that there was something different about me. My body, or rather a subtle and less dense part of my being that was located in my body, had the sensation of an unfamiliar force or energy in it. I would say that it felt good and benevolent, because it did, but *natural, clear, and vibrant* feels like a more fitting description.

PEBBLE

Oddly, this is the first pebble that has not come to me while writing the chapter. This visitation was so profoundly life changing and otherworldly that I could not think the pebble into existence. It had come to me, like The Presence did, of its own accord and in its own way.

The pebble here is that grace just comes to us, and I do not believe it has anything to do with how hard we may pray to feel it, or how much we need it, or how badly we have messed up. It comes for its own reasons. It simply sweeps through our lives and leaves us to determine what it is and how to make sense and/or use of it. As you will see in further chapters, and in how this story ultimately ends, it took years to weave its meaning and potency into my life.

Chapter Fifty-Three

PRESENTS FROM
THE PRESENCE

∽

*A*lthough the meaning of The Presence visitation took years to understand, some of the effects of its impact and a few early experiments I engaged in to discover what its purpose might serve, occurred shortly afterward.

For months after the experience, I often felt energy (like a mild electrical current) moving through parts of my body. I also noticed that at times, when I stood with my arms hanging at my sides, the energy would tingle my hands and then move them back and forth. *Fascinating,* I would think to myself. I became curious about what, if anything, the energy might be used for.

One day I was on my way to the refrigerator and thought to myself: *I'm going to ask this energy a simple question to see if it answers.* I closed my eyes, opened the refrigerator, and said, "Okay, please tell me what would be the best thing for me to eat right now." As I asked the question, I could feel the electricity flow and the energy push my hand toward something (I do not recall what). "Cool!" I exclaimed. I soon began to ask it other questions like, "Please tell me which is the better movie to go to." Or, "What would I find more satisfying to do, A or B?" I knew that the energy's purpose was much more significant than telling me which movie to attend, but I also had a feeling that starting small was the thing to do.

After several months of working with the energy in the simple ways I mentioned, I began to feel drawn to put my hands on friends. I wondered if perhaps the energy would enter into them and do something good for them as it had for me. Most of my friends welcomed my touch. Some of them said things like, "Your hands are hot," or "It feels like electricity is going through me." Whether or not they felt a physical sensation, everyone I touched felt that something "good" had happened—although what, specifically, most didn't know.

As time progressed, I noticed that occasionally my hands would throb when I was around someone. If it was someone I knew well, I would ask if I could rub his or her shoulders or just touch or hold them for a moment. If I didn't know them, I would just say a short prayer or focus my attention on them for a few moments. At times when I laid my hands on people, I could hear or see in my mind's eye certain things about them: how they felt underneath the surface, often before they were even aware, or issues that were affecting them or merited their attention. I wouldn't say I was getting psychic impressions, because I couldn't tell people specific things about their lives or about their futures. It was more like intuitive hits for the purpose of helping them heal their emotions or feelings about things. For example, I might see the person trying to hug something over and over, but with each attempt, nothing would be there to hug, and they would end up having to hug themselves. I would later find out that the person's parent was not emotionally available to them and that they felt they were always trying to get the parent to embrace them. After one of these intuitions—or insights—I might place my hands on them and focus energy. After one of these "sessions" most people experienced a deep state of peace, while some had cathartic experiences. For instance, a man with whom I was in a healing group was drawn to me one night. I could see his pain and asked him to talk to me as I pressed a spot on his arm that I intuited would draw out his pain. He began to cry uncontrollably for a long time until finally becoming calm.

When people asked what the energy was that moved through me, I replied that I wasn't sure, but it felt like the essence of Love.

"Whatever it is," I said, "I'm certain that its intention and purpose is to bring about joy, inner peace, and well-being." This I knew like the sun shines with each new day.

About a year after The Presence made itself known to me, someone told me about a clergyman who was gifted and well respected in a prominent church. Supposedly, the Force was strong with him. I became curious about the notion of a human as a conduit, or "middle man," between God and others less experienced with the forces. I decided I would ask him to meet with me so that I could see for myself what this might look like, sharing my experience with him to see what his response would be. I called him, and after a few messages back and forth, he agreed to meet me.

I arrived at the church in his office with an open mind and a hopeful heart, wanting to talk to him human to human: me as someone who felt she had had a direct experience of the Divine; he as someone who must have also had such an experience, or he would not be in the position he was in.

We chatted for a few minutes, and then he asked me to tell him what I wanted to speak with him about. I explained that I had had an experience and wanted to share it with him, not so much to get his opinion, but to talk about it in terms of what one might do with such an experience and its residual gifts.

As I told my story, I felt my heart expand as it had the night it happened. I became happier and more inspired relaying how beautiful The Presence felt and how its energy seemed to have remained with me. I relived the majesty and the healing I felt, and I quietly hoped that in some way the man would feel it, too. When my story came to a close, I noticed that his face appeared rather ashen. With a polite smile he said, "Is that it?" and I answered, yes. He then proceeded to tell me that he felt I was mentally disturbed, and that it was obvious to him that I either made the story up, or that I imagined it to fulfill some sort of emotional dementia or neediness. He added that I should probably seek professional help.

"Are you serious?" I asked, shocked by his response.

He replied with a solid yes and went on to explain why someone like me could not have such an experience—something to the effect that, in essence, I was not Godly enough; that those real experiences were reserved for people holier than I.

"Don't you think that Grace visits us at times for reasons we may not understand," I said. "And although we may not understand the reason, isn't it still real and potent?" He shook his head and stayed fixed in his position.

I thanked him for his time and left his office. I felt dirty—like someone had just called me a liar and attempted to wash my mouth out with soap and water. Then I got angry. *How dare he suggest that I'm lowly or delusional? How dare he assume that only people like him are granted, ordained, or given permission to have such an experience?*

I took a deep breath, shook my head, and promised to never again speak of my experience with someone of the clergy.

PEBBLE

What angered me most about the clergyman's response was that if I had trusted him to guide me, or if he had power over me, or I had been less confident in myself, my sanity, and my experience, I might have allowed him to convince me that something was wrong with me. He might have coerced me into believing that I was not worthy of such a divine visitation and that I must have imagined the whole thing.

In a way, this experience reminds me of the game Telephone. I said what I said, and he repeated back to me what he thought I said, but they didn't match. His beliefs acted as a filter, and because they didn't support what he heard, he discounted them as not being real, making up a scenario that would fit into his belief system. Many staunch Christians and Catholics I have encountered are fearful of others' experiences outside what the church declares acceptable and safe. They cannot help themselves, really—it's what they're taught and they're not encouraged or empowered to think for themselves.

Another analogy is the story of the Native Americans, who allegedly didn't see the newly arriving European ships because they had no frame of reference or understanding of their existence. Perhaps this man had no frame of reference to see my experience as being real, and therefore could not see it.

I suppose a fair question of someone without faith would be: "Could I have imagined my experience?" But it never entered my mind that I would be doubted and called delusional by someone of a "higher" position. My meeting with this man cemented my feeling that I had no place in most, if not all, organized religions.

The pebble was the realization that my experience of the Divine and its teachings live within me. I didn't need to seek outside validation or approval from him or anyone else. I set myself up for his response because underneath it all, I was looking for validation. Because of his status, I wanted the man to agree that my experience was as special as I thought it was. I didn't doubt that the visitation was real, but I wanted someone to share in it with me and say, "Yes. Isn't it great that this can happen and that it happened to you? Here's what you might do with it." I saw from my encounter with the clergyman that it was best to find my own meaning in matters of spiritual importance and potency, at least until I had a strong support system in place of similar and more open-minded people.

ADDENDUM

A note on my feelings about religion: I am not opposed to organized religion as long as it, and those in leadership positions, do not attempt to prevent its partisans from having a direct and personal experience of the Divine, and that all concerned refrain from telling others that their religion is supreme, or that those who practice their religion are superior to others, or that they are the only ones who are good and/or "saved."

Many find comfort, community, and profound love in their religions, and this is a good thing. What I'm saying is that religion should not be a place to hide, or something to fulfill a need to be superior or safe because a person has not done his or her own emotional healing and spiritual exploration. Nor it is something that one should use to replace one's own path of personal growth and development.

If we are to grow out of the unconsciousness, ignorance, judgment, and fear that have plagued our species for years upon years, we must think for ourselves and act from the deep sources of divinity within each of us.

Chapter Fifty-Four

NATIVE AMERICAN
RITUAL

∽

*T*he next several years were nothing less than one marvelous adventure after the next. In the remaining chapters, I will give a broad-range view of the magic and wonder that ensued from my ongoing choices to let go, trust, and take action from my intuition.

My father's father was half Osage Indian, and according to my grandmother, our heritage also includes Comanche (although because of my grandmother's recent death, I cannot confirm from where and when the bloodline flowed). Given my affinity for the earth and because of my heritage, I felt drawn to explore my devotion to prayer and God through Native American ritual. After asking several friends, I found Lynn, a local "medicine woman" and sculptor who hosted sweat lodges in her backyard on new and full moons. Simply put, a sweat lodge (a more updated term for an Inipi ceremony) is a purification ceremony traditionally practiced by the Lakota (more commonly known as Sioux) in an Inipi lodge made of a willow branch frame and wrapped in hides or blankets. People sit reverently around a sage-lined pit of fire-heated rocks onto which water is cast to create hot steam. Then the people sweat, sing, drum, and pray. In these lodges, a chanupa (pipe) was traditionally filled with flat cedar (nowadays, tobacco is also used) and passed around as each person prayed. The smoke, it is said, carries the prayers up to Wakantanka (The Great Spirit—or Great Mystery). It is an ancient practice and is considered quite sacred.

Lynn's lodges were non-traditional in that she was not Lakota, but she ran her lodges with deep heart. After I had attended her ceremonies for a year or so, I began to lead some of the songs in the lodge. Eventually, I helped wield the hot lava rocks from the outside fire to the center pit. It was an honor to be given the opportunity to take part in these rituals.

Before entering into her lodge, those present sat in a circle and passed the talking stick while stating what they were grateful for, sharing what they wanted in prayer. On a cool winter's night, a worn and sad looking woman shared that her teenage child, who had had some psychological issues, had been missing in the forest for a couple of days. She asked for prayers that he would soon come back home. I had an odd feeling about what she shared, and I asked The Presence if the child was all right. The Presence told me that the child was dead and that I should offer my prayers and comfort for strength and healing rather than encourage her hope. Without telling her what I was told, I did as I was counseled. Within a week, they found the child's body. He had apparently been killed in a fall. This experience deepened my appreciation of the wisdom of The Presence.

In the spring, I told Lynn that I wanted to go on a sort of Vision Quest so that I could deepen my conscious connection with Spirit —and the earth—and to get further insight into the purpose of and opportunities for my life. She sent me to a cabin in the woods where I was to perform a Flowering Tree ritual. I was tasked to find a group of four trees, one standing in each direction—South, West, North and East. I was to then sit with my butt and spine against each tree's base and meditate, connecting to its spirit. Then I was required to ask a series of questions from the four directions of each tree: Who am I? Where did I come from? Why am I here? Where am I going? and/or, What is my path of heart?

I arrived at the cabin later in the day than I expected and wasn't sure I would return from my quest before the sun set. I had never used a compass before and wasn't sure how, but I had an instinct to bring it. I set out and after forty-five minutes or so, I found the perfect set of trees. I sat down at the base of the south standing tree. Through my spine, I could feel subtle electricity coming from the tree. I felt welcomed by the ancient being and a gentle, grandmother-like encouragement to open and surrender to my writing process. I began to write feverishly.

Journal entry—

South Tree-South

Who am I? *You are the heart. You are humor at the place of joy. You are a vision of light and of love. You are an inspiration to those around you who seek the path of love eternal on the earth plain. You are a keeper of truth, of lighting the path, the way. Songs are your path. Sing to us now. You are one who brings music to the children, to the hearts of many, the wounded, the dancing. You are sunshine that burns for eternity. You dance, you play, you create joy with your very being. Hear us now. Oh hey, ah hah, hey oh, hey. Sing a song to us tonight. Hey oh, hey ah, ho, oh hey. Sing of peace to set yourself free. Your humor is your joy. Let it in, let it flow, set it free. Ah ho.*

Where did I come from? *From the light of a smile from the new fallen snow. The moon all aglow on the snow. The sun through the trees, the shimmer, the glow. You walked on the ray of free will seeking play.*

Why am I here? *To bring light into the hearts of others. Through your smile, through your touch, and through the song. To sing Hallelujah. To give praise. To walk the path from dark to light. To discover truth, under truth, under truth. To laugh, to dance, to rejoice at being one of the few to begin.*

Where am I going? *To the bathroom. Let it flow.* (I laughed out loud. I paused and took a quick break...) *To a place where the sun always shines. Do not fear, the time will come. Just open now to sing and sing, and jingle jangle your pots and pans, shake and pop your toys, your toys. To the bright side of the moon. To ring the chimes.*

South Tree-West

Who am I? *One who needs to discover patience to receive illumination. You are lovely and bright, but you need to learn to sit still. There is a peace in stillness if you can trust long enough to let it in. You are one who worries about so many things. Calm yourself dear. Remember to be present and the next moment will take care of you and your worries. It will take care of itself. You fly with us often and run with the deer. You are one we call Runs with Deer and Flies with Heart.*

Where did I come from? *From the ever-present illumination that surrounds you even now. She asked to give you birth and teach you the depth of emotion, love and femininity. She taught you well. Thank her and move on.* (I thanked her.)

South Tree-North

Who am I? *Walk the path and you will see. You are one who talks with the four legged, with the winged ones, and with the silent critters that know nothing but now—this very moment. They teach you with their play, their song, and their being-ness. They know nothing but now, right here, the sun and the moon.*

(I am not wise, I say.) *You must be completely present to see the truth in the moment. You are wise when you are present and your ego is standing aside.*

Where did I come from? *From your mother, who came from her mother, who came from her mother, who all came from the Great Mother. All things come from The Mother. The Great Spirit—one you cannot see but always feel, breathed life into all things and continues to shower you with the will to continue this journey.*

Why am I here? *To play and sing love into the hearts of others. It is indeed a wise one who can see the humor and light in all situations. They are nothing but other steps on the path to illumination.*

Where am I going? *To find your humor. Learn this and your path will be more complete than you thought possible, more fulfilled than you dreamed. Laugh and smile. Everything truly will be okay. We assure you. Now continue.*

South Tree-East

Who am I? *You are an ancient one who carries the energies of many times before. As we bring our history to this time, so do you. Keeper of heat, sharer of the flame, you pass it along. You cast out possibilities for all to see. You are a keeper of energy.*

Where did I come from? *From the depths of the sea. From the highest of peaks. From the heart of the mother and father, sister and brother. You are fed with possibility and pushed out for others to behold. Constant and stable for you—know who you are. Do you see you came from inside me?*

Why am I here? *To throw stones to those who will catch them, so they, too, may hold the truth, the energy that love created. To show how bright we can shine with the discovery of truth. One must listen to hear the answers to the questions one is asking. Tell them.*

Where am I going? *To the top of the mountain, to the depths below, and all around…until you understand it well enough to give it away. Tighten up your hiking shoes, get water and food to nourish, and continue on.*

(Any particular path? I ask.) *Create your own.*

And now, skipping to the fourth tree, fourth direction, and last entry—

East Tree-East

Who am I? *You are love.*

Where did I come from? *From the Great Mystery.*

Why am I here? *To love and be loved.*

What is my heart path? *Whatever you want.*

Then it/they asked me, *What are you willing to give away?* The truth as I know it.

As I wrote, I heard my mind say things like: *I know you say this is possible, but how can it be possible for me? Given all the mistakes I've made, how could I be taken seriously as someone who knows anything?* It felt as if I was hearing my parents give me a pep talk and that I was having the child's response, "Yeah, but you have to say those things because you're my parents!" Still, I listened to what I was hearing —that even though I might have made many mistakes, I had also taken responsibility for them and learned from them. I wondered if maybe, just maybe, this process is what one does on the path of becoming someone who shows the way for others. I knew that regardless of the answer, everything that had transpired would have to have time to settle in and to germinate.

As I sat giving thanks to the trees and all others for guiding me, and feeling gratitude for the opportunity to commune with nature, I realized that the sun was setting. It had taken about an hour per tree to complete the process.

I quickly began heading back in the direction of the cabin. About half way back, it turned completely dark. At one moment I flashed on the teenager who had died in the forest and felt fear, but then I heard myself say, *Death is not my fate, not yet anyway.* I looked at my compass and to the trees and asked, *Please lead me back.* I walked and walked, tripping from time to time on unseen obstacles since there was no moon. Nothing looked familiar yet I kept on, trusting. Then finally, just when I began to wonder if I would have to sleep in the forest until daybreak, I came upon my cabin. Elated, I gave thanks.

I lit a warm fire and laid next to it for hours reflecting on the day. The light from the fire flickered on the trees and their rustling leaves above me. I imagined them laughing and talking amongst themselves, celebrating my successful journey and my daring adventure back to the cabin. I felt their life, and I loved them. I was utterly content.

Through a friend I also met Michael, a half Lakota/half Celtic shaman, who ran traditional Inipis in the local desert, and I began attending his ceremonies. I enjoyed his lodges and felt his depth and sincerity from a more male and traditional perspective. I also learned of White Buffalo Calf Woman, a supernatural messiah to the Lakota people. She came to the Lakota, and brought with her the sacred pipe. Her messages of purification, honoring the mother (earth), prayer, ritual, devotion, and the interconnectedness of all things struck a deep core of recognition within me. I recalled how much closer I had felt to God up in the mountains of Lake Tahoe than in any church I had ever attended, and now understood why. I embraced her teachings with reverence.

It was during Michael's Inipi ceremony that I first encountered the statement "Mitakuye Oyasin," which means, "All My Relations." This was said aloud before entering the Inipi lodge, during the ceremony, and any time one wanted to honor the fact that we are all related. This struck a deep chord within me that I experienced as my being connected and related to all things—not only the obvious living, but also plants and supposed "inanimate" things—the earth, rocks/minerals/metal, water, air, weather, fire— and, of course, the Spirit that runs through them all. I began to reflect that even though they may not have the type of consciousness that we do, these things give to us on a continual basis, and this makes them worthy of my gratitude and honoring.

Although I usually prayed before I ate, my prayers began to feel incomplete. In time, I realized that it was not enough to thank only God/Goddess for my food and to pray blessings on those who were not as fortunate as I. It seemed appropriate to also thank those who died so that I may live. In my prayers, I started calling them out by name, "...I give great thanks to the fish and plant beings whose lives were taken so that my body could be nourished and my life sustained..." It felt deep and good, and more complete to pray in this way. I have continued this practice to this day.

It was summer, and Michael offered private visioning sessions to some of us who had attended his lodges. I signed up, having the feeling that something potent would be revealed from my work with him. During this process, I was to show up at his home in the evening and be prepared to stay up the entire night meditating (in and out of the Inipi Lodge) and asking for guidance.

At one point while in meditation, I remember sincerely asking why I had not met a human I could consider my spiritual teacher. I grappled with my disillusionment with the church, as well as the fact that even though I had met and known some very wise people, none of them had the breadth of spiritual understanding that I sought, nor did they seem devoted to walking their talk sincerely or in a way that inspired me to adopt them as my teacher. I asked if I would ever find such a person. It was then that I understood the following: Love itself is my true teacher in this lifetime. (Remember my epiphany as a child that Love was all we needed, and then my later epiphany that Love is really the essence of everything? Well, here it was again, only phrased differently.) When this awareness hit, all my questions, confusion, and pain around this issue ceased. I then understood that there are many pieces of the puzzle to learning how to live a life of fulfillment and peace. No one person, or teaching, carries all the answers. It is up to us to forge our own path and find our way through, then offering our insights to others, if it is our calling.

This time I asked, *Why was I born into my particular family? I have always felt disconnected from and alien to many of them. I would like to understand why they were given to me.* I felt a deep peace run through me as the answer came. *It would have been easy in my adult years to create a controlled environment from which to live. It would have been free of most suffering and consisted largely of joy and happiness. My family kept me in the practice of forgiveness and compassion. Through them, I was able to see first-hand how much of the world lives and operates. My family was important for my growth and what I would later offer others.* With this, I surrendered my lifelong resistance to who they were and what they represented. This realization was pivotal. First, it helped me embrace the part of myself that I felt was flawed. Then, of course, I was able to forgive my family for their foibles. This led me to a deep sense of compassion for those in my—and for the rest of the world—all of us making it through life the best way we know how.

At the end of the session with Michael, we lay in his Inipi lodge, him by my side facing outward, like a bear protecting his family, me curled up behind him. Peace and understanding were momentarily mine.

I followed a quasi-Native American path for a couple of years while meeting and participating in ceremonies with many people, including full-blooded Lakota elders. This was always a profound experience. I also attended powwows in the summers. I recall the beauty of the colors, sounds, and the dancing. The pride of the Native Americans was palpable.

PEBBLE

The first pebble for this chapter is Mitakuye Oyasin, All My Relations—The Native American's version of the truth that there is no separation. There is only one heart, one mind, and one world. This understanding resides deep in my bones, and it is good. Ah ho.

Sharing the details of my Flowering Tree ritual has felt very risky to me. I have never spoken much about my own spiritual process. My feeling has always been that it is personal to each person. What Spirit says to one person is for their heart only—it is what he or she needs to hear, given where they are in the moment. If one shares their process with others, even with the best of intentions, it can give rise to the ego's habit of comparison. The other is that as far back as I can remember, I have had a strange, deep-seated fear that I will be persecuted for my spiritual insights. Regardless of its origin, my fear has no truth in the here and now. So, the reasons I shared a portion of the details of this ritual is threefold: 1) to press through fear; 2) to show that spiritual growth and insight takes focus, attention, and time; and 3) to share my hope that something in this process will cause a pebble of insight for you, the reader.

Oh, one more thing: With regard to what I heard and then wrote during the Flowering Tree ritual…I hope I am fulfilling who I'm meant to be and of what I am capable; based on the answers I received to those questions, we shall continue to see. What I do know is that none of us truly knows what we are made of until we do what we are capable of.

To use the immortal words of Marianne Williamson: "Our deepest fear is not that we are inadequate. Our deepest fear is that we are powerful beyond measure. It is our light, not our darkness, that most frightens us. We ask ourselves, who am I to be brilliant, gorgeous, talented, and fabulous? Actually, who are you not to be? You are a child of God. Your playing small doesn't serve the world. There's nothing enlightened about shrinking so that other people won't feel insecure around you. We are all meant to shine, as children do. We are born to make manifest the glory of God that is within us. It's not just in some of us; it's in everyone. And as we let our own light shine, we unconsciously give other people permission to do the same. As we are liberated from our own fear, our presence automatically liberates others."

An interesting point that I made note of while transcribing the Flowering Tree ritual from my journal was that some of what I wrote in that process is now coming to fruition by my writing this book. In 1994 (fourteen years ago), when I did the ritual, I had not yet conceived of writing a book. Yet, in some of the passages I can see how this book fits in nicely to what was being created.

The realization that Love would be my teacher was another foundational insight. Reaffirming that Love is simply everything was…everything. I saw, even more clearly, that it is the essence of what we need and what we want. It is our teacher and it is the only real truth. With this understanding, I have been able to walk these last many years with a deeper experience of peace and resolve.

∽

I would like to take this opportunity to honor both Lynn and Michael for their individual contributions to me, for their devotion to their path, and for honoring ritual in a way that has positively affected those around them.

Chapter Fifty-Five

I AM LOVE

∞

From a friend, I heard of Patrick the Storyteller, a man who was great at telling Native American stories. I contacted him and set up a time to do a storytelling for a group of my friends. He showed up wearing a t-shirt that caught my eye. In gold leaf it read I AM LOVE and underneath the lettering was a large Aztec-style image of the sun with a pyramid in the center. I asked him about his shirt, as I wanted to buy one. He told me that he got it from a friend of his who was in an alternative dance music band with that name. This made me think about how much I missed having music in my life and how I wanted to get back into it. The band I had been in previously and recorded a demo with had broken up. I wondered if by chance this new band needed a backup singer.

Patrick was delightful. His stories were sweet and lighthearted. His cadence made people feel as if they were sitting inside an ancient teepee listening to the elders share wise and wonderful tales. I had never known that Native American humor was so funny: "What do you call a boomerang that doesn't work? A stick." This one had me laughing so hard I embarrassed myself.

After the storytelling, I asked Patrick for his friend's contact information. I called Roy the next day and introduced myself. I told him that anyone with a band named I AM LOVE was someone I wanted to know. We spoke a long while about Patrick, the shirt, his band, and my music background. I asked if by chance they were looking for a backup singer and percussionist. We agreed that he would first send me a demo so that I could hear whether his music and my voice would be a match.

I very much liked the production of the music. Roy was not only the lead guitarist, but he also wrote a fair amount of the music and engineered and produced the songs. I called to tell him that I thought we could work together and we set up a time for me to come to a rehearsal.

I practiced and practiced to the tape to be sure I got the nuances of the songs. The week before the rehearsal, I was so nervous I wasn't sure I would be able to go through with it. My friends encouraged me saying, "Just give it your best shot. That's all you can do." I took their advice and showed up with all my percussion toys, my nerves, and my enthusiasm.

It ended up we sounded pretty good together, and Roy, Victor (the lead singer, who had been lead singer for a well-known British Gothic Rock group in the eighties), and I got on well. We seemed to be on similar wavelengths in many ways. The next day I got a call from Roy, inviting me to join the band. I was ecstatic.

We practiced often and had gigs around L.A. We attracted all sorts of interesting people who wanted to know the band called I AM LOVE. What I remember most about this time was the fun and love we all seemed to enjoy while in the creative process, and that everyone who visited us got swept up in the "vibes" as well.

Roy told me about Tek, who ran Share the Warmth—a part of Sacred Hoop of America—which is an organization that provides blankets to tribes in the northern plains reservations. He brought to my awareness that Indians froze to death each year on the reservations, and they got little to no help from the government. I was touched by Tek's efforts to bring comfort and warmth to these people. Roy said that he was thinking about doing something to raise money for them. "Perfect!" I said. "I know how to plan events!" With all the concerts and parties I had produced with Sean, I knew it would be a breeze for me, and so Roy and I decided to co-produce a fundraising event. Alexandra, a close friend of mine, and a fan of I AM LOVE, joyfully clamored to be a part of the event and declared herself our production assistant.

We heard that Eric Wright, the grandson of legendary architect Frank Lloyd Wright, lived with his wife, Mary, high in the hills of Malibu on the family ranch. They sometimes had gatherings and private functions on their property, and they also had a sweat lodge on their land, so it seemed a natural fit for us to ask them if they would allow us to have our event there. We approached the Wrights, telling them of our intentions to raise money for Share the Warmth, and to our great delight, they agreed. We scheduled a date and began the months of preparation.

I called the local newspapers to see who might be interested in our event. Nick, who wrote for *The Outlook*, our local daily newspaper, called me back to say he was interested in doing a story. Nick came and interviewed Roy and me. He was a gentle, intelligent, and articulate man who was touched by what we were doing and promised to do his best to give the event as much exposure as he could. Within a few days, a large article appeared in the paper. He kept his word, and I kept him as a lifelong friend.

Roy and I knew our event was catching momentum and we continued planning feverishly. We had to secure a sound system, bathrooms, a first-aid station, and food for five hundred to eight hundred people. Then we put the word out to dozens of vendors to come and sell their wares. We extended invitations to many prominent Native Americans to emcee and perform at the event. Everyone was clamoring to be a part of it. We invited a Lakota elder to be our honored guest and asked him to give a talk. Even he agreed. After producing so many events, I knew by how things were shaping up that it was going to be a successful and well-attended affair. It was getting so big that we needed many people to staff the entrance gate, the parking lot, the set up, the tear down, the clean up, etc. We also needed walkie-talkies so that I could keep track of everything.

It all came together in the end and the event was a smashing success. Everything went smoothly—even the parking (the volunteers never took a break, God bless them again—and the love that circulated was palpable. I ran around most of the day like a crazy person, hardly stopping, but I didn't want to miss a minute of it. It was a day of utter joy, and I felt like the luckiest person on the planet to be a part of it.

As the producers of the event, Roy and I scheduled our band to be the last act. I vigorously tried to clean off the layers of dirt and muck caked on my skin, under my nails and in my hair before going on stage, but to no avail. It didn't matter, though. With the glow of the day emanating from my face, our show went off flawlessly, and we ended the event with our gratitude to all who attended.

After the guests and vendors had left and much of the teardown was complete, Wallace offered to hold a special Inipi in our honor. Wallace, his followers, and Roy, Victor, and I all filed into the lodge, and we sweated and prayed together. In the middle of the ceremony, something happened that I had never encountered before in a lodge. An eagle (or rather the spirit of one) flew from the back of the lodge through to the opening. Many of us witnessed it, and Wallace told us that this was a good sign. We took it as such and ended the day as we had begun—with prayer, the heartbeat of the drum, and reverence.

We were thrilled to have hosted approximately eight hundred people throughout the day, and we netted $9,800—enough money to make four hundred and seventy two heavy woolen blankets. They were shipped to the reservations a few months after our event, just in time for winter.

PEBBLE

Producing this event remains one of the highlights of my life. Almost everything about the day was flawless. I say almost everything because the person who was asked to videotape the event ended up bolting with all the footage. He seemed to believe that because he filmed it for us, it belonged to him. I regret that no one will be able to revisit this day as we had hoped, but at least we got some beautiful photographs.

The pebble here has to do with how every contribution matters. If each person whose basic needs were met gave $1, $5, or $10 a month to a worthy charity, or if they gave a few hours to an organization that was doing good in the world, what a difference it would make. Our individual contributions may not solve problems completely, but they will definitely make an impact, and when combined with hundreds, thousands, and hundreds of thousands of other people doing their part, great change can take place.

Chapter Fifty-Six

SEDONA CALLS

∽

uring this period, I read books on female shamanism and on the feminine aspect of the Divine. I discovered Marianne Williamson and read or listened to her extraordinary works on spirituality and empowering women. These and other books deepened my awareness of the power inherent in women and of the feminine essence. I welcomed the notion that women have great power and abilities to facilitate healing and change in the world, and I looked forward to seeing how I might be a part of this process.

Victor from I AM LOVE and I had become close friends. He and I regularly attended group meditations and other spiritual gatherings. In 1993, Victor and Paul, a gifted pianist friend of his, decided that they were going to Sedona, Arizona to camp over the long Easter weekend. They wanted to meditate in this supposed spiritually potent place. I wasn't sure I agreed with the notion that one place on Earth is any more spiritually potent than another, but I knew when they first mentioned the trip that I wanted to go. I felt somehow that I was "supposed" to go. For some time I had been engaged in the practice of following what I felt inspired or guided to do. Half joking, I told them that whether we drove there together or I drove by myself, I was definitely going. They took me seriously and were happy to have me go along, especially since I offered to drive us in my new car.

Each of us was to bring something for our meditation circle. Victor brought his crystals, Paul brought his portable piano, and I brought my heart and love of Spirit. I felt that these were the most powerful gifts I had to offer.

We set out on Friday morning. The miles and hours of travel flowed easily past as we made our way eastward and through the desert, stopping from time to time along the way. We reached Sedona in mid-afternoon. When I got out of the car, I noticed that the ground under my feet felt like it was vibrating. *Interesting*, I thought to myself. I lifted one of my feet to see if the foot I lifted would still vibrate (thinking that maybe my feet were vibrating simply because we had been driving for so long). The foot I had planted vibrated while the one I lifted stopped. When I returned my foot to the ground, the vibration began again. It was as if I could feel energy emanating up from the earth. While noticing this, I felt a subtle invitation from the unseen realm to just relax into the vibration.

Victor had done homework on the various places to visit. Certain locations, or vortices, supposedly emitted high levels of energy. We decided that we would visit each one of these locations and meditate. We first went to Bell Rock, named because it looks, well… like a bell. We settled in and meditated for a while. Although it was quite beautiful there, I didn't feel anything otherworldly. After we finished meditating, Victor and Paul went on and on about how amazing their meditations were and how they felt all sorts of energy in the place. Although I chimed in on their experiences, I was quiet about my own. I thought to myself, *I must not be in tune enough to feel what everyone else feels when they come here. Okay then, I'll just bring my love wherever we go and leave it at that.* We went to a couple more places and meditated before we went to get dinner. We camped the first night among the trees and rocks.

When we awoke the next day, Victor laid out his crystals, Paul played his piano, and we all meditated again. I remember wondering if perhaps, like the men, I should have some "thing" to do or offer. I thought, *Am I doing enough? It seems like they're offering so much more than I. Maybe so, but I'll just keep offering my heart. That's what I have.*

We continued to go from place to place, meditating and communing. And as we did, I felt deeper and deeper levels of gratitude for the opportunity to be in such a beautiful and serene place. This began to extend outward, and as it did, I started to feel a profound love for Sedona. Victor and Paul were having similar experiences, and we began to feel the desire to pray for the earth, for peace, and for healing.

Late in the day, we decided that we wanted to camp at the top of Cathedral Rock. Set atop a tree-covered mountain, a majestic collection of massive red rocks shot up toward the heavens. A high ridge, or saddle, connected the peaks. We would be camping on the ridge, which was about a three-quarter-mile hike up the steep rock face.

As we reached the parking area at the bottom of the mountain, the sun set. We wondered with the light almost gone how long it would take us to get up there. None of us knew, but we decided to go for it anyway. It took us a while to get our things packed and it was getting darker by the minute, but we felt no need to rush.

We set out in the general direction of the rocks. With our unfamiliarity of the way up, and with Paul carrying his piano, the going was slow. The light now was completely gone, and we were hiking up the face in utter darkness; we could barely see our shoes. Victor and I put on our headlamps, but Paul hadn't even brought a flashlight, so one of us had to stay with him. The lights helped us see where we were walking, but they didn't shine brightly enough for us to see which direction was the safest to take.

At nightfall, a strange sound began calling out from the top of the rocks. We all heard it—it sounded like a bird, but not like any we had ever heard before. As we listened to it, we all agreed that if we followed the bird, it would lead us to the top. Slowly we made our way up the rocks, joking that the bird was there solely for the purpose of helping us get to the top, and for two hours it called out to us. The moment our feet hit the ridge at the top, the bird stopped.

We could see the city lights far below. It was magnificent: the gentle breeze, the silence, the stars—oh my Lord, the stars. It felt like we were being held in the palm of the rock's hand, holding us high, offering us up to the starry heavens.

Searching for a place to camp, I found a tree that immediately struck me as what the Bible's "burning bush" would look like. I claimed the spot just next to its trunk and set out my sleeping bag. Lying next to the tree, gazing at the stars and the tall rocks, I felt like the luckiest person on earth.

We explored a bit and then gathered for another meditation before bed. Victor and I settled in to a beautiful state, each of us with our eyes open and taking in the stars above and the sparse lights in the city below. We felt warm waves of peace flowing through us when Paul started to play, and then something extra-ordinary happened: Each time he pressed his fingers onto the piano keys, a beautiful white light shone on the massive rock on the opposite side of the saddle, about forty meters away. It was not bright, but it was clearly visible, and it was definitely *not* a flashlight. We looked at each other in awe at what we were witnessing. It was as if the rock was responding to every chord Paul played with a corresponding and pulsating force of life, perceived by us as light (and without drugs mind you!).

The next morning was Easter Sunday. We arose to a gorgeous, clear morning. In our bliss, we all felt very close to The Christ force on Cathedral Rock. We sat together, had a long meditation, and then explored the rocks and the surrounding area more thoroughly. We wanted to stay longer, but we began to get hungry. We had neglected to bring food with us, but as we were saying we should pack up, a beautiful young couple walked around a ledge and offered us their leftover food. They said they were on their way down for brunch and didn't need it. We gratefully accepted, and after snacking on fruit, bread, and nuts, we spent a couple more hours communing on the rock. Before we left, we offered our gratitude for having a truly blessed Easter.

We hiked down in less than half the time it took us to get up there. We were astounded to see where we had hiked up in the dark; we actually weren't sure how we did it. At that moment, we paused and offered thanks to our guiding bird.

We hopped in the car and drove to the local health food store to stock up on food. We then drove on a dirt road for eight miles to see the Palatki cliff dwellings and petroglyphs. *Palatki* means red-house in the Hopi language, although evidently many different cultures inhabited the area over a 3,000 to 6,000 year period. We happened to be the only people on the site, and we thoroughly explored the amazing dwellings, rock art, and spots where supposed portals would take you into other dimensions. We meditated next to one of the portals. I didn't travel anywhere, but I felt my heart sink deep into the place, and I prayed for love and consciousness to prevail there, in all of Sedona, and outward.

Again, it was getting late, so we drove to the parking lot near the Boynton Canyon trailhead. We chose to camp up Boynton Canyon because it was considered a sacred spot representing the womb of Mother Earth. The opening did remind me of the opening of a vagina. It was beautiful, luscious, and deep.

The hike into the canyon was two and a half miles. We knew we wouldn't reach the end before it got dark, so we agreed to find a comfortable place to camp when hiking no longer became feasible. I felt energized and strong with each step into the deeply feminine place. It seemed that as I grew stronger, Victor and Paul grew more tired. At one point, they were walking very slowly; they said they felt heavy and fatigued. I remembered a song that I used to sing in the Inipi ceremonies, one that gave thanks to the trees and to the earth. As I sang it and then taught it to them, it seemed to give them energy—enough anyway to enable them to travel another hour farther up the trail.

As the sun went down, we intensely felt the life of the canyon around us, so much so that we resorted to reverent hushed tones as we walked. Eventually, we found a huge flat rock that was exactly big enough for three bodies to sleep upon. The silence was enormously loud with the thousands of life forms we felt surrounding and watching us. The energy was so strong that I slept very little. Mostly I just gazed out into the dark and up into the starlit sky.

The next morning we continued our hike to the end of the canyon. We climbed up to a flat area of rock where we could see the lush canyon below and the high rim of the canyon surrounding us. We made preparations, and I slipped into a deep and powerful meditation. I sat in wonder at the depth of love that I felt for the place. So much love was moving through me that all I could do was sit back and let it flow. And then something happened; I began to hear singing. It was the most beautiful symphony I had ever heard. It was deep, rhythmic, and proud. It grew in volume until I could clearly hear the song. I had never heard it before, but I knew without question that it was Native American. I began to hear drums weaving their collective heart through the song. I wondered where the sounds were coming from and looked up. In my mind's eye, I saw the entire upper rim of the canyon surrounded by Native American peoples, with their beautiful black hair and brown skin and in full regalia—feather headdresses and leather clothes, fringe swaying with their moving bodies. The song grew in energy, and as it did I started to cry uncontrollably. Their song entered my heart as my prayers had entered theirs. I looked around at the spirits of hundreds of people singing a song of thanks. It was profoundly beautiful. This went on for some time. Then, as the music faded, my mind and attention brought me back to the rock on which I was sitting, and to Victor and Paul. When I opened my tear-filled eyes, I could see them looking intently at me. Once I was fully back, they asked me about my experience. They too had had powerful meditations, although very different.

We spent a bit more time appreciating the canyon's beauty, and the wonderful trip we were graced with. We then began our trek back down. Just as we started to head out of the densest part of the canyon, a hummingbird began to follow us. It stayed with us for quite some time, darting back and forth around us, mostly around Paul. I delighted in its ability to fly in any direction. We laughed, joking that we weren't sure if it was happy to see us, or if it was happily pushing us out the door.

A few months later, I traveled to Sedona on my own. The first night I was there, I planned to camp next to the bush on Cathedral Rock. The moment I stepped foot onto the base of the rock, I felt like I was home. It felt natural and effortless climbing up the large face, like the way a child climbs up her parent's body to be held. I was completely happy.

While I was on the rock, I asked Spirit to help me with a logo that would be used for my healing work. I immediately saw it in my mind's eye and drew it as best I could. As I drew, Spirit explained to me what everything meant.

The outer circle represents heaven, and the inner, Earth. The four diamonds are the four directions. The triangle is the strongest shape, and the three triangles represent the strength in the triple trinity—the body, mind, spirit connection; the father, son, and Holy Spirit; the mother, daughter, and Sacred Feminine. The two triangles facing down represent bringing heaven to earth. The one triangle facing up represents humans striving toward our highest ideals. With every effort we make to attain these ideals, the heavens more than meet us. The winged heart represents the limitless potential of the open heart. Its position suggests that it brings all things into union.

After I was finished drawing the logo, I chuckled to myself, *Spirit gave me my logo. I like it! I never knew Spirit was into marketing.*

The next day, I hiked up Boynton Canyon. It was a lovely trip. I meditated while walking and gave thanks for the opportunity to be there. That night, my sleeping bag was atop the same large rock at the end of the canyon where I had heard the song. The view was magnificent, and the canyon, trees, rocks, sky, and scent of the place were full of life. I lay down under the moonlight and gently glided off into a peaceful sleep. Hours later, I woke with a start to something in my head saying, *Wake up!* I opened my eyes and looked around to see who was talking, but no one was there. The moon was no longer visible, so it was quite dark. I then heard, *Look up.* As I gazed into the massive collection of solar systems, I saw a light traveling straight across the sky. I thought for a moment that it might be a satellite, but it was moving too quickly. Then, even though it was traveling in a straight line, I wondered if it was a shooting star. As I thought this, the light shot straight down, then left, then up, and then all at once it shot to the left again and disappeared. I felt my eyebrows rise as I said to myself, *Hm, no, that was no shooting star.* Then I said out loud, "Okay. I saw it. Is there anything else?" Nothing. "Okay then, thank you." I lay back down but before I went back to sleep, I smiled to myself and said, *I have no idea what that was, but I'm really happy to have seen it.*

PEBBLE

The common thread through these, and several other experiences about which I have written, is when I walked without assumptions, kept my ears and mind open, did my best, and brought my heart with me wherever I went, the outcome was fulfilling and insightful. Actually, now that I think about it, this book has been written in the manner I just described.

As I write about these Sedona experiences, I am reminded of a few things Spirit told me:

1. *Know where your heart beats and you'll know where your answers lie.*
2. *Heed your intelligence, but follow your bliss.*
3. *Offer your own unique gifts, and you will be rewarded with beauty. This beauty will help carry you through challenging times.*

∽

To the spirits of Sedona...
O Mitakuye Oyasin

Chapter Fifty-Seven

MOUNT SHASTA

∽

I felt called to visit Mount Shasta for the Thanksgiving weekend, having heard it was another hot spot for mystical energies.
The cone of an extinct volcano, it's located about forty miles south
of the California/Oregon border. It was supposedly a long drive—
nine hours without bathroom, gas, leg stretching, or meal breaks.
All told, it would take about eleven hours, but still I wanted to drive
to take myself out of my comfort zone. After meditating on this, I
realized that I had some cherished friends, Selene and Gary, who
lived in Menlo Park, about halfway to Mt. Shasta from Los
Angeles. They just so happened to celebrate the holidays with as
much gusto as I did. *How perfect!* I thought. So to make the
beginning of my journey more enjoyable—and more manageable
—I made arrangements to stop there on Thanksgiving to have
dinner and to stay the night.

My excitement at seeing Selene and Gary made my trip to
Menlo Park seem easy and quick. These two were as good as they
come; Gary was one of the most ethical people I knew, and Selene
the definition of vibrant and jovial. Oh, and did I mention she was
an excellent cook? So, not only was my heart filled to the brim by
seeing them, but so also was my stomach. We had a grand night of
merriment, and the next morning I was roaring and ready for the
next leg of my journey.

I had been on the road for a couple of hours and was in the
fast lane, traveling up Interstate 5, when out of the left corner of

my eye I noticed something rise up and down from the ground. As I passed it, I realized it was the wing of what looked like a dead owl being moved by the gusts of wind from the cars passing. I felt a tug at my heart. Then, as always when I passed animals likely killed by humans or our machines, I said a prayer. I noticed that the tug at my heart didn't stop. Then I heard in my mind's ear, "Go back." *What?* I replied in my head. "Go back to the owl," I heard again. *Oh, no. I'm sorry, but I don't do dead animals,* I replied strongly. *No. I'm not going back.* Then I thought. *Okay, this is weird. I'm arguing with the voice in my head.* Uncomfortable silence. *I don't even know where it is now!* As the tug at my heart turned heavy, I knew that following what I was guided to do could include not only things I was comfortable with, but also things that made little or no sense. So I gave in. *All right. I'll do it. But if I don't find it with my first pass, I won't go back again.* The heaviness in my heart immediately began to lift.

There was no exit within miles, and I feared that if I went too much farther that I would have no chance of finding the owl. So, in the name of Spirit, I slowed down and turned my car to the left, traveling across the center area. Bump-bu-bump-bu-bump-bu-bump-bump my car went as it crossed over the uneven ground, shrubs, and rocks. I turned again to the left and got back on the highway facing south. I traveled a couple miles and again crossed over the center area, part of me hoping I had gone far enough, and part of me hoping I hadn't. I drove as slowly as I could while looking to my left for the bird. I didn't find it and half wondered if I had actually seen it correctly. *Maybe it wasn't dead and was just standing there,* I thought. But sure enough, a bit further up the road I saw the dead barn owl. I pulled off the road and looked around, hoping a highway patrolman wasn't anywhere nearby. I looked at the owl. It hardly looked dead, except for the fact that it was lying on its back. *How sad,* I thought. *It's such a beautiful bird. It must have just happened.* Then I said out loud, "Okay, now what do you want me to do?"

"Take the bird with you," the voice replied. *Oh no, I was afraid of that. Nope. I don't do dead animals.* I knew there was no use in arguing, but still I protested. *I have nothing to take it in. I cannot just put it on my seat!* "Open the trunk." it said. *Fine,* I said, knowing that nothing was in there. As I opened my trunk I thought, *See? There's nothing in…oh, crap. I forgot about that bag.* There was an empty brown paper bag lying right on top of my things. *But what about the body decomposing—won't it start to smell?* I thought. "It's cold enough in Shasta that it won't be a problem," I heard. *Right. Okay, I'll take the bird.*

I looked around again for a highway patrolman. I was pretty sure that barn owls, like other birds of prey, were protected. I wasn't sure if what I was doing was legal.

As I gently lifted the bird into the paper bag, I prayed my apology for its death and honored its life. Then I rolled the end closed as best I could. *Okay, I did it. Is this it?* A light feeling came over my heart. I took that as a *yes* and placed the owl in my trunk, then continued with the rest of the trip.

Mount Shasta was beautiful and majestic, and the town was sweet. Although I had never been there, it felt familiar. Like Sedona, there was a welcoming feeling to the place.

I found the youth hostel where I had reservations and brought my things in. After I was settled, I asked the owner what there was to do at night. "Well, tonight there's a Christmas tree lighting ceremony."

"Perfect!" I replied.

As I walked downtown, I saw the early stages of a winter scene: The sun was setting, the sky was trying to snow, the city's people in their bundles mingled around City Hall happily communing, children were running around, dogs were barking, and the nip of cold bit at my nose. There was an aura of family and celebration. I chatted lightly with people as the time neared to light the large tree that stood in the center of town. Before the ceremony, they passed candles around to everyone; we then sang several old-fashioned Christmas songs. Given my love for Christmas, I knew the words to all of them and sang loud and strong. After we finished the songs, we lit each other's candles until the entire community was a sea of flames. Then, with great anticipation, the grand tree was lit and met with "ohhhhhs" and "ahhhhhs." People lingered for a bit longer, then slowly dispersed with many well wishes and hugs. *Now this is my idea of a spiritual sojourn,* I thought.

The next couple of days were spent exploring the mountain and meeting all kinds of interesting people at the hostel. The most common questions upon meeting were: "Where are you from?" and "Why are you here?" Many of those I spoke with had come to Shasta for spiritual awakening or insight; they hoped that being on the mountain would give it to them. While I didn't believe, as some did, that the Lemurians (a mythical group of highly evolved people of a lost land) were secretly and invisibly living in the heart of the mountain, I did feel that there was a potency to the collective spiritual life there. I felt moved to meditate often and to tap into the life there, adding my own energy to it.

Upon my leaving, nothing struck me as extremely memorable but being there had definitely been nourishing to my soul. (By the way, during my two days on Shasta Mountain, I checked on the owl a couple of times. It was fine, like the voice in my head had said. The trunk of my car was like a refrigerator—probably colder.)

My journey home began at around noon, after a hearty breakfast and a host of goodbyes and blessings with those at the hostel. The drive was uneventful until I got about a third of the way home—not far, in fact, from where I found the owl. While driving, I began to have visions of things I had not yet experienced but apparently would. I had to pull off the road several times so that I could record on paper everything that was downloading into my head. What I was seeing were complete scenes. Much to my surprise, I saw myself in front of groups, talking and putting my hands on people and loving them. I was working with them, using The Presence and the energies. I saw myself singing in front of these people as a means of raising the spirits of those present. I was in awe of these visions and puzzled as to how they might be brought into being. I had no frame of reference for this, nor did I understand why these visions were coming to *me*.

About two-thirds of the way home, I became tired from driving and from the intensity of the visions. I pulled over to take a nap and to pray thanks. When I awoke refreshed about forty-five minutes later, I finished my drive while pondering all I had seen.

Upon my return home, I shared my visions with a few of my friends I knew would welcome such experiences, and they all thought it was fascinating. I had no insight, though, as to how to put my visions into motion anytime soon, and I went back to my day-to-day life trusting that if the visions were meant to be, the opportunity would find me.

I called a friend of mine who made dream catchers (a Native American object—made with willow twigs, leather, twine, feathers and beads—that hangs over one's bed to catch the bad dreams and filter the good ones through) and asked him what to do with the owl. I told him I didn't really want it, but that perhaps I should keep the wings to make fans for smudging (another Native American ritual to cleanse one's energy by lighting sage, cedar or sweet grass and allowing the smoke to pour over themselves). He told me how to preserve the wings, and then we arranged to meet so he could take the body from me. As difficult as it was to dismember the owl, I also felt reverence while in the process. I prayed over it, thanking it for being and for the opportunity to have part of its body for my spiritual rituals.

My friend made dream catchers with the feathers from the owl's body and gave me one to keep.

PEBBLE

It felt great living in what I considered the spiritual flow. I was living in the way I believed I was meant to live—in harmony with the earth and with those around me. I was not thinking about the past, nor was I fretting about the future. I was loving my life as it was. So, one pebble is appreciating the feeling of ease and flow while it is present. I saw how several events had led to, or culminated, in this experience. I set a new standard for what I considered to be a centered and harmonious life. This is how I wanted to live the rest of my life.

You may wonder if the opportunity will find you, or if you will find the opportunity. I have since learned that with these visions, or moments of guidance, it is often a more potent choice to be proactive and find the opportunity, rather than to wait for it to find you. Many of these visions have a window of opportunity, as most things in life.

What I have also found is that the more "in tune" I became, the more readily I received insight, inspiration, and visions of opportunities. Since insights and visions can fade quickly, I learned that it was in my best interest to record these things as they occurred to me. That way, they could be revisited once the initial insight had passed' otherwise, I might lose the insight and allow it to travel back to the vast and limitless realm from which it came...ready for someone else to act upon.

Upon my return from Mt. Shasta, I typed up a three-page account of the vision I received. If I were to live into this vision one day, I wanted to make sure I remembered it as clearly as possible.

Chapter Fifty-Eight

HEALERS HEALING

∽

*T*hroughout this time, I continued to work with The Presence, the energies, and doing healing work on friends. Through this, I started to meet people who did healing work for a living.

I was introduced to Chuck, a man dedicated to helping people heal themselves. Chuck lived in the Seattle area and often traveled to Los Angeles to work. He seemed to be fairly adept at tuning into people and helping them with issues, and he and I traded sessions on each other and I attended a couple of seminars he gave. I watched how he used his gift, and we worked on people together. He commented several times that he thought I was a natural and encouraged me to continue.

I signed up for a seminar which supposedly taught people to do healing work, and at the end they gave certificates that claimed we were trained "healers." We were instructed to wear all white: "To keep the energy pure," they said. I thought it was rather silly. I thought, *If one's heart is of pure intent and one's own energy is clear, does it really matter what color one wears?* I didn't voice this, as I figured that maybe they knew something I didn't.

I showed up in the whitest clothes I owned, and I participated fully and listened intently. After a full weekend, I left the seminar with three things: 1) a thought that I was already doing what they were teaching; 2) a feeling that I could have worn purple with pink and green daisies and I still would have had the same experience; and 3) a certificate that said I could officially work with people in a healing capacity, which felt odd once I had it in my hands. *Did I really need this piece of paper to tell me that it was okay for me to work with someone?*

I continued with my exploration, having private sessions with people who worked in various healer capacities, and I participated in other seminars and workshops on healing people and on following one's intuition. I also continued my work on healing myself, which I felt was as important—if not more so—than the work on others. It felt vital to do this for my own self-awareness and to maintain equanimity. I wanted to keep the balance between being the teacher/healer and being the healee/student. This was crucial, I felt, to staying out of my ego.

PEBBLE

The pebble for this chapter has been offered previously, but I've reframed it a bit. When we make choices (whether positive or negative, pleasurable or painful, life-affirming or life-diminishing), the Universe will align itself and rise up to meet these choices. I made the choice to continue to do something that felt good and right to me. The Universe gave me all sorts of opportunities to learn what I needed and what I didn't need. My choices gave the Universe a chance to teach me what I needed to know about what I was interested in. This is why I consider life a Ph.D. program. If we are even somewhat conscious in our day-to-day lives, we can learn so much about how to live and love, and how to give back. Life is the university of all universities, and the Universe is the teacher of all teachers.

Of course, it's important to get training in the field we are interested in mastering, and it can be important to those using our services that we have degrees and certificates that prove we are trained. I would hope, however, that what is also valued is the training we put ourselves through, and how we 'show up' with what we know. Personally, I am more interested in how someone shows up, and if they 'walk their talk.'

Chapter Fifty-Nine

FEELING THE POWER

∽

On January 17, 1994, at 4:30 in the morning, a large earthquake awakened me and couple of million other Angelinos. It was recorded at 6.7 on the Richter scale, which is quite strong, but what made it so powerful was the ground acceleration. It was the highest ever instrumentally recorded in North America.

I was practically thrown out of bed. All the lights in the city had gone out, so when my roommate Anna screamed for me, I ran to her in the complete darkness, tripping over objects that had fallen.

After making sure Anna was all right and then tending to my neck (I had strained it falling on my shoulder when tripping over Anna's bike), I lay back in bed. Then the aftershocks started. As I started to fall back to sleep, I would see in my mind's eye what looked like a bolt of lightning appear from above, and every time the bolts hit the earth, an aftershock occurred. I lay in bed, amazed at what I was witnessing. This occurred over and over again until I eventually fell back to sleep.

PEBBLE

I have no idea how to explain what I had experienced during the earthquake, and I never felt like I needed to figure it out. It was enough just to know that it had happened, that somehow I was able to feel or tap into the immense power of the earth.

The pebble for this chapter is appreciating the earth in all its magnificence. Witnessing the earthquake and aftershocks was not unlike witnessing the mighty waves of Hawaii or Niagara Falls, or a hurricane or tornado, or a glacier, or Mount Everest or the Grand Canyon, or, of course, the universe itself. In addition to seeing who I am, knowing what I am capable of, and the contribution I'd like to think I could make, I also value the feeling of how minuscule my existence is in the larger scheme of things. It brings a sense of perspective to my day-to-day experience.

Chapter Sixty

A ROCKY ROAD AND
AGATE BEACH

∽

*M*y thirty-seventh birthday was approaching. In numerology, the number 37 is reduced to a 1 (3+7, then reduce it to one digit). In the Tarot, the ten marks the coming of a new cycle and/or renewal.

I felt the potency of the coming year, with or without its numerological significance. I wanted to enter into it consciously, so I called an astrologer who specialized in Astrocartography—the astrological science used to find the optimum place, given one's goals for the coming year, to begin the year's journey. (It is also used for finding the optimum place to live, given one's goals.) Although at times one's optimal place might be in the middle of an ocean or in Greenland, usually there are two or three livable places to choose from. After all the options were presented, Agate Beach, Washington, was the place I decided on. The astrologer didn't know much about the place; he just knew that it was ideal for me. Upon further research, I discovered that it was located at the very top of the state, along the coast of the Strait of Juan de Fuca, a bay that separates Washington from Vancouver Island and British Colombia.

I began to make my arrangements to fly up to Seattle, and then to drive three hours to Port Angeles, which was thirty minutes east of Agate Beach. I figured that once I got up there, I would find accommodations.

To embark on such a journey, one should spend the three days prior to one's birthday, and the three days after, focusing on the quality of life that one wants to live. This can include having gratitude for what is, focusing on what one wants to manifest, changes one wants to make, etc.

Before I left, I stated to the Universe that I wanted to have a fabulous trip, full of wonderful adventures. I also stated that I wanted to meet people who recognized me, and I them. What this meant was that I wanted to be drawn to people of like spirit, heart, and mind. These thoughts fed into my affirmations for the next year—to be led to charming places, to meet wonderful people, and to offer myself as a loving presence. I also affirmed that I wanted to get an idea of how I could be of service.

After landing in Seattle, I began the process of renting my car. The price they charged was fifteen dollars per day more than I was quoted over the phone. I told them what I had been quoted, but the counter person said that the price was the price. The man checked the records of my reservation, but there was no mention of my conversation or of a quote. He said he was sorry, but there was nothing he could do. He suggested I call their consumer affairs department on Monday.

I walked away from the counter to calm down and think for a moment. I had a tight budget and this would take me over what I could charge on my credit card. I thought to myself, *I could either go back and make a stink, or be patient and wait to see what happens during my trip.* I chose the latter and turned to walk back to the counter. *Maybe there will be a windfall somewhere else,* I thought.

A new shift had started while I was gone, and a different counter person waited on me. We completed the contract, and I got the keys to the car. The counter person asked if I wanted help to my car. I answered yes, and we walked outside together. She asked if I was happy with the service. I hesitated and then told her of my unfortunate experience. When I finished, she said cheerfully, "Oh, I can help you with that! I'll just adjust it in the computer." She walked me back to the office and not only gave me the cheaper rate, but also upgraded me to a much nicer car. As we walked out to the new car, I expressed my gratitude to her and silently asked that she be blessed many times over for her generosity of spirit.

The car was very comfortable and roomy (with eight different speeds for the windshield wipers!). Not only was I on a wonderful adventure, I was doing it in great comfort. I noticed that I had not yet affirmed traveling or living in comfort in my earlier declarations, so I added that desire to my list.

Journal Entry –

When I arrived at Chuck's home, he, Sharon (his girlfriend), and I started right in and did some wonderful work on each other. We worked late into the night until it was time for Sharon to go home.

Chuck and I awoke the next day and continued. Earlier, I had taught Chuck some powerful work that is done in the shower. The person being worked on stands, clothed in a bathing suit, in the shower while the one in the healing position gently scrubs their body with mineral salt placed into a washcloth. (Certain salts can be used to pull out toxins in the body.) While they scrub, they energetically cleanse the person. It was Chuck's turn to do the process on me. He knew my history of being molested and that I was still affected by those experiences. He asked if I would be willing to clear more layers of this from my cellular memory. "Absolutely!" I replied.

As Chuck began, I felt wonderful and light. At some point, he warned me that he was going to begin to work in my genital area. He told me to let him know if I began to feel any emotional or physical discomfort. His hand and the mineral salt were close to my genitalia when I began to feel lightheaded, hot, and nauseous. I couldn't hold myself up. All the strength went out of me. I propped myself up so that I could put my head down below my hips as he continued to work. For a long time I continued with this process while burping up putrid smelling gas. He kept letting me know that he would stop if I needed to, but I wanted to continue; I wanted to go as deep as I could. I could smell sex and the taste of semen. I actually had to spit it out of my mouth. Then, I felt like I might vomit or lose control of my bowels. My stomach cramped. I started to groan and then to cry. Chuck reminded me to breathe as I began to cry harder. We continued. In a somewhat lighter moment I said to Chuck, "Some kind of healing, Chuck. Thanks!" We laughed until the next wave of sickness hit. At one point I felt a strong urge to scream at the top of my lungs. Chuck said to go ahead, so I did, two or three times. We continued clearing for what seemed like forever. In actuality, it was probably another fifteen minutes or so. Then, the symptoms subsided, and I felt the session was complete.

After the shower, I was very weak. Chuck put me on his massage table and continued to work on me, although it was much less dramatic. When it was over, I felt like I had just cleared something monumental. Chuck agreed. I also felt like I had just been through major surgery. "This kind of work can feel like that," he said. "Over the next few days, it will be important to take it easy."

We both felt that our sessions had been powerful and quite deep. I momentarily hesitated before leaving that evening, feeling tempted to have more time with Chuck and our work. But in the end, I decided that we would most likely have more sessions with each other; I would not, however, have another thirty-seventh birthday trip. I took him out to dinner as a thank you and then left.

I had reserved a motel room in Port Angeles. It was not optimal, but I wanted to be sure I had somewhere to stay. If it was comfortable, I would stay there for the rest of my trip. I was running late, and I called to confirm that I was coming but would arrive at about nine or ten p.m. The woman wasn't as pleasant or kind as I would have expected her to be in her position. I thought to myself, *Hm. Not sure this is the place for me.* I confirmed that I would stay there one night and then decide about the rest of the nights.

While on the road, I was thoroughly enjoying myself. There were varying degrees of mist resting on my windshield, and the smell in the air was sublime. I felt free, open, and inspired. I was humming a song to myself when out of nowhere I heard a voice in my head say, "Eat a hamburger."

"What?" I said out loud. I had been a vegan for a couple of years when I was cleaning my body of toxins, but found that that diet didn't serve my body. Even though I was no longer a vegan, I didn't eat beef, so I ignored the voice and jokingly claimed it was some sort of auditory apparition. Then I heard the voice again, "Eat a hamburger, Donna. Your body needs it. Don't worry. It won't hurt you." *Okaaay.* I thought. *All right. I'm listening. I guess someone knows better than I.* I pulled into the next hamburger place I saw and ordered a big one with all the trimmings. Oddly, as I carefully unwrapped the bulging creation, dripping with cheese and sauce, it looked delicious. While trying to hold it together, I felt the juices running down my hands. I took a bite and felt as if I had been transported to heaven. *Oh my gosh!* I thought. *I don't remember hamburgers tasting this good—correction: incredibly good!* With my body humming, I prayed thanks to the cows, to the people who made it, and to the voice in my head.

Then things went from odd to just plain ridiculous. Some time after I finished my burger, I heard another thought in my head. "Okay, now eat a candy bar." *That's it! No way! Ain't gonna happen!* Again insistent, the voice said, "EAT A CANDY BAR." *Oh, all right,* I said, resigned, then thought sarcastically, *I'll get one. And by the way, what kind of candy bar would you like me to eat?* "A Rocky Road," the voice replied. *A what?!* I contested. Now, there are a couple things I have to establish for this to make sense. First, I didn't eat candy and hadn't for years. Second, I never liked Rocky Roads, even when I ate candy. They were probably my least favorite of them all. My brother Stuart loved them, but I always thought they were disgusting with their marshmallow and cashew inside and milk chocolate covering. They were way too sweet for my taste. I respectfully said to the voice, *No, thank you. I don't like Rocky Roads.* Silence. *But I can't. It will give me a horrible headache, and I won't be able to think.* It replied, "It won't hurt you. Eat one and you will see." *Jeez, I'm arguing with the voice in my head again.* I chuckled to myself. *This can't be good.* But as I was the one on the spiritual trek, I thought I should heed any message I got, no matter how bizarre.

I pulled into the parking lot of a liquor store and got out of the car as I kept thinking, *Are you sure this is a good idea?* Silence. Still, I went in and asked for a Rocky Road. I wasn't even sure they still made them; I didn't remember seeing one for years. Sure enough, though, the cashier pointed to them, shiny red plastic packaging and all.

I got back into the car and opened the wrapper. The sickeningly sweet aroma attacked my senses. I took a deep breath and ate a bite. Expecting to be repulsed, I was surprised to find that it actually didn't taste so bad. With each bite, it seemed to taste better and better. By the last bite I had a big smile on my face. *That was GREAT!* I thought. I waited for the aftereffects to hit, but I never felt a thing. The voice was right.

It was about ten p.m. when I showed up at the motel and checked in. I went into my room and confirmed that this would definitely not do; the next day I would look for another place.

I stayed for a few minutes, then left and drove to where I expected to find Agate Beach, but I couldn't find it in the dark. The only thing I could see was a sign that said, "Road Closed." I got out and walked around a bit until I found a log that looked inviting. I sat and meditated for a few minutes. Before I left, I gave thanks for the adventure I was having and acknowledged that it had been a great one thus far.

The next morning I looked for a new place to stay. I reiterated my goal of wanting a place where I felt recognition both ways— where I felt I belonged there, and they felt the same way. I had three bed and breakfast establishments on my list. Although it would be a huge stretch for me financially, I "interviewed" the first two and finally went to the one that was first on my list. After talking to the owner on the phone, I felt this one had the best feeling. I knocked on the door of the Tudor Inn, and a pleasant looking man answered.

"I'm the one who called you about the small room you have available," I said.

"Good, come on in. I'm Jerry. My wife's busy right now, but I'll show you the room. We'll charge you forty-five dollars per night, which is half of what we usually charge. This is off-season for us."

Forty-five dollars was a great rate—still a bit more than I wanted to spend, but I was interested. He took me upstairs to the room. As I followed him, I noticed the décor—tasteful antiques, books and statues everywhere, captivating paintings and lithographs of people and scenery, hardwood floors and big stuffed chairs. The room was tucked away, separate from the others, and very cozy. I thought to myself, *Yes. This will do nicely.* I breathed deeply and told him that it looked good. As we walked out of the room I noticed a beautiful picture in a large frame. It was a brown, two-toned print of the bust of a woman gazing up, as if she were looking for guidance. She had a look of deep sincerity and surrender.

"That's how I feel when I work," I said, surprising even myself. "Where did it come from?"

"It's something my wife found and framed," he said. "What kind of work do you do?"

"I help people with the energy that comes out of my hands."

"Oh, my wife definitely has to talk to you! She's very into that kind of thing." He disappeared to the back rooms and returned with Jane, his wife, excitedly telling her about what I had told him. Jane was in her fifties. Her face was open and interested, and after a few minutes of talking to her, there was no question that this was where I was going to stay.

I was hoping to visit Agate Beach at least twice during my journey, so after I brought my things upstairs and settled in, I made my way over to the beach.

Journal Entry –

I drove to Agate Beach and discovered that the beach was private and closed. This is just great! I thought. I've come all this way and I can't get onto the beach. I decided to see how closed the beach really was and drove back to a local market to see what I could find out. I asked the market clerk if she knew where the owners of Agate Beach lived. I told him that I had traveled a long way to see the beach and saw the sign that said it was closed. He suggested asking the owners if I could just take a quick jaunt on the beach. "They sometimes allow people to do that," he said. He wrote the owner's name down for me and told me how to get there. I drove to Marilyn's home, thinking on the way that I could talk her into letting me walk on the beach for just a while.

I knocked on the door and a younger woman answered. "I'm looking for Marilyn." I said. Looking at me suspiciously, she said, "Just a minute." Marilyn came to the door, and I briefly asked my question. She responded saying that the beach was closed, period. I explained that I had come a long way just to see her beach and walk on it for a few moments. She wanted to understand why it was so important for me to do this. I gave her a watered down version of the truth. She was hesitant, explaining that people try to get onto their family beach all the time. She spent her childhood there, and over the years she has had to turn many people away. She then asked me why she should let me go onto the beach. I said, "Because I've come so far. I just want to be there, if even for a short time, just to see it and walk on the sand." She looked at me squarely and then agreed to let me go as her friend, but first she wanted to get her car so she could lead me there herself.

Before she left to get the car, she asked if I wanted a cup of tea. I said that I would love one. Her daughter came into the room to bring my tea, but wouldn't make eye contact. Marilyn later told me that her daughter had warned her that they didn't know what kind of energies I was bringing there. Heeding her daughter's warning, she wanted me to talk more about what brought me there and who I was. She seemed very interested and encouraged me to go into greater depth. I recommended a new book I had been reading, The Celestine Prophecy. *She wrote the title down, but as she wrote I started to sense fear in her. "Do you attend church?" she asked. I then understood where her questions were coming from and gave her a watered down version of my history while reassuring her that I had attended churches for much of my life, and that I was in alignment with the fundamental teachings of The Christ.*

Her son came in as I was talking and stood for about a minute staring at me. He loomed over us, like a watchful keeper, obviously not trusting me. Marilyn asked him if he wanted anything, and he said that he needed to take care of a few things for her. He went into the office and reluctantly closed the door. Marilyn and I spoke for a few more minutes, but I felt a fear come over her again at his presence. After a few minutes, she said that she should check in with him before we went to the beach.

I put more water in my teacup and waited. When she returned, her face was gloomy. She said she was sorry, but she couldn't let me go onto the beach. She sincerely apologized and said, "I'm not strong enough." How odd, I thought. I wonder what that means?

The potency of the moment almost had me in tears. We sat in silence for a moment, her eyes no longer able to meet mine. Finally I said with a smile, "I understand. You have to do what you have to do." I began to get up, and she asked me not to go until I had finished my tea. I drank a few more sips and said that I had finished. I went to the door as she apologized again, and I reiterated that she had to do what she had to do. As I walked out, I saw both fear and regret in her face. For whatever reason, she couldn't follow her own instincts.

I left there stunned by the experience. I had no idea what kind of web was woven in that family, but I felt its power. As I drove past the beach, I thought, *I wonder if there's a beach next to Agate I can walk on?* I got out of my car at a beach that looked accessible and started to walk toward it. Almost immediately a car drove up alongside me and a man got out of it. He asked what I was doing, and I said that I was going to walk on the beach for a few minutes, asking him if it was all right. He said yes, but warned me not to walk too far to the west because it was private property. I said I understood and promised that I would stay where I was.

I spent about twenty minutes walking on the beach and meditating on how I wanted to transform this trip from an apparent failure to finding the good that had come out of it. I felt that, although I had not reached my intended destination, I had gotten darn close. I realized then that what I went away with would be my choice, so I chose to view my trip as a success. I gathered a few rocks to remind me of the beach and walked back to the car. While driving away, I giggled to myself, imagining watchers of surveillance cameras saying, "The intruder has left the premises. Hear this: The intruder has left the premises."

My first night at the inn was wonderful. Jane and I thoroughly enjoyed each other's company while talking late into the night in her small study, fireplace ablaze. A friend of Jane's was there, too. Jane wanted her to meet me, and it all felt so familiar and comfortable, like we had done this before, with them asking questions about the power of love and the healing that ensues when one surrenders to it. During our conversation, I mentioned to Jane that I noticed Jerry coughing. She said he hadn't felt well for some time, and I offered to do some healing work on him the next day. She gratefully accepted on his behalf, although she wasn't sure how he would react. "He's a bit of a square peg," she confided.

"I think he'll be fine." I said.

A bit later in our conversation Jane said that she wanted to cook me dinner for my birthday. "I would be so honored," I said. Then she asked if she could ask a couple more friends over to meet me.

"Of course," I replied. "This is what my journey is about—following Spirit and meeting wonderful people!"

Before retiring for the night, I wrote in my journal (the entry that you, the reader, have now seen) and then did some automatic writing. I felt very connected as I surrendered to the love and support around me. The sweetness of the room, and the coziness of the bed, invited me into a peaceful sleep.

The next day was my birthday. I saw Jane the next morning, and our conversation started again, this time about energy work, divination, and connecting to Spirit. A bit later, I worked on Jerry. He was willing and open. We worked for about one and a half hours, and after the session, he said he felt great as he bounced out of the room. Jane said later that he seemed happier than usual. She thanked me again, and I thanked her for the opportunity to be of service.

My birthday dinner was lovely, and Jane's friends were delightful. It was strange to realize that I had just met Jane and her husband only two days earlier.

My prayer before retiring that night: *Thank you. Thank you. Thank you. Thank you for this experience. I am grateful for my life, my abilities, the opportunities for growth and partnership, and mostly for your love. I pray for vibrant health and well-being for all who played a part in this trip.*

The next day as I opened my door, ready to bring my things down to the car, Jane handed me a package she had wrapped up.

"What's this?" I asked.

"It's the print that was on the wall in front of your room."

"No! Is it really? I love that print. Every time I went into my room I coveted it!" Tears were streaming down my cheeks.

"I know." she said. "Take it. I appreciate all that you've brought to me." As I settled up my bill, I saw that they had charged me only half the rate they had quoted.

PEBBLE

I never found out anything more about the people who owned the beach. It was obvious to me that Marilyn and her family could not move past their fear. It was interesting and somewhat painful to watch, and not only because it impeded my journey. I wanted to say to her, "Fear is something to embrace and then move past. You can do this now. It is safe." But I knew well enough not to try to help unless I was asked. The pebble here is a variation on a previous pebble—patience for others' processes and timing. Everyone has their own path and their own timing. It is not our place to judge another person, but to have respect and patience for their timing and to have compassion for their suffering.

All in all, my birthday trek came in under budget, and it over-delivered in personal significance. Setting my best intentions (this could also be called creating a vision); listening to and trusting Spirit—and having the willingness to follow its guidance—even though it may not make logical sense; and navigating with ease and grace through detours on the path that I hadn't expected, were more pebbles for my path. One may not know the bigger picture of what Spirit has in store... until one sees it. So, we may as well not worry about it and let it unfold on its own and in its own time.

∽

I would like to take this opportunity to honor Chuck. You know who you are. For a short time we embarked on a remarkable journey together. I am grateful for your wisdom and encouragement, as well as your integrity as a healer and way-shower. We discovered some wonderful things together and for this I am grateful.

Chapter Sixty-One

PERMISSION GRANTED

∽

$\mathcal{U}$pon my return from Washington, I did a meditation that had a strong effect on me. It had to do with seeing the darkness (that I translated to fear and pain) that still resided in my body and emotions. It was very evident to me during my session with Chuck that I still held onto these feelings. *Given that there was so much to be cleared,* I thought, *how much more is there that I'm still not aware of? Even if I have a certain amount of dedication and insight, how can I help others if I still have places in me to heal?* In the meditation, I saw myself trying to break away from the lurking darkness, but no matter how hard and how many times I tried to break free from it, it was always there. I also saw how the darkness shrouds this entire planet. I saw interwoven threads of gold and lightness melting away the darkness, but the darkness was immense and overwhelming.

I decided to have a session with Ron Scolastico and The Guides. I received an answer for my question that was very simple, yet it knocked my socks off. They knew of my strong belief that love is what ultimately helps, guides, and heals us. Given this, The Guides simply said, "You don't have to be perfect to love." As I heard these words, I stopped cold. I felt forgiveness flow through me for my imperfections, and gratitude for my love, insight, and good intentions. They also reminded me that everyone with a body has issues to resolve, and physical and/or emotional healing to do.

As far as the darkness in the world, the answer is always the same. Yes, it is prevalent, and yes, it is destructive, but it is not more powerful than goodness, truth, and love. I have experienced this personally and have seen it in my meditations many times. As more and more people wake up, as each of us does our best for ourselves and for others, and as we continue to hold a vision for a peaceful and loving world, we have a good chance of turning things around.

PEBBLE

You don't have to be perfect to love. 'Nuf said.

Guidance and support systems are other pebbles for this chapter. Even those with the strongest faith and conviction need support at times. The Guides, as well as other forms of divination, have provided two things for me. First, they reminded me of the power of my essence when I forgot. And second, they gave me perspective and context. Having access to these was—and continues to be— invaluable.

Chapter Sixty-Two

A MULTIFACETED
RELATIONSHIP

∽

I met Randy while attending a seminar on strengthening one's intuition. We both felt a connection and soon started seeing each other. He also did a type of healing work with people. He used a pendulum to find out where blockages were in people, and then he attempted to help clear them using meditation and past life regression.

He had been a long-time follower, and for years had been on the staff of a prominent Indian Hindu guru. Randy had adopted the tradition that to find enlightenment, one must meditate to empty one's mind; it was not until then that one could be set free. He and I meditated together daily, often for an hour in the morning and another hour in the evening.

This relationship had its share of issues (which I will briefly touch on later). One thing is for certain, though: while I was with Randy, I experienced some wild mystical experiences and profound insights.

We did healing work on each other fairly often. When he worked on me, I was able to get into a state where I saw images from what I perceived as being other times and places (not in this lifetime). I had a series of visions over the course of our sessions that showed me where I had been taught to do healing work. The visions usually came in small clips after I had attained a deep level of meditation. During one vision, I saw a tent at night with light glowing from it. I wondered about its significance, but decided that the less I attached meaning to what I was seeing, the better it would probably be. At other times I saw groups of people gathered together—some sitting on rocks, some on the ground—waiting for something. After Randy and I had worked together a few times and we were able to go to deeper levels of trust with one another, I saw something that changed me. As I felt myself go into my meditation, I opened my heart and mind and said: *Whatever would serve me most to see or feel, I welcome it.* I released, and as I did, I saw the tent that I had seen before, only this time I was inside the tent with a group of people. I couldn't see them all, but it appeared that there were thirty or so of us. I was in the front row with my eyes closed, and I could feel warmth, but not from the earth's temperature. It was emanating from something or someone, and it traveled through my heart. I felt my utter surrender and trust, sensing the presence of everyone in the tent. A strong and pervasive love was all around, palpable and inviting.

In my vision, I felt an impulse to open my eyes. My head was facing the ground, and as I opened my eyes, I saw my feet, and then I saw someone else's feet—*his* feet—in sandals come to stand before me. With this, I looked up and saw *my teacher.* His eyes were dark and clear with a Divine intensity that could have made me swoon. But there would be no swooning. I was to stay conscious and receive his teaching. There were no words spoken; it was as if what was being said was transmitted through his eyes into mine. As he gazed into my eyes, I understood that he was teaching me how to wield energy and infuse love in a way that could help heal people. In current time, I began to understand what had been re-awakened inside me, and how I naturally knew how to do this type of work. I had been taught by this beautiful, radiant, resplendent man. As he lingered, I felt a depth and breadth of love that transcended anything I had ever experienced with another. It was as if I was looking into the face, heart, and mind of love itself, and I received him.

As the vision left me, his eyes burned themselves into my consciousness. I came out of the session feeling that as I continued to work with people, I could go with confidence that I had been trained well.

In a later session, I saw people gathered together listening to his teachings. I also saw him and me walking and talking together. With each session, I felt his presence press itself deeper into me, and as it did, I felt more and more confident of the power and energy that resided in me.

These visions affected me quite strongly. A part of me said, *Who am I to have such capabilities?* while another part said, *Why not you?*

When I thought about having access to so much power—and seemingly having power over people—I wondered if I could unintentionally hurt someone. I came to understand that back when this teacher was alive, the human mind was not as developed as it is today. Back then, he and others could cause large shifts in people's consciousness and physical processes. Nowadays, people's intellects are quite complex and our wills are strong. Whatever changes occur now are *co-creations*, healer and healee working together. I understood that if my intentions were pure, I didn't need to worry about hurting anyone.

Then I had the question: *Does anyone heal people now as it was done back then, with such dramatic results?* I knew it was quite rare for that kind of healing to happen in this day and age—as was mentioned, when healing does happen it's usually a co-creation. Overriding peoples' will and personal choices rarely happens; the work now is to learn to heal oneself. The job of the healer or healing conduit is to offer their "patients" new, healthier paradigms of thinking, and to help clear emotional and energetic obstacles so that the patients can more easily discover the process of healing for themselves.

You may be asking (as I did) that if this amazing teacher taught me, could I work with people in a larger capacity? Good question. I will speak to this soon.

In the Pacific Palisades there is a beautiful temple called The Self-Realization Fellowship Lake Shrine. It was built in 1950 for Paramahansa Yogananda, an Indian yogi and guru. The stunning grounds include a Court of Religions honoring the five principal religions of the world with their symbols—a cross for Christianity, a Star of David for Judaism, a Wheel of Law for Buddhism, a crescent moon and star for Islam, and an Aum symbol for Hinduism. Also on the grounds is the Mahatma Gandhi World Peace Memorial, where a portion of Gandhi's ashes is enshrined.

When I heard of this place, I mentioned to Randy that I wanted to attend a Sunday service. Because I had left organized religion, I was curious about what would be taught in a place that honored several religious traditions.

As we sat in the beautiful little temple, I gazed at the framed prints of Paramahansa Yogananda; his teacher, Sri Yukteswar Giri; guru Lahiri Mahasaya; and Jesus, The Christ. Every time I looked at one of the photographs of Paramahansa, I started to cry. He looked utterly effulgent. After the service, I walked up to the photograph and stood in front of it for some time, feeling my heart open while tears streamed from my eyes. I had never had such an experience before from looking at a photo. I asked someone about it and was told that this picture had been taken just hours before his death.

Randy and I were talking on the way home from the temple about how wonderful the service had been and how connected we both felt to the photograph of Yogananda. As I was talking, I had a strong stabbing feeling in the palms of my hands. "Ouch!" I said out loud, and as I did, Randy spontaneously started to cry for no apparent reason. We asked each other what the other had experienced. Then it happened, again and again—the stabbing pain that changed location from the palm of my hands, to my sides, and to other parts of my body, and each time Randy began to cry. It eventually stopped. All we could do was look at each other in awe at what had just occurred.

Experiencing another example of something I knew I couldn't explain, Randy and I resolved that our deeply felt connection with Yogananda included strong bodily reactions. Ever since this day, a copy of the photograph of Yogananda has remained on my puja table (meditation altar).

One evening, Randy and I saw a movie called *The Little Buddha*[1]. It's a sweet film about the quest of a group of monks seeking the reincarnation of their spiritual teacher, the Lama Dorje. The monks find Jesse, a young American boy, who they believe could be the one. Because Jesse's birthday is March 1st at 6:30 a.m., the same that the Lama's had been, he's perceived to be their teacher. When Jesse's birthday and its significance were revealed, Randy and I looked at each other incredulously. "Wow! That's my (your) birthday and birth time," we both said at the same time. I was born just a few minutes after 6:30, but this was close enough! (Randy knew of my birth time because he was also an astrologer.) We laughed after the movie that it was too bad I missed the boat. As we joked though, I felt something tugging at my heart.

I did a fair amount of reflection about the movie afterward. What struck me strongest was: *What happens when a group claims that a child is born a holy person or a reincarnated teacher?* I imagine that child grows up being respected and told that he or she is special, spiritually advanced, and will be a potent teacher. They are likely taught great secrets and told they have the potential to change the world. I reflected on how I, like many—if not most—came into the world being told what my place was, to fear God, to think like everyone else and not for myself, to act "normal," and to not rock the boat, etc. Even though I understood what I believed were spiritual truths, no one saw me as anything special. My father certainly never acknowledged the truth of Love that I attempted to explain to him. So, the question is: Is being a spiritual teacher usually dependent on whether someone *recognizes* you as such, or that you are born into a specific country where spiritual teachings and teachers are abundant and accepted? I'm certain that being a spiritual teacher has much more to do with an inner dedication to God and Love than having agreement around him or her, but as I continued to reflect, I came to the questions:

What if we treated our children as if they mattered, and as if they were deeply special whether others recognized it or not?

What if we treated them as if they had the ability to create great change in both themselves and in the world if they focused their attention and energy to do so?

What if we truly listened to the profound things that are expressed through their minds and hearts?

What if we validated that they had the ability to tap into grand states of consciousness if they chose to?

Then I asked, *Why don't we do this for our children?*

Because we do not know any better...

Randy and I had the good fortune to meet and study under a Buddhist monk, His Holiness Orgyen Kusum Lingpa. I was struck by the monk's obvious goodness and moved by his utter dedication to helping uplift humanity. Buddhism, for those of you who don't know, teaches that the root cause of unhappiness and dissatisfaction (i.e. suffering) is our habitual tendency to see our world and ourselves in a narrow and limited way. If we could free our minds, our bodies, and our environment of this mental conditioning, we would find ourselves enlightened and our world transformed. Being freed of suffering, we would then be able to extend ourselves to others.

I attended both talks and empowerments (initiations) given by His Holiness, as well as with His Holiness the Dalai Lama. (A master gives empowerments so that his students can participate in particular meditation practices designed to free their minds.) During these empowerments, the master shows the student a glimpse of a pure realm that is beyond the habitual patterns of the mind. Based on their experience during this sitting, students learn to sustain and expand that initial experience through the continuing practice of the meditation. I found these practices to be expansive as I integrated them into my other rituals.

Although I believe in reincarnation as the Buddhists do, the one thing I could never quite go along with was the notion that if one had a bad thought, they could stack another five hundred or so lifetimes on top of what was already planned, depending, of course, on how bad the thought was. Maybe this is true, but if it is, I didn't want to know it!

One cherished memory of Orgyen Kusum Lingpa was when he took the money he had raised from the admission price of an empowerment down to Marina del Rey and bought as many just-caught fish as his money could buy. Then, he freed them. (Buddhists, by in large, eat no meat or fish.) Of course, he chanted a beautiful Buddhist message as the fish were being released. While watching him, I imagined that he was saying something like, "Aum. Little fishes, I bless the water you swim in. I am glad to free you! Many blessings on your new journey, and may you never be caught again! Swim away now in all happiness. Aum." After all the fish had been released, several students donated more money and, sure enough, he freed more fish and chanted for them, too.

Other loving memories I have are of the private audiences His Holiness gave me, always generous with his spirit and with his blessings for my prosperity and well-being.

His Holiness Orgyen Kusum Lingpa made his transition in February of 2009. For the wisdom and blessings he brought to my life, I am forever grateful.

Randy and I were a part of a group that did some cutting-edge meditation and emotional clearing (healing) work. During a meditation with this group, I had an epiphany that left me dumbfounded. As if someone were speaking directly to me, I heard in my mind's ear, "Mary Magdalene was not a prostitute." When I heard this, my mind momentarily froze. Finally I thought, *Okay, and what about this?* "The one you know as Mary Magdalene was of his cherished inner circle." Then, in my mind's eye, I saw a woman walking with The Christ, looking radiant and self-possessed, not at all like someone who came from a gutter or fresh out of a man's bed, but like someone who was a respected confidant. I thought it was very strange, given that I had been taught that Mary Magdalene was stoned and cast out because of her sexual practices, and then later became devoted to Jesus as a sinner he had saved.

I did a fair amount of research after my meditation and discovered that in some more esoteric writings, Mary of Magdala, a wealthy and respected woman, was a devout member of Jesus' inner circle— not as a result of her penance, but rather because of her stature and her devotion to his teachings. She had not been a prostitute, as was portrayed in the Bible. Some also wrote that after Jesus' death it was Mary who went on to hand down his teachings in their purest form. These people believed that Mary was the mother of true Christianity, which included the feminine aspect of God that was not represented in the Bible—either by design or by omission. It has also been suggested that this Mary is a composite of several devout female members of Jesus' inner circle, intentionally portrayed as one woman within the myriad allegorical stories that make up the Bible. Others have asserted that Mary may have been Jesus' wife, as marriage was the norm, especially for rabbis. Scholars who believe that Jesus spent time with the Essenes, a group who chose celibacy so as to focus entirely on their spirituality, have challenged the assertion of his marriage.

Whatever the truth, from the perspective I was left with, this woman's persona had been transposed in the Bible into an unholy character to serve someone's agenda and to create fear and judgment around feminine sexuality.

Obviously, no one knows the true relationship Jesus had with Mary, but given that I had no reason to question what the Bible said, *someone* went to an awful lot of trouble to tell me that Mary was not who the Bible portrays her as. I came away from this having a vague sense, and a seed planted, that there was a message for me about embracing my own femininity, power, and sexuality.

∽

While I have some potent memories of my time with Randy, our romantic relationship was one of the strangest I had ever had. When we met, we felt very drawn to each other, and we both assumed this meant that we should be in a relationship together. But from the very beginning, I felt something inside me that said, *I'm not sure about this … I don't know if this feels right.* Even though we seemed to be a match on many levels, and we were extremely compatible on a spiritual level, I often felt an underlying anger and resentment coming from him. In the beginning it was very subtle, but later it became more pronounced. I was never one who enjoyed disagreements and usually did my best to diffuse them, but I often found myself at odds with him.

Our relationship was eventually resolved, as you will see.

PEBBLE

First, I was grateful for the time I spent with Randy, as I was for all the experiences I had while I was with him. They have made my life richer and deeper.

What I had begun to realize with Randy was that just because I may have felt a connection, or chemistry, or had really intense spiritual experiences while I was with him, it didn't mean that I should necessarily be in a romantic relationship with him. Also, not all relationships are necessarily meant to last a lifetime. And because my goal was to find the man I was going to spend the rest of my life with, all relationships I put myself in had that question looming overhead.

Two things I have learned since my time with Randy are that relationships have purposes and that chemistry is usually memory. As you have read and will continue to see in upcoming chapters, my time with Randy was full of potent experiences and insight. Many of the experiences were important for my spiritual development, yet because Randy and I kept trying to push each other into the relationship box, it caused friction. We weren't emotionally compatible.

I didn't understand this until years (and a book) later. Suffice it to say, each relationship has its own purpose.

If you agree with the notion of past lives, I will say this. Just about everyone we meet, we think we have met before (déjà vu), and just about everyone we have relationships with, we have been in a relationship with before (in some capacity). So what is called chemistry is actually memory, with some pheromones thrown in. Who knows, perhaps pheromones are triggered by distant and unconscious memories, drawing us to each other for a purpose. One thing that has worked for me in more recent years is to ask myself early on in a relationship: If I had something to work out with this person from before, what might it be? I often get an intuitive hit that ends up being spot-on. If you do not believe in the past life theory, you can ask the same question. It might be phrased more like: Given my history, and given the sense I get from this person, what issues might we bump into? Conversely, one might also ask, what possibilities for goodness do I sense here? With either of these questions, questioners must be cognizant of what their actual inner sense is, and what might be projection of their personal fear, desire, or agenda. Practice helps one differentiate between the two.

∽

While in meditation one day, I was reflecting on Love and its healing power when another realization came to me. I understood that many humans are waiting for what is commonly called The Second Coming—the time when Jesus returns to earth. Then, after Judgment Day and a lot of people dying, the Kingdom of Heaven will reign on earth. What I understood in the meditation is that the Second Coming would actually be a shift in our collective consciousnesses, or rather, when the largest mass of people shifts into The Christ Consciousness. (For clarification, The Christ Consciousness ultimately means Love Consciousness and is secular in nature.) This will happen when the critical mass comes into a certain level of self-mastery, creating a tipping point, and this will occur from many spiritual orientations. There will not again be one God-man or Goddess-woman sent to "save" humans. Instead, humans who have mastered certain aspects of their humanity, and disembodied beings who have already mastered earth life, are guiding us through this process. There are way-showers, and some with great insight into the process of consciousness and illumination, but not one person. The good news is that we have evolved to a level of consciousness where our freedom of choice will not be taken from us. It is our collective personal journeys that will lead us there.

I reflected on The Presence and how it had made itself known to me, loved me, and helped me heal, but it didn't overtake me. It was I who chose to continue to invite it to guide me, and it was I who continued to access its wisdom and power. This meant I could see that The Presence and its love had a profound impact on me, but it didn't take away my choices for growth. That was always up to me.

I sat quietly, affected by my newfound understanding. I spoke of this to only a few people, for it seemed radical. I found out later that other people had similar insights, and I began to speak of it more freely.

Chapter Sixty-Three

TALES OF TWO HEALERS

✍

Randy and I first met Earl at a seminar on conscious evolution. Earl opened up to me immediately and told me he was a local body worker who had had some unexplainable occurrences having to do with blistered hands and lights malfunctioning around him. He noticed that after these occurrences, when he placed his hands on certain people, they would start channeling. He was at the seminar hoping that the channel could help him understand what had occurred, and how he might make use of this newfound ability.

By this time, I had been working with the energies for a couple of years and was familiar with how they worked through me. I gave Earl my number and told him that I would be glad to help him however I could. He called a few weeks later as I was planning an event, and I invited him to attend. Spiritual friends I knew were traveling up to Banff, Canada to take part in a four-day conclave, whose purpose was to help bring healing to the planet. To honor their good intentions, I planned my own event to coincide with the conclave, and I extended an open invitation for people to come meditate, make music, and commune.

Earl came over and took part in the weekend, and while he was there he asked if I would work on him. He wanted to see what I did and how I worked on people. He also wanted to know if I could help him, as he had been on strong anti-depressants for some time and wanted to get off of them. I worked on him during the weekend and then several more times, teaching him how I worked.

I also introduced him to Chuck, the healer, when he was in town from Seattle. Eventually, Earl was able to go off the anti-depressants. He turned his bodywork into a healing practice and has since become a renowned healer, traveling the world teaching.

A bit later, Randy and I met Lawrence, an energy worker (one who manipulates the body's subtle energies to promote healing and higher levels of consciousness) of extraordinary ability. He had recently come to California after having lived on an ashram (a spiritual community) in Oregon while studying under his guru, as well as working on her body. After talking about what kind of work each of us did, we decided we would trade sessions with each other.

In one of my sessions, I was in meditation while he worked me. He suggested that I stay in as deep a meditation as I could while breathing deeply, as one does with this kind of work. I was on my stomach as I felt him placing things on my spine and using his energy to move energy around in my body. Then, the oddest thing happened. My body began to involuntarily undulate (kind of like a fish). It started with me feeling little bits of energy pulsating at the base of my spine, and then a subtle but strong energy began moving my body as that energy flowed from my lower spine up to the base of my skull. It was powerful. I continued undulating for several minutes, and then finally the movement ceased.

This was called a Kundalini experience. Kundalini is a Sanskrit word for "coiled" and it describes an unconscious, instinctive, or libidinal force as a sleeping serpent coiled at the base of the spine. With meditation, Tantric (sacred) sexual practices, breath, yoga, visualization, or chanting, one can awaken this Kundalini energy. Once it is released, the energy travels through the spine and at times up and out of the head, rendering the person in a state of illumination. When this is experienced in sexual practice, it can create a spiritual union between lovers.

The energy didn't travel out through the top of my head, so it seemed I didn't have the *full* experience, but it was still quite powerful. I guessed that this was probably due to the fact that I thought too much, so the energy couldn't get through my thick skull. I heard in later meditation, *Not to worry, your illumination will come in time.* Still, even with a *partial* Kundalini experience, I felt quite luminous afterward. I also felt that some sort of shift had occurred in my ability to wield energy during my sessions on people, and I felt more confident using it.

P E B B L E

It was interesting to see Earl on television and to see his work become well known. Part of me wondered if that was a path I should travel. A larger part of me, though, wanted to stay out of the public eye. It seemed safer to me to work with people under the radar, so to speak. By safer I mean less tempting to the ego. I had seen too many people become warped with notoriety and the power that comes with it. I also had a feeling that my time would come to touch people in perhaps larger ways. After several years and countless experiences, and after working with many people, I was led to write this book. The pebbles for this chapter are, again, patience and trust. I needed to have patience for my own process, and I needed to trust my own timing. For me to push myself, so that I could feel perhaps more worthy, would have only backfired in the end. Instead, I trusted that my time would come, when and if it was right. In the meantime, I just wanted to do what I loved to do.

With regard to Lawrence and my partial Kundalini experience, what can I say besides: Grace guides the thickheaded it its own way and in its own timing. I have since then had other Kundalini experiences, but that's for another story!

Chapter Sixty-Four

WAVERLY SPEAKS

❧

I met Waverly through Lawrence. He said that she was a gifted channel and he thought I would benefit from a session with her. Given my relationship with Ron Scolastico, I didn't feel the need to see someone else, but thought I would talk to her to see if I felt drawn to have a session. We spoke on the phone and had a wonderful conversation. She seemed to be grounded, while at the same time able to access broader realms of understanding. I felt she had something to offer me, and she felt I had something to offer her, so we decided to have a session.

When I arrived, Waverly and her assistant eagerly met me at the door and welcomed me in. Waverly and I sat together on the couch in the bright and airy living room and chatted for a few minutes while her assistant sat in a chair watching. The level of love and devotion I felt from them while we spoke struck me. Then, very casually, with her left foot tucked under her right thigh, Waverly went into her trance. She began to breathe deeply and rhythmically, and I watched as her body transformed itself in gesture and stature. Her eyes began to twitch slightly, and her head moved from side to side. After a moment or two of this, it appeared as if some invisible force "stepped" inside her body. As this happened, her posture became straight and somehow larger and majestic. She then opened her eyes and began to speak. It felt odd, after years of sessions with Ron, who always spoke with his eyes shut, to see a person's eyes open while in this process. I wondered how she could stay in this state. I gazed at her with this question, but the energy coming from her was so strong that the question was knocked out of my head. She/the being coming through her began to confirm much of the spiritual life that lived within me. As she spoke, I felt waves of recognition and expansion with her reflections. She then began to ask me questions about what my intentions were with regard to sharing my knowledge and understanding. I explained the work I did with my hands and briefly mentioned The Presence. She then went on to tell me the path they felt it was time for me to take. She explained that the knowledge I had should be shared with others, and that with the large amount of love and healing energy that I wielded, I should be working with groups. As I listened to her, I felt two primary things: one, shock that someone would suggest I had the ability to do such a thing; and two, gratitude that someone would have confidence in my ability to be of service in this way. She went on to tell me that I should begin with having a Darshan for people. She recognized that I might not think I was capable of doing this, but she said that I should know I had done it before (in a past life) and that I was, in fact, quite capable. She then said that the first two Darshans would be held at the house where our session was taking place. The first Darshan would be for Waverly's group of followers; the second would be with those from my circle. Even though what I was hearing was in some ways hard to believe, it also felt somewhat right.

When she came out of her trance, something seemed to overtake Waverly and her assistant. They looked at me and both broke into tears. They said that they had never been in the presence of someone who emitted so much love. Waverly's assistant, in particular, seemed to be affected. As I watched this scene, my mind was quiet while my heart seemed to expand outside my body. It was not unlike when I first realized I could love another, in that it was magnificent to see my heart and consciousness become so vast that it entered these two women, unlocking something deep within them.

At the end of the session, Waverly and I discussed when the two gatherings would occur. Because of her travel schedule, we decided on the following Sunday, which was a few days away.

I was so overwhelmed by the experience that I neglected to ask Waverly what a Darshan was exactly, for I had never heard the term. I got the gist of it, but wasn't sure of the details. I drove directly over to Randy's apartment and proceeded to tell him everything that had occurred in my session. When I told him of the Darshan that I was to have, he looked at me as if to say, "Really? Okay then."

I looked at him square with what felt like a fair amount of bewilderment and said, "Randy, I don't know what a Darshan is. Do you?"

"Sure," he said. "My guru used to do them all the time." He went on to say that the word Darshan is a Sanskrit term meaning "sight"—having a vision of the Divine, God, or a holy person. He went on to explain that the usual process of a Darshan includes a guru sitting at the front of a room either meditating or talking to the group about being at one with the God-force. Then, after some music and more meditation, people come up one by one and are blessed by the holy person after bowing, prostrating, and/or touching the guru's feet. Sometimes the blessings came after being touched on the head by the guru's hand or by an object he was holding. Sometimes people would swoon after such a blessing, while others would involuntarily vibrate or bounce while sitting in their seats.

"What?! I can't do this," I exclaimed. "I'm not a guru! I'm not qualified to lead a Darshan. And I wouldn't know the first thing about helping others have an experience of God. I only know how I do it." I had a sudden feeling that I was being led to a den of lions.

"Relax, Donna," he said. "The point is for people to have epiphanies and insight, not experiences of enlightenment. "And besides," he added, "you can do this your way." I remembered what The Guides had told me: *You don't have to be perfect to love,* and its meaning sank in.

"Well," I said, "what I have to offer is unique to me. I'm not a guru, but I do love deeply."

"Right!" he confirmed. I still felt daunted by the notion of leading a Darshan but was also yearning to offer Love and my devotion to God through working with people.

"Okay then, tell me what your guru did so that I can know what a real Darshan looks like." He proceeded to give me a picture of these elaborate gatherings of hundreds of people. As I listened, I began to form a picture in my mind of what I might be capable of doing.

Over the next couple of days, I meditated for guidance and called friends and acquaintances of mine who I thought would welcome being a part of this gathering. Shockingly, most eagerly said yes.

As the weekend drew near, I often felt reverence for all who put themselves out to offer others their insights, hearts, and knowledge, and in some cases their illumination. I began to get a glimpse of the feeling I wanted to create with my Darshan and meditated into it.

The day before the Darshan was to happen, I heard from Waverly that about thirty of her followers would be there. Some would come to the earlier gathering and some to the later. About fifteen of my circle of friends intended to come. Upon realizing how many people would be present, I sank into my heart trusting that my love would carry me through. I began to imagine in my mind's eye being in front of these groups so that I could get used to it. I imagined loving every person who was curious enough to come. Still, I had a small, nagging worry (although I didn't express it to anyone) that I might not be qualified to lead the Darshans. The Buddhists and Hindu monks who led these sorts of things had spent years dedicating themselves to their meditation practice and their studies of God. I had not followed this kind of devotional practice. I kept reminding myself, though, that I was not attempting to do what others had done and what tradition had dictated—there was no way I could. I was just going to go there and offer myself.

That night I had a dream. I don't remember now what the dream was, but what I do remember is that just before I awoke, I saw a man with wild eyes and with intensely powerful energy come up to my face, look deeply into me, and then bless me in a way that felt like an initiation. He said that with his blessing, I was now ready to hold a Darshan. The moment was so powerful that I awoke with a start. I felt myself in a unique state of awe, excitement, and peace, and I realized that I was ready. I woke Randy and told him of my dream.

"Randy," I said. "Do you have a photo of your guru?" He went over and took a picture out of his drawer. When I saw it, I gasped.

"This is the man who blessed me in my dream!"

He looked at me with intense eyes. "This is a really auspicious sign!"

"I got something else just now," I said. "I'm to give a rose to each person who comes forward today."

"It's Sunday," he said, as both of us realized how difficult that task might be. Most florists were closed on Sunday.

"Well, there will be a flower shop open," I said. "There has to be. I saw it."

Sure enough, on our way over to the house where the Darshan was to be held, a flower shop was open and I purchased a few dozen roses. I prayed over the flowers for the rest of our drive.

When I walked into the house, I noticed that it seemed to sparkle. The house felt clear and vibrant. I asked Waverly what she had done and she said that she and her assistant completely washed it down. She said she wanted to have the house as clean as possible for me and for what I was about to embark on. I expressed my thanks, and then we spoke briefly about how the day would go. I lovingly placed the flowers in a vase next to the small sofa where I would be sitting, and then sat in meditation while waiting for the first group to arrive.

At this point, my memory becomes a bit blurry. I could feel people begin to enter the room, although I didn't open my eyes to acknowledge their presence. Instead, I stayed in the love that I had generated while in my meditation. At some point, Waverly tapped me on the hand and I knew it was time to begin.

I opened my eyes and was struck by the look in the eyes of every person gazing at me. I could see nothing but love in their eyes, their hearts, and in every inch of the room. I began to speak, of what I'm not sure, but the words were of the power of love and of the presence of the now. The more I spoke, the more expansion I felt. It was very much the same feeling that came over me during my session with Waverly. After I had spoken for a while, it felt like it was time to invite people to come up and spend a few moments with me. One by one, each person took their turn as they sat or knelt in front of me. I was overcome by the fragility of their hearts and the strength of their hope for goodness and for grace. Whatever came to me, I said. Some I held close to me, as a mother does with her child, while others I touched where The Presence suggested I should. Other times I gazed into a person's yearning eyes while holding their hand and simply told them what I felt moved to say. The flowers felt more like hearts as I handed them to each person. There were tears and there was laughter, and with each one who bravely stepped forward, the love in the room seemed to grow. Once everyone had come forward, I said a blessing and thanked everyone for coming. I then got up and left the room.

I went into the bedroom, cleared myself, and waited for the next group. I stayed connected to various levels of meditation as the house cleared and as more people began to arrive.

The next group went quite the same as the previous, the difference being that most of this group was composed of people I knew. I expected to feel nervous or awkward, but it felt as comfortable as it had felt the first time. My friends and loved ones were supportive and open. They were as fully engaged in the process as those who didn't know me. Other than the love, which was palpable, the moments I remember most clearly were when I held my young godsons in my arms. They were so utterly trusting in their natural state of openness.

Upon the completion of the gatherings, I reflected with Waverly about my feelings during the Darshans. The whole experience felt oddly natural and comfortable, like putting on a favorite pair of old, perfectly fitting shoes and getting on a bike again after not having done so for years. Then the question came out of her mouth: "When will your next one be?"

I began to plan the next Darshan, which would take place a couple of months later.

PEBBLE

The pebble for this chapter is that this was the time when most of life's crucial pebbles had finally been laid and that the culmination of all the pebbles had become the pathway for my life. This is not to say that I would not gain more pebbles, but rather that those yet to come were not so much new contributions, but ones that would augment what had already become my foundation, therefore making the path stronger and wider.

I am moved to thank Randy for his contribution to this experience. I want to also give thanks to Waverly for her vision. I thank God and The Presence for their constant companionship and guidance through the gatherings. I am grateful to Randy's guru for visiting me in the dream world, and for his blessing. Lastly, I am grateful and give thanks for the experience of Love that I was able to have, and of the power that lived intrinsically within it.

Chapter Sixty-Five

CALLING ANGER TO THE MAT

⌀

$\mathcal{I}$t was late June of 1993, not too long after the Darshans, when I had another vision while housesitting again for Joe and Cara. It was during a meditation in the same room where I first encountered The Presence that I saw myself traveling to Sedona and camping on top of Cathedral Rock. I heard my inner voice say that it would be good for Randy to come with me. I asked what the purpose of the trip was, and I heard that all would be revealed in time. I knew better than to press, so I decided to trust that all would, in fact, be revealed.

That evening, I let Randy know that it was suggested we both go to Sedona. "Are you nuts?" he said. "It's mid-summer right now!"

"I know," I said. "Don't worry. We'll be fine. I was told in my meditation that there will be a rainstorm when we go, and it will cool things off."

He looked at me as if I had finally gone cuckoo. "I'm going to check this out, but I don't think we should go." Then he walked away in a huff. He later came back to me and said that his sister who lived in Phoenix told him that there were record heat waves, and that people were having heat stroke and dying. He said it was definitely NOT a good time to go to Sedona, and then he reiterated that he didn't want to go.

After listening to him, I gently said, "Randy, if you don't want to go, it's all right. But I have to go." I understood that it might be hard for him (or anyone, for that matter) to trust my visions, but I trusted them. Randy, however, wanted me to trust *him* more than my vision.

This was an example of the rifts that we had. About a month earlier I had done a meditation and asked to be shown why he and I had so much love yet so much strife between us. I also asked why I felt a sense of heavy responsibility for him. This was not something I normally felt for a lover. I wasn't getting an answer in the meditation, so I let go of trying to figure it out. Then, all of a sudden, and very vividly (while still in meditation), I saw myself on a large battlefield. The sky was darkened with gray clouds; the scene felt heavy and grim. I was sitting on a proud black horse, wearing a suit of armor. Trying to get my bearings, I looked up and saw a large wall made of stone or brick. It looked like it could have been a fortress. Then I looked down and scanned a sea of death. Blood, bodies, and their parts were strewn all around me. I was struck by a grief that yanked my heart out of my chest. Intense guilt overcame me, because I knew I had led these valiant men into battle and to their demise. Tremendous anger boiled through me with the realization that I had been vehement in fighting a war I thought was worthy, for God and country. But even those things couldn't justify the scope of death I was seeing. Something caused me to look down, and as I did, I saw the body of a man lying face down, a man I knew as my most trusted comrade. "Noooo!" I yelled as I leapt off my horse and fell to the ground, praying that he was still alive. I gingerly turned him over, but he was dead, his eyes still open. To my horror, it was Randy's face I was looking at— his startling blue eyes staring blankly at me. I wailed, knowing that my misplaced passion had killed this man who had greatly revered me and trusted me with his life. I came out of my meditation sobbing.

I went to Randy and told him of my vision. He looked at me with a shocked expression. "That's exactly how it feels! I feel resentful of you all the time because I believe you'll destroy me." It felt like dominos were falling on each other in a long line as I recalled the myriad times he had gotten angry with me. I saw the string that linked all those events to the vision I saw in my meditation. Even though I had no way of proving that what I saw was true, it resonated for both of us. I realized that there was nothing I could do to change whatever had happened between us, so I asked for his forgiveness. "Whatever it is I have done to you in the past, I'm sincerely sorry." My apology eased things between us for a short time, but the resentment never left. It seemed to invade many of our days, to some degree or another.

Another byproduct of this meditation was that it strongly re-kindled my fear that if people trusted me (with my energy work), I would somehow hurt them. I worked with this fear, and it took time as well as trust in myself and my sincere intentions to make headway.

He decided he would go to Sedona, I believed, in part so that he could prove me wrong. He was angry when we packed the car and angry as we drove east. We made small talk, and as we got into Arizona I offered to drive the rest of the way. As I began to drive , he fell asleep. I listened to music on my Walkman.

As we traveled north from Phoenix, I saw massive, beautiful, and very dark thunderheads making their way toward me. *Uh oh,* I said to myself, *Randy's not going to like this.* I turned the music off and asked my inner guidance if it would let me know why I was asked to go to Sedona. I expected to hear nothing or a *Not yet*. But what I heard was, *You are going to Sedona to confront and clear anger, for you and for others.* "I understand," I said, and I welcomed my "mission" without resistance. I wanted to have deeper under-standing of anger, and I felt that my relationship with Randy had something to do with teaching me this. Just as it began to rain, Randy awoke. Sure enough, he wasn't happy.

It rained off and on as we approached Sedona, cooling the temperatures as I was promised. Once we got there, the rain stopped. I hoped for Randy's sake that it had stopped completely. We parked the car and got our gear ready. I helped him put his backpack on. (He had never camped before.) The moment we stepped foot on the path, it began to rain again, lightly at first. But by the time we began our climb up the mountain, the light rain became a downpour, complete with thunder and lightning. I welcomed the rain. It felt like a baptism of sorts, and I took off my hat to let the pure water wash over me.

I seemed to glide up the mountain. Every step felt effortless and light. Randy, on the other hand, was almost in tears. His anger was pulsating at such a rate that I could almost hear it coursing through his veins. I kept encouraging him, saying that we would be there soon, and I reassured him that we were perfectly safe. I knew that without question, but he couldn't let himself believe me and didn't want to hear anything else, so I just stuck close by to be sure he didn't fall or hurt himself. The rain continued to come down hard.

I saw the mountain's ridge coming up and pointed to it. As we approached, the rain seemed to lighten up a bit. With our first steps onto the ridge, the rain stopped completely. We stood on top and looked around us in awe. It was raining and lightning was striking 360 degrees around us, but where we were was perfectly still. "Good!" I said. "We should pitch our tent while the rain has stopped." We got our tent set up and our things settled, and I wanted to meditate for a while to center myself and to ask for guidance. I asked Randy if he was all right with that, (I hadn't informed him of what I had learned about why I was there) and he said he was fine, so I found a nice big rock with a breathtaking view of the valley. I took a few minutes and gazed out at the view, the warm wind gently massaging my face, and then I closed my eyes.

I went into meditation and was shown the complexity of anger. I was shown how it always begins with fear. I saw how this planet is shrouded by a thick matrix of fear and anger, and how anger is ingrained and running rampant in our culture and in Randy. I saw how I drew anger into my life so that I could work it out; I also saw that the one thing I could do to help was to love. So I sent my love to Randy and out as far as I could imagine so that it would join with others, and as it grew in intensity, I prayed that it would help to release all humans from anger's grip. I prayed that we be healed from this affliction—this *disease*—and that it melt away like wax on a candle. As I sent out more love, I sank deeper and sent out more.

I had been in meditation for over an hour when Randy called to me. I could barely hear his voice. "Donna, can you hear me? You have to see this." I slowly started to come back into my body.

"What is it?" I said with my eyes still closed.

"Open your eyes." I did, and Randy's face met mine. There was no anger in his eyes. He actually looked peaceful. "Look," he gently insisted. I glanced around and saw one of the most amazing things I had ever seen. As the sun had started to set with its color and splendor, the lightning and thunder still struck in the distance around us. It was ravishingly beautiful. The clouds were thick, dark, and ominous. Then, I looked straight up above my head, expecting to see more clouds, but instead what I saw was a perfectly round hole in the clouds, which appeared to be about twelve inches in diameter. And through the clouds I could see the stars. I looked around to see if the clouds had parted anywhere else, but they had not. I gazed up again, looking through the hole. "Look…at…that." We sat there in awe. I gave thanks—thanks for the moment and thanks for the message I took from the clouds: If you focus on love enough, it will clear away your clouds of anger.

After several minutes, I felt an opening to tell Randy what I had been told on the drive and what I saw in my meditation. He sat next to me and we talked about anger and fear in a way we had not done before.

The rest of the trip went more smoothly, except when Randy accidentally stepped into a cactus bush. Unfortunately, it took a long while to get the thorns out, and this trigged his anger again.

While in Sedona, I felt I had crossed some sort of bridge, and as we drove home, I hoped Randy had done the same. It seemed like he might have, but within a few days, we had the biggest upset yet. He thought I didn't trust him about something (I cannot recall what) and he became livid. He was yelling at me from the hallway and then suddenly rushed toward me. I thought he was going to hit me. He got within a few inches of me, his face contorted, yelling and screaming. Then *it* hit me. It hit me so hard, in fact, that I almost fell back. I finally understood the reason I had brought Randy into my life. *Compassion heals anger. You fear anger. Cultivate compassion now, for his anger and yours,* I heard a voice say. I had always been uncomfortable with anger being expressed toward me, and it was not an emotion I relished feeling. But in that moment, anger seemed like a lost and scared child that desperately wanted me to hold it tight. I looked into Randy's out-of-control angry eyes and realized that my relationship with him was complete. Something had shifted. I had no more anger toward him. A wave of compassion rolled through me, bringing me to peace and balance as I resolutely let Randy know that I could not and would not argue with him again.

Within a few days I had moved into the second bedroom of his apartment, and within a few months, I was sharing a home with Roy (the guitar player from I AM LOVE) and his younger brother.

PEBBLE

"Compassion helps heal anger" is the pebble for this chapter. This is not to say that anger will magically disappear with compassion, nor am I saying that in the name of compassion one should subject oneself to another's rage. What I'm saying, however, is that through the practice of compassion, I was able to see how Randy's anger was torturing him and sabotaging our relationship. I understood that the anger came from deep pain within him, and that I was acting as a trigger. It wasn't personal to me, and once I understood this, I could see that underneath his anger, what he ultimately wanted was to be loved and to be happy. He just didn't know how to get himself there because he wasn't ready to leave the anger behind.

Of course, applying this to oneself is crucial. In order to heal anger, one must take responsibility for it. When I began the practice of loving and having compassion for myself when I felt anger, as a parent would for a young child, I could feel calmness set in. It was an amazing practice: to feel compassion run through the body at the same time anger flowed. The compassion seemed to intercept the anger, and it usually ceased—if not immediately, then almost.

With this insight, I saw that because of Randy's inability to take responsibility for his anger and heal his own pain, he blamed me for it. When I saw this and realized that it would likely continue, I had to remove myself from the relationship for my own well-being.

Things may happen to us that are extremely painful. Does this mean we have the right to get angry? Absolutely. Does it mean that it is conducive to our health and happiness to carry anger, rage, and resentment? Absolutely not. These things only fester, creating an emotional consciousness that looks for every opportunity to express itself, or it implodes inside us and causes ill health. It's insidious.

To revive a previous pebble: People always do the best they can; otherwise, they would do better. Again, this does not absolve those who have done wrong. This does, however, allow us to come to compassion and peace.

About the clouds parting: The universe works in mysterious—and sometimes wild—ways, I always say. Though at times I'm at a loss for understanding its magic, I always do my best to be grateful for it.

Chapter Sixty-Six

UNCONVENTIONAL SUPPORT

❧

I had not shared the Darshans with some of my friends because I hadn't yet fully embraced the scope of them and the transformation that seemed to be happening in my life. Cara and Joe, who I was still working for, were two that I could not quite wrap my mind around telling. With them, it would be more like telling my family (who I had also not told). I couldn't imagine them aligning themselves with my new life, but I intuited that they sensed something was going on with me, and after I returned from Sedona, they were particularly curious. They would ask a question here and there (I think they were trying to be respectful of my privacy) that I managed to avoid fully answering.

As I was leaving work one Friday, Cara and Joe met me at the door to say goodbye, and Cara asked what I was doing over the weekend. My mind was already out the door and I was caught-off guard; I knew I was spending the weekend planning the next Darshan. I must have stuttered when I answered with my distilled, Reader's Digest version, because Cara looked at me and said, "Donna, what's going on?" I looked at her and Joe and admitted, "Well, a lot is happening in my life right now. I promise to tell you more about it once things have settled down a bit more." I shyly looked at them, hoping my answer would appease them. Then, all of a sudden, a hailstorm started, but not just any hailstorm—this storm was heaving down golf-ball-sized ice. Cara looked at me as the entire house sounded like it was being attacked with rocks and said, "You aren't going anywhere until you tell us what's going on!" I laughed, realizing that I was caught, and began to carefully explain many of the footnotes of the stories they had already heard. I did leave out some of the parts that I have now admitted in this book—the clouds parting, the Native American spirits singing around me, and so on. Unexpectedly, and to my relief, they were fairly open to what I told them, and they requested that I let them know how things progressed. I wasn't entirely sure why they wanted updates. I could feel their reserve and their desire to keep a close eye on me, but it seemed they also sincerely wanted to know what was unfolding so that they could support me.

As soon as I finished telling Cara and Joe what I had been keeping secret, the hail turned to a light rain.

One of the questions I often heard from people was, "How do you not take on negative energy from people you work on?" My first response was always that I didn't *believe* I took on people's energy. My understanding was that their energy passed through me and didn't cling to me. Second, I was never afraid of anyone's energy, because I knew that *negative* energy was based in fear, and I was not afraid of people's fear. While working on people, I prayed that all such energies be released and then be transmuted into neutral energies as they went into the ethers. I always trusted that this worked, and I never felt the heaviness after my sessions that some energy workers do. Still, one day while I was in meditation I inquired: *My belief is that energy is transmuted as it leaves me, but can you tell if there's a way I can be sure? Maybe you can give me a sign?* I received a *Yes*.

The next time I worked on someone I got a large gas bubble in my stomach and I had to burp. I couldn't hold it back. The burp was large and it felt satisfying. When the gas bubble went away, right away another came and I burped again, followed by another. I would like to add that these were not small, dainty "girl" burps— these were full-fledged sailor belches! As this continued, I was told that this burping would be my way of being sure that the energy had left my client's body and mine.

After the session, I laughed to myself, realizing that this phenomenon was one that would continue. I considered it my own little cosmic joke. "You asked!" I said out loud to myself.

PEBBLE

Is honesty always the best policy? Usually. It depends on the timing and the audience. What I will say about telling Joe and Cara is that it gave me the opportunity to have a reality check, and it gave them the opportunity to support me. It served me to have a broader support system, and a structure of checks and balances in place during that time of expansion and transition.

As far as the hail goes, whether it was just a coincidence or well-timed help from beyond, who knows for sure? Again, the Universe works in wondrous ways —and, I will add, with impeccable timing.

To this day, my clients laugh the first time they hear me roar. In further sessions they look forward to the burps, then eventually they often begin to do it themselves. It was somewhat embarrassing at first; I had never burped before unless I ate onions. Also, I had never heard a woman burp so…enthusiastically. As I said, I have to take it as a cosmic joke. When I explained the burping once to one of my clients, they had the perfect response: "At least the gas gets released from the right end!"

Seriously though, as ghastly as this sounds, the burping has been very useful. It not only allows me to know that something is being released, it also tells me the magnitude of the energy that is releasing. It is not unlike an erupting volcano. The more the build up, the larger the eruption.

As previously stated, I believe the Universe is always conspiring for our highest good, for our success, and for our well-being, even if the ways are at times a bit unconventional…and loud.

Chapter Sixty-Seven

BOUNDLESS LOVE

∽

I realized, as I was planning the first Darshans, that I had seen a vision of them while driving back from Mt. Shasta. In my vision, however, I was working with larger groups and singing. So for the next Darshan, I decided to invite more people, include music, and create it more like what I had seen in the vision. I booked a room that would accommodate one hundred people and began getting the word out.

A large difference between planning this Darshan and the previous ones was that this one felt more expansive and joyful. I felt confident in what I was to do, and I welcomed more people and more energy to work with, and of course more love. And while in the back of my mind I knew that what I was doing was not a true Darshan, and therefore was not entirely comfortable calling it that, I embraced what I was doing.

While planning, I researched the music used in a traditional Darshan, one hosted by an East Indian guru. The instruments most often used are sitars and tanpuras (strings), tables and dhols (drums), harmoniums (similar to an organ, but smaller), and such. The music begins slowly at first and then builds, increasing in volume, intensity, and rhythm to a crescendo just before the guru enters. The music is played to raise the energy level of those present so that they can receive what the guru is going to offer.

Although I appreciated East Indian music, I felt it would be inauthentic for me to use it for my Darshans, given that I had virtually no personal spiritual experience with it. The music I saw in my vision was intended to uplift spirits and open the hearts of those present; it was music that was personally meaningful to me and close to my heart. Feeling that it was more appropriate to choose this music myself, I chose "Conviction of the Heart," by Kenny Loggins[1]. I would sing the song at the end of the Darshan while accompanied by guitars, a violin, and percussion played by the most loving and open musicians I knew, as well as a few others they invited.

I contemplated what topic I would speak about and landed on *Living in Trust, Living your Dream.* I didn't wish to prepare what I was going to say. I preferred to simply know that I was speaking about something in which I had a certain level of mastery, and then be sure I was open to allow Spirit to work and speak through me. I trusted that together we would know what wanted to be said and what needed to be heard.

For the flyer I was preparing to send out, I asked Spirit what I could say to give people a glimpse of what to look forward to. Here is what I heard and what was included on the flyer: *"When one opens to deep trust, a multitude of possibilities begin to unfold. Blockages become bridges, and miracles, dormant within us, become realities."*

My most cherished intent for the Darshan was that every person who attended be given the opportunity to open to unconditional love, the fabric from which we all are created. I wanted the attendees to understand that trusting God/the Universe/our personal Guidance and acting from love was the ultimate daily practice. Everything I did to prepare for the event was within this framework.

Because I believed so strongly in the power of intent, I created a question sheet that was to be distributed to all attendees. The question was to help them focus and be open to receive what they desired. The question was, "What do you hope to gain, clear, or experience from your presence here today?" There was room for their answer and a signature. Then at the bottom of the sheet it said simply, "And so it is…" The participants could either turn them in for me to read and pray on, or they could keep them.

I wanted those who were in attendance to feel comfortable and supported during the Darshan, so I worked with volunteers (a collection of friends and acquaintances who had previously attended one of my Darshans) to create such an environment. They were to be helpful, kind, loving, and centered and had be available to the attendees for their needs. It was their responsibility that the space feel safe and secure.

The day of the Darshan, I felt well prepared and organized. I walked out in front of the seventy-five or so people and sat on the comfortable chair next to a beautiful arrangement of flowers, feeling a combination of things: struck by the beauty I saw in the faces looking back at me, the privilege it was to be in that position, the responsibility the position held, the desire to open the hearts of all present, the sense of trust in my inner guidance, and sheer and boundless love. As people came forward one by one—some falling into my arms, some weeping, others hesitant, and still others laughing with joy—I held them and loved them. Although a part of me had little practical experience with this type of gathering, another part of me felt I had done it hundreds of times. *At last*, I thought, *I'm home*.

After the Darshan I felt exalted. I had lived out a dream I didn't know I had, yet at the same time believed it was something I was destined to do, as if every moment of my existence had culminated at the Darshan. At that moment, my life felt complete —as if I had again surpassed my vision of who I was and of what I was capable.

P E B B L E

For me, the Darshan was a pivotal experience—the answer to the question of why I was born and why I was protected from harm so many times throughout my life. I knew now beyond question that I was meant to help people. The

Darshan was the culmination of all that I knew intrinsically, and all that I had learned and cared most about in life, woven together by a vision—in this case, the vision I had while on my way home from Mt. Shasta—of bringing people together for the sole purpose of loving them.

My experience of Grace is that it is always, always, ALWAYS waiting for a sign to rush forward on our behalf. Certainly Grace had caught me on several occasions when I was falling, but in this case it came to champion my vision. There was clarity in my vision, yet I was open to guidance of how to bring it into being. That opening was Grace's cue to step in to help me realize it.

So, what happens when all of one's pebbles finally come together? What happens when one realizes their biggest and most outrageous visions? First of all, I hope we make time to feel joy. After that, one makes a choice to either continue realizing those visions... or... he or she creates a new vision to live into.

Chapter Sixty-Eight

A CHANGE IN COURSE

∽

*A*s usual, when one believes that their life is full and complete and they couldn't want for more, Spirit gives a gift—it reveals where one can find the next level of depth and fullness.

I had met Jay, a massage therapist who also did hands-on healing work, while preparing for the large Darshan. He was one of the musicians who accompanied me while I sang. He played guitar and was dashingly handsome. He had a quirky sense of humor, which I liked. Some time after the Darshan, I realized I felt quite drawn to him. He seemed to feel the same, and after detangling ourselves from the people we had been seeing, we had our first date. He wanted to take me to dinner, but I had been on a grape fast (a fast to cleanse the liver and clear toxins from the stomach) and I wasn't ready to break it, so he decided he would eat before coming over to my place. Once arriving, he fed me grapes while we got to know each other better. We talked for hours. The intensity of the evening was extreme; I had not felt drawn to someone like this for some time. At some point, he began massaging my feet, and as he did, a word came into my awareness— from where I do not know—and that word was *yes*. It seemed that my head and entire being could feel nothing but *yes* and I proclaimed it out loud. He may have thought my *yes* was an exclamation of passion, but it was much deeper than that. I spoke it out loud over and over.

As we continued with our non-sexual intimacy, an epiphany struck me hard. I realized that I would have a child with Jay some day. I gasped at this, but said nothing. I had not thought about being a parent since I had been with my husband, Sean. This was a powerful realization, but I thought it wise to keep it to myself. The evening was a lovely first exploration into our intimacy, and it eventually went into our history books, affectionately known as Grape Day.

On our second date, a couple of days later, we drove up to Topanga Canyon State Park and hiked up into the hills. It was clear that we had chemistry. I wanted to know more about Jay and to get a sense of how he lived his life. In particular, I wanted to know some of his goals to see if his were in alignment with mine. We lightheartedly asked each other questions like, "Who do you want to be when you grow up?" and "What's your favorite dessert?" But we also asked questions like, "Where do you see yourself in five years?" "What have you still not done that's on your 'bucket list'?" and "What makes you most happy?" Although we differed in some areas, we seemed in alignment with others. It was on the top of one of the beautiful Topanga Mountains, with the autumn sun shining radiantly as far as we could see, that we decided we would begin to explore a relationship.

Although the large Darshan was a magnificent experience, I didn't want to hold Darshans of that scope regularly. I began to also hold smaller Darshans, which I chose to call Gatherings, and these were less structured. I spoke about what it is to walk alongside Spirit in life, and I did healing work on people when it felt appropriate. I enjoyed the Gatherings because they felt more authentic to me.

As I continued to hold Gatherings, however, I began to feel a sense of unease. On the surface, it seemed all was well—people were coming to me for guidance, and they seemed to get what they needed. Going deeper though, I had conflicting feelings. Some people attending the Darshans had placed me on a pedestal and began to treat me like a guru, including Waverly. Early on she asked me if I would take a different, more spiritual name. She came up with the name *Mother Gloria*, Gloria being short for glorious. People would call me by the name from then on, she explained. She went on to say that all people who hold Darshans use their spiritual names. I didn't feel altogether comfortable with this; it felt a bit self-indulgent, but in the moment I allowed myself to be swayed. I reasoned that perhaps taking on such a name would be appropriate for the new path I was traveling.

For a short period I used the name, but I noticed that I felt uncomfortable when people addressed me in that way, sometimes calling me simply *Mother*. I tried to convince myself that my new name was something I would just have to get used to, but it didn't happen. Because of this, and my discomfort about people treating me as a guru, I began to doubt whether this was a path I wanted to continue traveling. I felt that other than God, I had no one to talk to. Those who helped me with the Darshans and Gatherings were also looking to me to guide them. I thought about speaking to an outside source but felt that those who didn't attend the Gatherings or Darshans would not understand the work I was doing. As a result, I felt quite on my own.

I meditated and asked for guidance, and it always seemed to come down to this: there was no right choice and no wrong choice. The Darshans and Gatherings were potent opportunities to be of service. Given this, it was up to me to work things out within myself.

Over time, and after a fair amount of introspection, I decided that I would continue to do one-on-one healing work and to hold the smaller Gatherings, but I would stop holding the Darshans altogether and stop using the name. My internal resolution was that, until I had a stronger group of peers around me—ones that I could keep counsel with—I would not put myself out into the world in this way.

Although my choice to stop holding the Darshans felt like the choice with the most integrity and authenticity, I felt a fair amount of sadness about it. A part of me felt that the Darshans had been given to me as an opportunity and a gift, and that by choosing to stop them, I was letting someone down, although I didn't know whom. But, even with this, I felt I was doing the right thing, for me. My final words to myself about this were: "I trust that if and when I choose to come back to the Darshans, there will be new opportunities to do so."

PEBBLE

First level of insight, early on—

If I had had a strong support system and/or or a stronger sense of Spirit, could I have weathered my conflict and continued with the Darshans? Perhaps. As I reflect back on that time, there was a deep-seated fear that I had begun to glimpse in my meditation, seeing myself as a warrior with Randy. If I were given power to influence people, I would somehow cause them pain. Given that I had this belief (even though I wasn't fully conscious of it at the time), my subconscious created a mechanism to keep me from doing damage—the strong impulse to find a group of peers to keep me on a righteous path.

A pebble for this chapter is that we must not only follow our bliss and internal guidance, but also honor our sense of personal integrity. The results in the moment may not look expansive or grand, but we will feel we did the right thing. And no matter what we do, isn't it important to feel good about ourselves and what we are doing? For me, it was more important to feel I made the best choice, congruent with my instincts and ideals, than to follow someone else's visions of grandeur.

As far as whether or not I did the right thing in ending the Darshans, I must again quote Maria Rilke who so aptly wrote: "…Live the questions now. Perhaps you will then gradually, without noticing it, live along some distant day into the answer."

The second level of insight, a later and deeper interpretation—

Over the years, I struggled with my thoughts on how the Darshans came about and the reasons I let it all go, as I truly wanted to be of service in larger ways. I didn't fully understand until recently, when I was fortunate enough to personally experience Mata Amritanandamayi—known to many as Ammachi or Amma, the hugging saint—a true modern day guru.

After spending time with her and reading her biography, Ammichi: The Life of the Holy Mother Amritanandamayi[1], as well as, Autobiography of a Yogi[2] by Paramahansa Yogananda, I came to understand that my lack of comfort with being a guru was not because I didn't have a strong support system, although they and organizational support are important to have; it was because I knew I didn't have the consistent God identification that a guru has. I understand this identification, or consciousness, as the ultimate example of connection and trust, translating into a unity of the person with God. To attain this unity, one would have transcended the human ego and fear, which I had not yet done.

Why then did I feel encouragement and receive assistance to realize my vision of the Darshan? I cannot presume to know what Grace was thinking, but I will say the vision I was given, in its original form, was of me talking to people as a teacher and giving them love through my words and hands. The title "Darshan" was attached later. My vision had no identity; it was simply a deep practice of love. My vision didn't include my being a "guru." It would appear that one has to be very conscious when bringing one's vision into the physical realm, and not to allow it to be altered by another's vision, unless the alteration acts to enhance and not distort.

One other point that I didn't understand in my earlier reflection, although I felt it tugging on my subconscious, was the significance I had put on being a teacher and in a position of leadership. For me, as relevant as being visible, available, a source of love, being committed to my personal growth, and knowledgeable of how to help people was, I had not yet mastered transparency, and the scariest for me, accountability. I can now see that part of my hesitation in taking on a leadership role was that I took that position very seriously. I would not allow myself to say one thing and do another, or act out of alignment with what I taught, as I had seen other teachers do. And although I lived most of what I spoke, I was not impeccable. I had a very high standard of what I thought a true leader should hold himself or herself to. I knew that I wanted the option of walking both paths, even if I chose to walk the higher one. There were times when I wanted the option to be unconscious. This realization has been an important one. I wanted to have the freedom to go see a movie and disconnect from the world and my responsibilities; to have a glass of champagne and eat bonbons if I felt like it; to have the freedom to have emotions, experience drama, and to learn from my mistakes; to be human and imperfect, to live life on my terms.

When I first started out on this path, one thing I was very clear on was how much I loved this world. My intention was to do what I could as a means of contributing to the uplifting of others. The direction I felt I was headed toward was separating myself from my own humanity. From my perception, the guru separates himself or herself from living a "normal" human life in their devotion to, and their dwelling within, the Divine. I deeply and profoundly love what it is to be a human being, with all our faults and foibles. My goal has always been to live fully in my humanity while infusing the Divine into my life, and to help people from this place. Although I was not conscious of this, I didn't want to become so immersed in God realization that I would no longer live a normal life. The closer I got to feeling that I was separating from humanity, the stronger my unconscious grip to the human drama became.

These realizations lead me to several points of growth: 1) I do not have God identification. What I have is Love identification. 2) My fear of being accountable was due to a lack of trust and confidence in myself, and not fully understanding where my true gifts lay. 3) Choosing "freedom" is not necessarily choosing consciousness or success. In fact, this form of freedom, the freedom that dissuades one from personal responsibility and committing to a path, keeps one trapped and small. 4) I have always cared deeply about my work with people and have trusted myself to walk a conscious path. I may not have been perfect at every turn, but I have always been committed. And 5) The fact that I was at this level in inquiry means I was on the path, otherwise my lack of impeccability would not have occurred to me.

I will say that the Darshan experience did change me. It allowed me to see the purity and power of Love. I witnessed the support that is always around me. I was blessed by being able to see, firsthand, the beauty in the hearts of people and their desire to be loved and uplifted. It allowed me to understand, in my bones, that someone, somewhere had confidence in me. All these things further solidified my commitment to fulfilling my life purpose. So, I was served very well.

By the way, as Rilke said I would, I did come into the answer ... in this case, how to be of service and give my love. You are now reading the fruits of my four-year labor. Through Grace and Divine Intelligence, I am learning to trust and surrender. Beyond this, we shall see ...

But there is still more to this story.

Chapter Sixty-Nine

A DOOR CLOSES, ANOTHER OPENS

∾

*I*t was a cool and cloudy day in late December when my brother Nate called to tell me that something was wrong with our father. "Dad has been acting stranger and stranger, he said. "He talks like he's drunk all the time."

"You should take him to the hospital right away, Nate," I insisted.

"He won't go. I've been trying to talk him into it, but he won't listen." I encouraged Nate to tell our father that they would go to the hospital just to run some tests, and afterward, Nate would bring him right back home. Our father finally relented, and Nate took him to Hoag Hospital in Newport Beach.

After many tests were completed, it was determined that my father had an advanced brain tumor. The doctors immediately scheduled surgery to see what they could do for him.

When I drove down from Los Angeles to see my father in the hospital, the man who was once strong and handsome was now withered, confused, and frightened. When I walked into the room, I wavered as I took in that familiar smell I recalled from when my mother was hospitalized. I felt like falling apart as I saw him lying helplessly in the bed, but instead put on a strong face and asked him how he was and what I could do for him. He looked so scared. I held his hand and gave him as much love as I knew how. Although he appreciated my presence, he was mostly concerned about purchasing a gift for Nate, who had just gotten engaged. My father was ecstatic because Nate was always the one he worried about most. He wanted to leave the hospital and kept attempting to get out of bed so he could go to the store. I promised to take him as soon as he was able to leave the hospital and that seemed to appease him.

The tumor was wrapped around the base of my father's brain, and although they were able to take out some of it, they couldn't get it all. After the surgery, the doctors informed our family that with radiation, he would live for twelve months at the most.

Denial—being the powerful stage of grief that it is—allowed me to temporarily disbelieve that my father would die, even though the doctors were certain about his prognosis. He was a strong man with a very strong will. I believed he would beat the odds and prove the doctors wrong. He believed this, too.

It was not until a few months later that I realized my father was actually going to die. One night while sleeping at Jay's, I had an odd dream. I had recently seen the movie *Junior*², the story of a scientist who impregnates himself for a research project. In my dream, Arnold was playing with children that were all around him, and I was pregnant and eating a smorgasbord of foods. I awoke from my dream perplexed as to what it meant. As I recollected the details of the dream, I began to get in touch with how much I had always wanted to be a mother. I then remembered the insight I had during Jay's and my first date. It occurred to me that I was thirty seven years old, and if I were going to have a child, I should do something about it. Jay and I had been seeing each other for five months and had several unresolved issues, one of which was that he needed a lot of time apart (which triggered my pain around yearning for the non-present male figure). I didn't think he was ready to be a father—or know if he even wanted to be one—but that morning, I decided to tell him that I wanted to be a mother and to ask if he wanted to have a child with me.

Jay was in the kitchen, and I asked if he would sit with me because I had something important to talk with him about. When he sat down, I blurted out something like, "I realized this morning that I want to have a family. I'm thirty-seven and I'm ready. Do you want to be a father, and do you want to have a child with me?" I'm certain this caught him totally off guard, because his face looked like a Mack truck had just hit him head-on. After a moment, he said something like, "Uh, I don't know, maybe some day." We talked about it a bit more without resolving the question either way, but I left the conversation certain that I was ready to be a mother. I also knew that if Jay didn't want to be a father, it would be a defining moment in our relationship.

A few weeks later I missed my menstruation. I had been using the rhythm method for years and could always feel a pinch when I ovulated. I remembered that I had felt two pinches the last time I ovulated. The first I felt three days before Jay had returned from a seminar—making me happy that the timing was such that we could safely make love when he came home. Then, the day before his return, I felt another one. I recalled thinking to myself, *Odd that I would feel another pinch. I know the first one was an egg dropping.* I then shrugged off my uncertainty, saying to myself, *This must be something else.* When I remembered this, I thought to myself, *Uh oh.*

The next morning on my way to work, I went to the drugstore and picked up a home pregnancy test. After I got some things done at the office, I told Cara—my friend and boss—that I was going to take a pregnancy test and asked her if she would look at the results with me. "Are you kidding?" she said. "Of course!" I carefully read the instructions, and after finishing the test, I placed the cap back on the tester as Cara and I anxiously awaited the results. Sure enough, the little window indicated that I was pregnant. I was shocked and stunned—but oddly, not scared. After the shock wore off, I became elated. Cara and I took pictures and jumped up and down in celebration of my news. Later in the day, we included Joe in our celebration by congratulating him on being an adopted uncle-to-be.

Upon reflection, I realized that either the second pinch must also have been an egg, or I misinterpreted the first one. Either way, the day I told Jay I was ready to have a family, I was already pregnant. Evidently, I was more ready than I thought.

I came to understand something else that day. I knew it was no coincidence that I got pregnant. I realized that my father was, in fact, going to die, and that as my father would leave this world, the child growing inside me would enter...at around the same time. I felt that this child was given to me as a gift.

Even though Jay felt he wasn't ready to be a father, he knew how much I wanted to be a mother, and because he loved me, he supported my decision to give birth to our child. Even though I hoped we would be able to work out our issues and become a family, I wasn't convinced this would be possible. Even so, I knew beyond reason that everything would turn out well one way or another.

I felt it was better not to do the Gatherings while I was pregnant, but I continued to build my private healing practice while working at the office part-time. My hope was to build up my practice so that when I went on maternity leave, I would still be able to bring in money.

When I found out I was having a girl, I was ecstatic. I wanted to bring an empowered child into the world, and I felt I most understood how to do that with a girl. Jay and I started going through the process of choosing names, but we were getting nowhere. One night, while at the Playboy Jazz Festival, Jay looked down at the little salt and pepper containers that came with our concession food and said, "We should call her Pepper!"

"That's perfect!" I laughed in response. The name stuck, and from then on as I talked to her and massaged her little body in my belly, I lovingly called her Pepper.

In July, Jay and I went to Sedona. While hiking up a few of the trails, we found ourselves bumping into the same man and woman several times. Each time we saw them, we had a short exchange. The final time, we stopped to have a more in-depth conversation to see if our encounters were coincidence or providence. It turned out that the woman, Alice, was suffering from a painful condition, and she asked if I would do some healing work on her. According to Alice, she had been experiencing a fair amount of pain for some time. Jay and I explained the mind-body connection and how many illnesses stem from a weakened physical state and immune system, often caused from strong emotions relating to unresolved issues. This made sense to them, and we offered to work on her. They accepted, so we arranged for them to come to the bed and breakfast where we were staying.

Jay brought Alice into a deep meditative state and did some guided regression work. While she was in that state, I began to put my hands on her and helped her through the rest of her regression. At the end of the session, she generously expressed her appreciation while claiming that the pain she had been experiencing many years was completely gone.

Herman, Alice's partner, mentioned that the two of them had a close friend, Celon, who had cancer, and he asked if Jay and I were available to fly to Florida to work on her. Herman said that Celon was most probably too far along in her cancer for us to help, but he wanted us to do whatever we could. We were able to arrange the time and finances, and within a few weeks, we flew out to the southern tip of Florida to try to help Celon.

We worked on her for five days, and although she wasn't healed from cancer, she felt much better. We also worked on Celon's friends so that they could better cope with her condition. When we left, they all thanked and acknowledged us for the work we had done on Celon, and on them as a group. I hoped for the best for Celon, although I knew that her passing would be just a matter of time.

Several months later, we learned that Celon had died. Herman said that she was at peace in her passing, and he thanked us again for our contribution to her and to them. Alice sent a bear in a beautiful southern-belle dress for Pepper; it had been one of Celon's favorites. I was saddened that I hadn't been able to help Celon more, but I knew that with any healing work, Western or alternative, there are no guarantees. I did my best and we helped bring her to a state of peace, and that was good.

The months to follow were quite challenging. With my surging hormones, I found it difficult to spend large amounts of time with my father. His mother and sister had rented him an apartment next to theirs so that they could take care of him. Every time I went to visit him, I became depressed, and it would take me days to recover. I visited him as often as I felt I could handle, crying all the way home each time, sensing the regret and fear he must have felt as he saw his life drawing to an end.

My father didn't know about my healing work; still, I thought of asking him if he wanted me to put my hands on him. But with his deeply Christian brothers, sisters, and mother, I felt the offer would not be welcome and decided to suggest other options.

I researched alternative healing practices and herbs for cancer patients and presented them to my father. He had never placed his faith in alternative healing, though, and didn't trust it. I think he took some of the herbs I brought to him, but one day when I questioned him about pursuing other natural remedies, he exclaimed, "What do you want me to do? Do you want me to stop my treatments?" The gravity of his illness hit me, and I knew I couldn't take it on. I muttered feebly, "No, Dad. I'm just trying to help." I felt myself cave in with the realization that there was nothing more I could do for him.

After the drive home and a good cry, I resolved to just love my father while he traveled down this final leg of his path.

One day, when I was about to leave my father's apartment, I turned to him and said, "Dad, I love you and want to thank you for being my father." He was dying, and no matter how good or bad a job he had done as a father, he was one of two who brought me into this world, and I knew he had done the best he knew how;

otherwise, he would have done better. I wanted him to know that after all was said and done, gratitude and love was what I was left with. His failings would not be what I remembered most, because I knew the scars would eventually heal. What I would remember was the love he gave me to the best of his ability, and that in his eyes I would always be his "princess."

One night after he had been transferred into a hospice care facility, I went to visit him. Jay and I were having challenges, and I wanted to be with someone I knew loved me unconditionally. Even though his health had declined dramatically, when he saw that I was sad, he got up out of his bed and invited me to lie down in his place. He sat down in a chair next to me and put his large warm hand on mine, patting it as he always had. I remembered how, as a child, this would make everything better, and on that night in late fall, it did.

Feeling little Pepper growing inside me while seeing my father slip away was quite powerful. It was as if I could see one door closing while another was beginning to open. I often reflected on the poignancy of this.

In mid-December, my father was entering into the final stages of his life. I had gone to visit him at the facility, and when I walked in, he was sitting up with his eyes closed and food running out of his mouth and down his chin. I called his name, but he didn't respond. I quickly called for someone. I felt so helpless. I didn't know if he was dead, in a coma, or what. It turned out that he had fallen asleep. I was concerned that he would choke and asked the nurse to check his mouth for food. Seeing him like this was too much for me, and I started to come apart. Before he awoke, I left to go back home.

While I was getting close to giving birth, my father was nearing making his transition and didn't appear to be conscious. On December 20th, at around nine p.m., I went into labor. My devoted friend, Alexandra, flew in from San Francisco to be with me through the process and to help me my first week.

I was weakened by the grief of my father's impending death, and I really struggled during my labor. Alexandra and Jay were close to me as I strained to keep breathing and to stay focused. After I had been in labor about fifteen hours, they took me to the alternative birthing center where I had planned to have my baby in water. But upon examination, the midwife told me that I wasn't dilated enough to be there and should take a long walk. She gave me a shot to relax, said it would likely be several more hours before the birth, and sent us home.

Unbeknownst to us, I dilated quite quickly after the shot, and soon after we got home I was contracting intensely. I couldn't imagine going through several more hours of that kind of pain, and after a couple hours had passed, I stopped eating and drinking. I felt I could go no further and asked to be taken to the hospital. Several times, Jay and the midwife (over the phone) tried to talk me out of going, but I begged them to let me go. I felt my weakened emotional and physical state and was concerned about my well-being. I felt I needed more care than I was getting. Eventually they relented, and Jay drove me to the hospital with Alexandra by my side.

Sean and Maura had been in touch by phone, and when they heard I asked to go to the hospital, they headed over there to meet us. I recall that it wasn't until I saw Maura's expression and the tears on her face what bad shape I was in. Shortly after I arrived, the doctor decided that I needed to rest, and I agreed to an epidural. I could have never imagined agreeing to such a thing, but in that moment, I couldn't imagine saying no. Within minutes, I went from thinking I was on a very grave path to being quite tired but truly happy to see many of the people I loved most in the room with me. Shortly after that, my brothers and Stuart's wife, Sandra, arrived. Stuart and Nate stayed outside the door, but Sandra joined us in the room.

A couple of hours later it was time to push, and at 8:58 p.m. on December 21st, my darling daughter, Noëlle, was born. Jay placed her on my chest, and as she made her way to my breast and latched on, I knew that my insight was correct. She was a gift of immeasurable beauty, given to me from Grace.

On Christmas day, I asked Jay to take me to see my father. Even though he was in a coma, I wanted Noëlle to meet him once before he passed. Jay carried her into the room and perched her on the bed in her infant seat. I talked to my father and introduced him to his only grandchild. I told him she was beautiful and that if he could see her, he would agree. Lastly, I told him that I knew he loved her. I then asked Jay to take her out of the room so I could talk to my father alone.

When they left, I held my father's hand and wished him his last Merry Christmas. "I'll miss calling you at midnight on New Year's Eve", I said, as I had every year. "I always think of you then." And then at that very moment, I could have sworn that I felt his large hand ever so slightly squeeze mine. I whispered into his ear, "I love you, Dad." I stroked his head, kissed him on his cheek, and said goodbye.

The night he was passing, I went to see him one more time. By then it appeared as if his spirit had left his body and that only the oxygen machine was keeping him alive. I kissed him on the forehead and on the cheek and then went home. At around midnight, I received a call that my father had made his transition.

One door had finally closed, and a new door was wide open. I had come full circle from being birthed, to experiencing my parents' deaths, to bringing into the world a new life—a resplendent being —precious and full of possibility. Life was beginning again, and with it, a new hope.

～

In Memoriam

George Holloway
August 24, 1927—January 3, 1996
Beloved Father

Your memory will always be cherished.
I have always loved you, and I always will.

～

EPILOGUE

✑

*J*ay and I were not able to resolve our differences, and when our daughter was a toddler, we decided to split. Beyond all the challenges of single parenting, one thing is crystal clear: I am truly blessed to be the mother of my daughter. The joy I have found in parenting, even when it's hard, is beyond anything I could have imagined. Every day, I'm acutely aware that my daughter is nothing less than a glorious gift.

Early on, I wondered if perhaps I unconsciously became pregnant to avoid being in front of people and teaching. Later, I realized that as much as I wanted to help people, I yearned to experience motherhood. I think the infinite wisdom of the Universe, and my body, knew this. The depth that has been cultivated from mothering has served to exponentially deepen my inner work and my work with people. It has also given me more impetus and inspiration to stay committed to doing my part to make the world a better place.

Now that I'm a parent, I can only imagine how challenging it must have been for my father to become a single parent of three in the sixties. I know very little about the dynamics between my father and mother, yet I know that my father pulled us out of a situation that was toxic. And although, because of his own pathology, he was not able to care for us the way that he "should" have, at least there was an attempt to improve our lives. For this, I am grateful to him.

Included hereafter are further applicable insights from this time in my life that didn't easily fit within the pebbles of my story.

This book is an offering from what I experience as Grace, and from me. Just as I realized early on that Grace is always here and willing to guide me when I allow it, I discovered as I began to write this book that it could only be a co-creation. Of the myriad stories I could have written, it was Grace that I trusted to guide me through the course. Each time I sat down to write, I made the same request —*I open myself to your guidance in this session and give thanks for your presence. May truth and revelation be easily and joyfully revealed through me. May the magnificence, power, and Grace that is you be woven together with my experience, insight, and wisdom to create a piece that will serve and uplift others.* When the going got rough, I would eventually realize that I had disconnected from Grace in order to fulfill a personal agenda. I would then close my eyes and re-attune, and the words and insights would flow again.

At some point in my writing, I began to reflect on the fact that there are *always* more facets to a story than the ones I see. As was adeptly shown in the film *The Upside of Anger*[1], we often don't know all the facts surrounding the situations about which we are resentful. With this perspective, and through forgiveness, I have been fortunate to achieve deeper levels of inner peace around experiences where I had previously felt residual blame or shame.

I ask for forgiveness from all those I have wronged in the past, and I forgive all those who have wronged me. I forgive myself, and I pray that you forgive yourself. May we release and move on.

We cannot bypass our emotional healing work, even if we have a strong spiritual practice. It is my testimony that emotional work is every bit as important as our spiritual work, and it is necessary for a fulfilling and potent life. When both are actively pursued, they act as doormen, gracefully opening doors for one another.

There is a great saying: "Change is inevitable, growth is optional."[2] Another is: "Change is inevitable, growth is intentional."[3] There is little question as to whether change happens or not. Here are the real questions: *What quality*, and at what level of *awareness* we will change, and *when* and at what *velocity* will it happen? With Buckminster Fuller's analogy of the trim tab, I assert that the speed and success of directional change is dependent on the stability of *the ship*. This is where emotional and spiritual work pays off.

In his compelling book, *The Tipping Point: How Little Things Can Make a Big Difference*[4], Malcolm Gladwell uses sociological terms to define a tipping point as: "the moment of critical mass, the threshold, the boiling point." In his "The green tipping point" article in *Time* magazine[5], Bryan Walsh describes them as: "the levels at which the momentum for change becomes unstoppable."

A tipping point is related to a trim tab, and both can be applied to the realms of *inner change*, as well as bringing one's vision into being (creation). A tipping point (and the experiences and energy that lead up to it) is what prompts the directional shift of the trim tab. It's fascinating, and I think valuable, to take note of our tipping point(s), both for inner reflection and plotting our changes of course. A few examples of powerful ones in my life were when the woman beat me, when I experienced the Presence for the first time, and, of course, the birth of my child.

There may be many thoughts and events that lead to the moment of critical mass, where inner change and creation occur, yet the thing that prompts the shift of the trim tab is the act of *taking a risk*—an intuitive leap of faith, stepping out of the known into the unknown. It takes courage to make change, as well as to create something new.

There is a great quote by the late Marilyn Ferguson[6] that states: "Your past is not your potential. In any moment you can choose to liberate your future." Tony Robbins[7] spins it a bit differently: "Your past does not equal your future." As we endeavor to co-create our futures, may we remember these rock-solid truths.

With my predisposition to believe in the past life theory, I have come to understand that our souls *choose* our lives before we take physical form, based on the lessons they want to learn next. The lives we choose then, and the probable experiences we will have as a result, support these lessons.

Of course, I would love to have had a happy family life and a stable childhood, but I realized long ago that that's not what *I chose*, and to have regret about my childhood doesn't serve me. It is wasted energy. Whether or not you ascribe to the past life theory, all of our experiences (the happy and the sad), and more importantly our *responses* to them, make up who we are today.

As previously established (but is so important that it bears repeating), fear is at the core of all emotional suffering and unrest in the world. It is the thing that keeps us separate from our individual and collective enlightenment. If we conquer our fear, we will conquer emotional suffering and, dare I say, planetary suffering.

Love is the life and breath of God, living through us as fully as we allow it. Love is the only real and lasting truth; it is the only answer. It's the one true power and the only true healer. It never ceases to exist, and we all need it. Love is the core of our existence. To love is to follow the highest path. When all is said and done, what is left? Love.

Choose love, release fear. Choose love, release fear. Choose love, release fear, over and over and over again until only Love remains. Then, you and I will know true freedom.

I am that I am. I am, as we all are, emanations of pure Spirit manifesting in the physical realm, at one with all things, in a state of constant evolution. This is *what* I am.

As far as *who* I am, I'm not defined by the choices I made twenty years ago, or ten months ago, or last week. Am I therefore defined by who I am in this very moment? Since this moment changes steadily, can I ever truly be defined? It would appear that we cannot be defined in static ways.

We can, however, be measured. But how? By the body of choices we have made up through today ... and by what is left behind in the wake of these choices.

> I know that I'm not always correct about what I am certain.
> Being right doesn't make me safe...or happy.
> It takes courage to practice compassion.

In chapter sixty-eight, I mentioned my desire to have a group of peers to walk with me through life. Nearly eight years ago, I met several people who eventually evolved into what has become my "Mastery Group"—a group of individuals dedicated to the empowerment of each member to live our highest ideals and manifest our deepest desires (i.e. to attain personal mastery over our own lives). We serve as mirrors, truth-tellers, cheerleaders, confidants, emotional fitness trainers, vision-holders, and ass-kickers to each other. Through my association with my Mastery Group, I have partnership in the process of personal evolution and expansion, as well as the earthly support I wanted while being out in the world as a teacher and guide. I highly recommend this type of group to all on the path of self-mastery.

When I endeavored to write this memoir as a contribution to others' health and well-being, my original thought was to recount things that happened in my life, give my insights about them, and then call it a day. What I wasn't aware of was the deeper level of healing and purpose that would ensue. What this book turned out to be was an exemplification of the process of healing through *self-revelation*. It is an extremely potent process, and I highly recommend it to those who are on a serious path of personal healing and self-mastery. I say serious, because this process is not for the faint of heart. There were times when the writing was grueling and all I could do was just keep going, one thought at a time. Other times, so many feelings were kicked up that I had to stop for weeks at a time to process them. The true peace of mind and sense of completion I now have tells me it was well worth the effort.

While delving into God, love, death and other matters, I have opened myself in writing this book to re-feel the pain, pleasure, struggle, and surrender of each experience. In the countless evenings and mornings of my writing sessions, my constant companions have been my soft, cotton "monkey pants," a large and well-worn shirt, a pair of cozy socks, and hot tea. By the way, I highly recommend Tahitian Vanilla Hazelnut^{tm8} and a few cookies (gluten and sugar-free, of course!). These simple things reminded me that, as always, I am surrounded and guided by goodness and Grace.

Life is full of pleasure and beauty, as well as pain and ugliness. It is in our ability to *live deeply, release fear, love profoundly, and receive Grace* that allows us to navigate effectively—and at times brilliantly— through it all. May we all live such lives.

Thank you for reading. It has been an honor to have you take this journey with me. May you be healed by love and freed of all suffering.

To you, magnificent Presence, I want to take this moment to thank whomever and whatever you are and for bestowing me with your Grace. It is true that the love I felt from you that night has never left me, and for this I prostrate my mind and heart to say thank you. On a daily basis I feel you, look to you for guidance, and trust you without hesitation. I gave thanks each time I sat down to write in this story and again each time I finished, for I know that without you I would not have had the impetus or the strength to forge my way through. Thank you for your love and for allowing me to experience your magnificence. I am so utterly grateful to know, firsthand, that you exist.

My most sincere prayer is, for those who would welcome it, that the love you bestow upon me be bestowed upon those who have read this book. May they be healed by love and freed of pain and fear. May they be brought into the awareness that all is good, and all is well. So may it be.

ACKNOWLEDGEMENTS

So many people have contributed to this book in direct and indirect ways. Of course, every person I have written about offered me grist for the mill. For the depth that they brought into my life, I am eternally grateful.

Then there are those in my life who push, prod, inspire and love me, and kick my butt. They must also be thanked:

John—For your constant presence and unending guidance, I am eternally grateful.

Mom and Dad—I bow to you. The profound lessons I learned from your love and your pain are with me always. They are a large part of what has prodded me to find deep fulfillment in life, and enabled me to guide, teach, and help others.

"Stuart and Nate"—For hanging in there with me since the beginning, I bow to you for your courage and strength.

Billy, the first member of my "chosen" family—For your love, wisdom and devotion, I am grateful. Let's go another 45!

Laura Ann, my first and most endearing sister in soul and emotional guardian—I have your back as you have always had mine. I love you for life.

"Sean and Maura"—You are part of my foundation. I am grateful for your constant love, support, and reality checks…and for your Christmas carol parties and our game nights.

"Cara and Joe"—Since I have known you, you have been on the lookout for the thing that would bring the most inner fulfillment to those on your watch. I am grateful to have you as noble confidants and as part of my adopted family.

Cindi Lyn, my younger sister in soul—À votre santé. I am grateful for the joy you bring to my life. You are always in my heart.

Ron and Susan Scolastico, P.J. Tyler, and Eileen Poole—Gratitude goes to you for your ongoing and profound guidance and support. It's a big job, and I'm glad you do it!

Wendy and Aleks, my trusted Mastery Group sisters—I bow to you for "seeing" me, for holding me accountable, for holding my vision, and for taking me to the mat when I need it.

Garrett—Our story will be told in the sequel … For now, I am grateful for your constant love and encouragement, and for your early confusion that inspired me to create the *pebbles*.

Stacey, my newest younger sister in soul—I bow to you in gratitude for your sensitivity, generosity, and talent in making this book ready for print. Your editing and design expertise boggle the mind. I can't wait for our next collaborations!

Elsa, Sandi, Donna, and Jeanine—Oh, how I appreciate the time and energy you gave to this book! Your collective suggestions and feedback are deeply appreciated!

"Kenrooding", my Fairy Godmother—I am blessed by your love, wisdom and magic fairy dust.

To my everyone on my "Loved Ones" lists—I offer my humble thanks for your encouragement and for your votes on various aspects of this book. Without your solid input, I'd still be swirling between versions 1, 2b, 4d, and 6c!

Greg—Thank you for the depth and breadth of your love. Your belief in me is humbling, and your strength, courage, love, and encouragement mean the world.

"Noëlle", my own personal lightning bolt—Day after day you show me what life is truly about, what is important, and what is real. You are my heart and my home. I am in awe of who you are and who you're becoming. You make a difference, and you matter.

QUESTIONS FOR DISCUSSION

∽

1. What was your favorite story in this book? Why? Did you have your own insight as a result? Was the journey interesting or fun? Were you inspired to do or create something new and exciting?

2. What was the hardest story to read? Why? Did it remind you of an experience of your own that you didn't want to revisit? Did it bring up feelings you're not comfortable with? If so, can you name it/them and find meaning and growth there?

3. Where do you think Donna was most thickheaded? Does it make you think less of her? If so, why?

4. Would you like to cultivate more self-love? If so, what belief(s) about yourself would you need to let go of in order to do so?

5. Where in your life is there room for more forgiveness and compassion? Where in your life is there an opportunity to cultivate more love? After reading this book, do you have a better idea of how to go about this?

6. Do you cultivate the spirit of generosity and gratitude with others—where do you see the value of others' contribution in your life?

7. Where in your life is there an opportunity to release fear, judgment, anger, or a sense of superiority?

8. Where in yourself is there an opportunity to release fear, self-loathing, or lack of appreciation?

9. Are you willing to stand up for what you believe in? To be seen? To contribute what you know and what you're passionate about? If so, what are you going to do about it…and when?

10. Where are you making a difference in the lives of others? What do you want to leave behind? Are you working on this now, or are you waiting for the "right time"?

11. Do you have a solid support system—a group who "sees" you and helps keep you on track? If not, can you cultivate the possibility inside you? Can you begin to look at people around you to see if any of them are contenders for such a group?

12. How is your relationship with God/Spirit/the Divine? Are you comfortable cultivating a personal relationship with him/her/it? Or does this feel intimidating or wrong? If so, why?

SOURCES

∽

INTRODUCTION

1. Fuller, Buckminster. *Buckminster Fuller's Universe: His Life and Work*, Lloyd Steven Dieden, Basic Books, 1989.

CHAPTER 31

1. Burmeister, Mary. *Jin Shin Jyutsu^{tm}*. www.JSJInc.net.
2. Poole, Eileen. Brentwood, CA, (310) 571-2377.
3. Ullal, Chakrapani. www.Chakrapani.com.
4. Tyler, P.J. www.CardinalStarSystems.com.
5. Scolastico, Ron. www.RonScolastico.com.
6. Schucman, Helen and Thetford, William. *A Course in Miracles*. Foundation for Inner Peace, 1985.

CHAPTER 35

1. Solandia. www.Aeclectic.net/tarot/
2. http://www.ojp.usdoj.gov/bjs/crimoff.htm. U.S. Department of Justice, Office of Justice Programs, Bureau of Justice Statistics. Criminal Offenders Statistics, Summary Findings, Recidivism, 1994.

CHAPTER 44

1. Ouija. Parker Brothers, Hasbro Games.
2. Ancient Ouija Boards: Fact or Fiction? http://www.MuseumOfTalkingBoards.com/ancient.html
3. Nichols, Sallie. *Jung and Tarot, An Archetypal Journey*. Weiser Books, 1980.
4. Blum, Ralph H. *The Book of Runes, 144*. St. Martin's Press, 1983.
5. Blum, Ralph H. *The Book of Runes, 12*. St. Martin's Press, 1983.

6. Wilhelmm, Richard, trans. Baynes, Cary F., rendered into English. *The I Ching or Book of Changes*. Bollingen Series X1X, Princeton University Press, 1950.
7. Dy, Manual B. Jr. *The Chinese View of Time: A Passage to Eternity*. http://www.crvp.org/book/Series03/III-11/chapter_xx.html.

CHAPTER 54
1. Williamson, Marianne. *A Return To Love: Reflections on the Principles of "A Course in Miracles,"* Harper Paperbacks, 1992.

CHAPTER 62
1. *The Little Buddha*. Starring Keanu Reeves, Chris Isaak, and Bridget Fonda. Miramax Films, 1994.

CHAPTER 67
1. Loggins, Kenny. "Conviction of the Heart", Leap of Faith. Sony Music Entertainment Inc. Manufactured by Columbia Records, 1991.
2. *Junior*. Starring Arnold Schwarzenegger, Danny DeVito, and Emma Thompson. Universal Studios, 1993.

CHAPTER 68
1. Amritaswarupananda, Swani. *Ammachi: A Biography of Mata Amritanandamayi*. Amritanandamayi Center, 1994.
2. Yogananda, Paramahansa. *Autobiography of a Yogi*. Self-Realization Fellowship, 1946.

EPILOGUE
1. *The Upside of Anger*. Starring Joan Allen and Kevin Costner. Newline Cinema and Fine Line Features, 2005.
2. *"Change is inevitable, growth is optional."* Attributed to Walt Disney.
3. *"Change is inevitable, growth is intentional."* Attributed to Glenda Cloud.
4. Gladwell, Malcolm. *The Tipping Point: How Little Things Can Make A Big Difference*. Little Brown, 2000.

5. Walsh, Bryan (2007-10-12). "A green tipping point," Time magazine.
6. Ferguson, Marilyn. 1938-2008, an influential author, and public speaker, best known for her 1980 book *The Aquarian Conspiracy* and its contribution to the New Age movement.
7. Robbins, Anthony. www.TonyRobbins.com
8. Tahitian Vanilla Hazelnut^{tm}. Yogi Tea. www.YogiTea.com.

ABOUT THE AUTHOR

Donna Thomas has dedicated her adult life to uncovering for herself, and then offering to others, insights on how to create deeper fulfillment in life.

At California State University Long Beach, Donna explored both psychology and philosophy as a means of understanding the human condition. She furthered this inquiry by attending myriad personal development courses and by spending time with numerous shamans learning their practices. She has trained in Holotropic™ Breathwork, Jin Shin Jytsu, energy healing, self-revelation, effective thinking, communication, meditation, and conscious relationships.

Her unique outlook stems from her journey through a somewhat challenging childhood, to the realization that she had control over her life and her experience, to the search for answers on how to create inner peace.

Donna extends her wisdom through writing and her work as an Intuitive Life & Empowerment Coach, Integrative Healing Conduit, and Personal-Mastery Group Consultant.

Visit Donna's website and join her email list for periodic announcements at http://donna-thomas.com/blog

Join the *From Pebbles to Pathways* Facebook Group at http://facebook.com/groups/FromPebblesToPathways